LOSING TIM

LOSING TIM

HOW OUR HEALTH AND EDUCATION SYSTEMS
FAILED MY SON WITH SCHIZOPHRENIA

PAUL GIONFRIDDO

COLUMBIA UNIVERSITY PRESS
NEW YORK

Columbia University Press
Publishers Since 1893
New York   Chichester, West Sussex
cup.columbia.edu
Copyright © 2014 Columbia University Press
All rights reserved
Library of Congress Cataloging-in-Publication Data
Gionfriddo, Paul.
Losing Tim: How our health and education systems failed my son with
schizophrenia / Paul Gionfriddo.
pages cm
Includes bibliographical references.
ISBN 978-0-231-16828-1 (cloth : alk. paper) — ISBN 978-0-231-53715-5 (e-book)
1. Gionfriddo, Tim—Mental health.   2. Schizophrenia in children—Patients—
United States—Biography.   3. Mental health policy—United States.   1. Title.

RJ506.S3G46 2014
362.2′6092—dc23
[B]
                                                        2014008507

Columbia University Press books are printed on permanent
and durable acid-free paper.
This book is printed on paper with recycled content.
Printed in the United States of America
c 10 9 8 7 6 5 4 3 2 1

Cover design by Jordan Wannemacher
Cover image is provided courtesy of the author

References to websites (URLs) were accurate at the time of writing.
Neither the author nor Columbia University Press
is responsible for URLs that may have expired or changed
since the manuscript was prepared.

*To Pam, my love, who supported me
—in every way—on this project; and to Tim,
whose courage always inspires me.*

I wanted the moments of my life to order themselves like those of a life remembered. You may as well try to catch time by the tail.
—JEAN-PAUL SARTRE, *NAUSEA*

Grant us wisdom to give priority to those measures of greatest urgency for the common good of all.
—TIMOTHY GIONFRIDDO, GUEST CHAPLAIN,
CONNECTICUT HOUSE OF REPRESENTATIVES, APRIL 10, 1995

CONTENTS

PREFACE

W HEN MY SON TIM was a very young boy, he knew
that I was an elected official, and he understood
that elected officials made many of the "rules" by which
people live. "My dad is important," he used to volunteer
to people when we were introduced to them. The problem was that he pronounced the word as "impotent," which
typically elicited a giggle that puzzled Tim. Giggles aside,
he had no idea how apt a description that would become
when it came to my helping to make his own life more
tolerable.

This book is in part a reflection on public policy and the
way public policy decisions I made in good faith affected
Tim's life. While it is mostly my story and Tim's, there are
some universal themes in it and plenty of other characters
who walk through its pages.

Some of these characters play big roles; others walk on
and quickly walk off. Some are real heroes; others, I am

afraid, may come across as villains. That is not my intention, and so, except for members of Tim's immediate family, I have removed or changed all the names and have even referred only generically to the schools Tim attended and to most of the providers who served him. There are a couple of exceptions when I couldn't really disguise a name—i.e., when there was only one provider meeting the description and it played an important role in Tim's life that only it could have played. But I believe that every person and every entity appearing on these pages had one thing in common: Tim's best interests. The problem, as you will see, was the rules.

As I imagine is the case for most parents of children with serious chronic illnesses, in the course of over two decades I amassed hundreds of hard-copy and electronic documents relating to Tim. They traveled with me from Connecticut to Texas and then to Florida. I saved all that I could, although there were plenty of times I wanted to burn the whole pile of paper or smash the computer in frustration. But after twenty years of storing them I decided it was time to make sense of them. So I began to do what I had been wanting to do for a long time— piece them into a narrative. I had no idea what the ending would be. I just wanted to understand better what had happened to Tim and me as we traveled his path of serious mental illness.

This book is the result. At first, it was all about Tim and not at all about me. But then I realized that I needed to describe better how I felt about what was happening to Tim. When I started to do this, it dawned on me that I also needed to write more about the role I played as a policy maker in determining what happened to him.

I proposed this to *Health Affairs*, the nation's leading health-policy journal. It liked the concept and invited me to write a short version of the story. "How I Helped Create a Flawed Mental Health System That's Failed Millions—and My Son" was published as its September 2012 "Narrative Matters" essay (Gionfriddo 2012) and became the journal's most widely read article that month. *Health Affairs* kindly consented to permitting the themes of that piece to appear in book form, and Columbia University Press agreed to publish it .

Before *Health Affairs* published the essay, Tim did something I found to be very courageous. He graciously gave his permission in writing for his story to be told. When he did so, I don't think that he admired policy makers as he once had or had much respect for the rules they've created that affected him most directly. But I think he understood that if his story could help change the way we think and move us to action, it was worth telling. Plus, he loves me, and I love him.

As it unfolds, this story may sometimes seem strange or surreal to parents whose children do not have a mental illness. I admit, some of the things that happened to us may be pretty hard to believe. But they won't be to parents of children who do have mental illness.

Part of the reason is that we don't usually get clean diagnoses from the start that we can then carry with us to schools or providers. Parents of children with physical disabilities, developmental delays, or genetic conditions often know where they stand. There are accepted treatments and services to mitigate the effects, and they can start treating those effects right away. Our kids' diagnoses often evolve over time, and it can be years before we get to the right one. That means years of uncertainty, years of the wrong drugs, and years of treatment that doesn't work.

Even our introduction to, and experience with, the special education system will seem unusual to many parents who are familiar with it. Special education opens doors to instructional programs tailored to an eligible student's individual needs for educational success. Many children (like my daughter Larissa) enter the special education system with a clear label, and that allows for the creation of a program with a clear set of instructional goals, objectives, modifications, and accommodations. The process is smooth, and these children thrive. But when the label isn't so clear, neither is the plan. And children with mental illness typically don't enter special education with a clear label. When a child is challenging behaviorally—and this is all you really can say—what is a school to do? And so when Tim first entered the special education system—probably already three years into his disease—it was with a "learning disability" label.

A reader may also wonder why Tim was in a regular classroom in a regular school when the story in the first chapter unfolds, months after his diagnosis of mental illness. Under the law, educational services are supposed to be provided in the "least restrictive settings." For nearly every child in special education today, that means instruction in a regular classroom first and the consideration of increasingly more restrictive settings only later. I had no quarrel when that standard was applied to Tim by our school district; in fact, I wholeheartedly agreed with it. Besides, Tim was legally entitled to it.

Finally, there is some chaos in the story to come, but chaos is an accepted part of life for every family dealing with a member's mental illness. Tim was raised by loving parents and, later, step-parents, around three siblings and later one step-sibling. We were no different from any other family in trying to balance Tim's needs with the needs of these siblings. Tim's mother and I ultimately agreed on nearly every decision we made on behalf of Tim. Not all parents do. Undoubtedly, we will be criticized by readers for some of them. But we made them in good faith at the time, on the basis of all we knew in the moment. We did not have the perspective then that anyone may have now. And criticizing anyone for circumstances outside of their control is really a dead end. In any event, I believe that this is a story that needs to be retold. And, I hope, it is a story to which all parents will ultimately relate at some level—one that reminds us how public policies also have consequences.

LOSING TIM

one

TIM BRINGS A GUN
TO SCHOOL

O N WEDNESDAY, November 20, 1996, my son Tim brought a gun to school. He thought he had a good reason—he was angry with another student. He was eleven years old and in the sixth grade. He had been diagnosed with a mental illness earlier in the year.

That morning, as he waited for the school bus, he pulled the gun from the bush in which he had hidden it the night before. As the bus pulled up, he put the gun in a brown paper bag inside his book bag. When he arrived at school, he went straight to his locker and put the gun inside.

Tim forgot about the gun as he went about his school routine. At the end of the day, he went back to his locker and grabbed his jacket, leaving the gun behind.

As he stood in line for the bus, he noticed the student with whom he was angry and remembered the gun. He quietly stepped out of line and bolted toward the school, ignoring the calls of the bus monitors to come back. Tim's special education teacher chased after him. Tim ignored him, removed the paper bag with the gun, and ran in the opposite direction. He exited the school through a side door, coming out beside a Dumpster. He had to think quickly. Students and teachers were standing around one corner of the building, and parents were gathering in the parking lot around the other. With no easy escape, he stopped in his tracks and threw the bag into the Dumpster just as his teacher emerged from the school.

His teacher looked at Tim, then peered over the top of the Dumpster, reached in, and retrieved the bag. He pulled out the gun. "Is this yours?" he asked. "Sort of," Tim replied. Then he explained. It was a BB gun. He was mad at the other boy because the gun was broken. "He sold it to me for twenty dollars yesterday and it doesn't work, so I want to make him take it back and give me back my money."

The teacher relaxed a bit and said, "You know it's against the rules to have guns at school, don't you?" Tim nodded. "For now," his teacher added, "this will be between you and me. Go back to your bus line. I'll see you tomorrow."

Tim went through his normal routine the rest of the day. When he came home, he did not tell me about the other student, the gun, or the encounter with his teacher. He played outside for a while, Rollerblading down our long driveway in the cool November dusk. He watched television and played video games with his younger brother, Ben, as I prepared dinner. He laughed and joked with Ben and his sisters, Lizzie and Larissa, over a supper of spaghetti with spicy calamari sauce. After dinner, he played with our dog, Peggy, and then worked grudgingly on his homework after failing to convince me that he had none. At bedtime, he relaxed with one of his favorite *Calvin and Hobbes* books until I came by to kiss him goodnight.

The next morning, Tim lay in bed for a while listening to rock music. It was a typical morning—I had to nag him twice to get up and get dressed so that he wouldn't miss his bus. When he finally came downstairs, he was too late to eat breakfast; he happily settled for a breakfast bar and milk. I checked his book bag for his homework, packed him a snack and lunch, and sent him out the door as the bus pulled up.

I had no idea how this day would change our lives.

The principal was waiting for Tim when he arrived at school. "Did you bring this to school yesterday?" the principal asked, holding up the BB gun. Tim nodded. The principal told Tim that he had broken the law and that the police were on their way. He also planned to suspend Tim from school for ten days.

Then the principal called me. He had left a phone message for me the previous day but had been unavailable when I called back. I assumed that he was calling about Tim's special-education-mandated Individualized Education Program (IEP), in which we had been negotiating changes for months.

I could not have been more surprised when he told me about the gun. I was momentarily stunned when he added that the police were on their way and that he was suspending Tim from school. Then I felt a rush of adrenaline. "You can't suspend him," I blurted out. Tim's IEP explicitly forbade Tim from being suspended from school for any reason. It was the principal's turn to be surprised.

This wasn't the first time he and I had battled over Tim's IEP. In fact, there were already armies of educators, administrators, clinicians, lawyers, family members, and advocates involved in Tim's life. Tim's gun-toting incident was just the spark that turned our cold war hot.

November 21, 1996—the day after Tim brought his gun to school— would be the day that changed the trajectory of his life. It was the day he was first suspended from school, the day the justice system first became involved in his life, and the day he first went sliding down the steep slope to failure.

It was not as if things had gone smoothly for Tim up until then. When he entered the sixth grade, he had already been diagnosed with language-based learning disabilities, attention deficit disorder, and clinical depression. He was receiving special education services in school, therapy from a well-qualified psychologist, and treatment from his pediatrician and a psychiatrist. He had a loving family and involved, well-educated parents. But none of this mattered on the day he brought his gun to school.

Tim fit a certain profile that was just beginning to emerge in the mid-1990s—that of an unbalanced young man who might do harm to innocent children. This was before Columbine, before Virginia Tech, and long before Sandy Hook, yet the public already connected mental illness with a propensity to violence. In "Violence and Mental Illness: The Facts," the Federal Substance Abuse and Mental Health Services Administration quoted a study that noted that between 1950 and the mid-1990s, the proportion of Americans who associated people who have mental illnesses with violent acts nearly doubled (SAMHSA 2011).

This perception has always been more wrong than right. The Institute of Medicine has noted that "the magnitude of the relationship is greatly exaggerated in the minds of the general population" (National Research Council 2006, 103). Others concluded that "severe mental illness did not independently predict future violent behavior" (Elbogen and Johnson 2009). In fact, people with mental illness are more likely to be the victims of violence than its perpetrators (SAMHSA 2011).

On the day he first tried to suspend Tim, the principal already knew that there was no chance Tim would have used the gun in school. By then—the day after the incident—the principal knew that the gun was broken and that Tim had no ammunition. And had he taken the time to check, he could have found good research to show that Tim's mental illness was not a significant risk factor, either.

So what risk factors are associated with violence and would have warranted a call to the police? A history of violence, substance abuse, and environmental stressors such as job loss, divorce, and becoming the victim of a crime are some (Elbogen and Johnson 2009). The Institute of Medicine (IOM) also singles out abuse, neglect, and living with parents who have been incarcerated (O'Connell, Boat, and Warner 2009). Tim had none of these risks; he was the child of a stable and loving family.

When the principal decided to call the police he was just following protocol. But when he treated what Tim did as a criminal act, he changed the conditions under which Tim was both treated and educated. And he fed the perception that Tim was dangerous—a perception that attaches itself to Tim and to so many others like him even more so today.

For years, both SAMHSA and the National Institute of Mental Health (NIMH) have worked to dispel the myth that more than a small minority of people with mental illness are potentially violent. In the aftermath of the Tucson shootings in early 2011, Dr. Thomas Insel, the director of NIMH, reminded us that "those with serious mental illness are eleven times more likely to be victims of violent crime than the general population" (Insel 2011). But every time a mass killing occurs, media coverage of the event tends to further cement the relationship in peoples' minds. In the wake of the Tucson shooting, the mental illness of the gunman, Jared Lee Loughner, was immediately identified as a factor in his actions, and a mental disorder was automatically presumed to be a factor in the actions of Adam Lanza, the Sandy Hook shooter. So, we begin to think, the association must always be there, especially in children like Tim, even though the experts reiterate that "the vast majority of people who are violent do not suffer from mental illnesses" (quoted in SAMHSA 2011).

But there is a clear connection between violence and mental illness, and it is the opposite of what many of us think. Exposure to violence can cause mental illness. The most vivid example? Exposure to violence can cause post–traumatic stress disorder (PTSD), a common mental illness in America. According to the National Center for PTSD (2014) of the U.S. Department of Veterans Affairs, 7 to 8 percent of us will have PTSD at some point in our lives. And we know that all violence — not just the violence of war — can cause PTSD and can contribute to depression, anxiety, and other mental illnesses. We also know that children are especially susceptible to its effects.

The Adverse Childhood Experiences (ACE) Study, an ongoing collaboration between the Centers for Disease Control and Prevention (CDC) and Kaiser Permanente, demonstrates the connection between abuse and neglect during childhood and adult dysfunction and depression. The ACE-affiliated authors Felitti and Anda (2010) noted that 54 percent of adult depression could be linked to adverse childhood experiences. ACE Study researchers have also argued that the more violence to which children are exposed, the more likely they are to experience depression, suicide attempts, obesity, alcohol abuse, and a variety of other adverse conditions.

Tim was diagnosed with PTSD three months after he brought his gun to school, and for a time it seemed that this diagnosis would explain many of his symptoms. But it would turn out that Tim did not just have PTSD, and the truth is that if the only thing ailing Tim had been PTSD, then with a proper response we might have been able to turn his life around in sixth grade.

What might this response look like? As a matter of public policy, we should address these causes of violence because addressing them will also address many of the risk factors associated with mental illness. In 2001, the U.S. surgeon general linked youth violence to poverty, weak social ties, antisocial parents, and peer conflict (Office of the Surgeon General et al. 2001, chap. 4). The 2009 IOM report linked mental illness to many of the same factors (O'Connell, Boat, and Warner). What we should not do is act out of fear or ignorance. We should not be so quick to blame violence on mental illness. And we should not blame children and their families for a disease a child can't help having. I was often put on the defensive about Tim by school principals and other parents, even though I had three younger children who did not have any of Tim's problems. "If he were mine, I'd keep him under control," was a comment I heard more than once. It is a comment to which all parents of children with mental illness can relate. And when I heard it, I was often both angered and bemused. I always wondered just how long the person making the comment would have lasted if they had had to deal with the symptoms of serious mental illness twenty-four hours a day, seven days a week while people told them what to do!

The day Tim brought his gun to school, I could understand why his principal didn't want to risk underreacting; he was afraid Tim might use it someday. But that fear was unfounded, and when the principal made Tim's illness a matter for the police instead of Tim's mental health providers, fear trumped reason.

I blamed him for this. When Tim was in the sixth grade, I still believed that we were just one good principal, one good teacher, and one good therapist away from forging a successful path in life for him. I was naive about that.

In fact, it was already too late. The deck had been stacked against Tim from the start. The people making the rules, not the people following them, were to blame. And I had been one of those rule makers just a few years earlier.

When my home state of Connecticut eliminated most of its state psychiatric hospital beds in the latter part of the twentieth century, we did not replace them with a well-conceived or adequately funded system of community educational, social, or behavioral health services and supports. I know this because I was part of this effort as a member of the Connecticut state legislature for eleven years.

Our goal in Connecticut—and throughout the country—was to move people needing treatment for chronic mental health problems from large psychiatric institutions into community mental health centers, halfway houses, schools, and supported workplaces. We also intended to provide supports to families so that family members with mental illness could live at home.

But we fell far short of the mark in building a coherent system of care and treatment. Part of the reason was budgetary. The recession of the early 1980s limited our tax resources just as we needed them for new community programs. Another part of the reason was political. It is always difficult to redirect funds away from existing services with strong lobbying efforts toward groups with little political clout.

But mainly, we fell short out of pure ignorance because we made two critical mistakes. The first was not noticing that while older adults were often the ones exiting the institutions, they had been children and younger adults when they first entered them. We paid too little attention to building the community-based special education system on which we would depend to provide the educational services these children and young adults needed in order to thrive. The second was believing that community-based services would always be better than institution-based care, whether or not we coordinated these services properly and funded them adequately. In both instances, our failure to integrate behavioral health care with health, educational, social, judicial, and correctional services was a policy blunder that magnified the effects of our mistakes.

We did not know better at the time because we had so little experience with deinstitutionalized populations. So instead of fixing the problems that were so apparent in our institutions, we unintentionally created a chain of neglect in which many people, like my son Tim, have been tangled for more than a generation.

A brilliant state legislator with whom I once served said that she came to politics believing that good ideas, good information, and good arguments would result in good public policy. She discovered she was wrong when her ideas, information, and arguments were beaten back by emotions, gut feeling, and rigid beliefs.

Like her, we are all disappointed when political leaders fall short of our expectations. We usually blame lobbyists and moneyed special interests, but we forget that the people we elect typically represent the thinking of the people in their districts. These elected officials do not have to be policy experts. In fact, we often idealize inexperience, electing "outsiders" with little knowledge of public policy in the hope that they will bring about whatever change we desire. The result is often the opposite of what we want. Outsiders too often build imperfect government systems and structures, and, where health and mental health are concerned, imperfect systems of care.

When I entered the Connecticut state legislature in 1978, I was an outsider who knew very little about health or mental health policy. I majored in philosophy at Wesleyan University. After graduating in 1975, I spent time as a community activist working on clean energy and energy-conservation policy. Then I joined the federal VISTA program, working with Connecticut Legal Services.

In the meantime, I took an active interest in local politics. Inspired by the Xaverian Brothers who taught at my high school to serve those in need as best I could and by the community activism encouraged at both colleges I attended—Middlebury College and Wesleyan University—I ran in a Democratic primary for the Middletown, Connecticut, city council in 1975, when I was just twenty-two. I lost that election, finishing last in a field of eleven. However, I was appointed shortly after that to the Democratic Town Committee and was given a seat on Middletown's Human Relations Commission.

In 1976, I helped organize the local campaign for Morris Udall for President. Relying heavily on Wesleyan students and faculty, a few progressive local Democrats, family members, and friends of my parents, our cobbled-together political organization won a surprise victory on primary day when Udall took Middletown. I had my first political victory and new clout in the neighborhoods that would become my legislative district.

I began to think seriously about running for the state legislature, and I got my chance two years later, in 1978. I won a contested primary for an open legislative seat and then took the general election with 70 percent of the vote.

I was sworn in as a member of the state House of Representatives in January 1979. At twenty-five, I was one of the youngest state legislators. My district included about half the population of Middletown. Wesleyan was geographically at the center of my district, as was Long Lane School, a state-run juvenile-justice facility. I also represented Middletown's downtown business district, some lower- and middle-class neighborhoods surrounding the city's center, and the wealthier, more rural Westfield section of the city.

Connecticut Valley Hospital, one of the state's three large state psychiatric hospitals, was in another part of Middletown, represented by an out-of-town legislator. I could see it off in the distance from the Wesleyan campus, and when I was sworn in I never expected to be heavily involved with what went on there.

My expectations changed during my first month as a legislator. I was assigned to the prestigious Joint Appropriations Committee through the intervention of a colleague and mentor. I was the low person on the totem pole when I was invited to meet with the committee chairs to discuss my subcommittee assignments. I requested Education, Regulated Activities, and Human Services, all areas in which I felt I had either some background or interest. "You're going to do Health and Hospitals," they said. "I don't want to do Health and Hospitals," I responded. "Neither does anyone else," they replied, ending the conversation.

A few weeks into my legislative career, with no background or training, I was the reluctant new "expert" on health, mental health, developmental services, substance abuse, and veterans services. I remained on the Appropriations Committee for ten of my eleven years in the state legislature and helped to fund every major health and mental health initiative that came before us in the 1980s. I also chaired the Public Health Committee for four of those years and managed the entirety of the state's health and mental health policy agenda as well.

There was a clear consensus about what to do with the state psychiatric hospitals back then. We believed that they were often no better than prisons for people with mental illness and that it was time to empty them. I helped close down a state psychiatric hospital in Newtown, start closing a second in Norwich, and reduce the size of the third one, in Middletown.

The same thing was happening everywhere; after decades of relying on institutional care, many people believed there were better ways to treat people with mental illness. According to the 1935 Statistical Abstract of the United States, in the depths of the Great Depression more than 300,000 people received mental health treatment in institutional settings (U.S. Census Bureau 1935). In those days, institutionalization was the primary strategy for treating mental illness. While the institutions housed people with serious mental illnesses like schizophrenia, depression, and what we now recognize as PTSD among World War I veterans and survivors of the Great Depression, without modern medications these institutions offered little more than custodial care.

Many of these institutions were like cities unto themselves. Both patients and staff lived and worked on the campus. Patients who were able to work were assigned jobs like farming and light manufacturing. Patients often stayed for years or even decades, and many died and were buried there. The institutional burial grounds at Connecticut Valley Hospital, for example, are a sad and moving reminder of those times.

The care and treatment of people with mental illness changed dramatically during the last fifty years of the twentieth century as new medications became available and the state hospitals were closed. Between 1970 and 2002, the number of psychiatric beds throughout the United States was reduced from 525,000 to 212,000. In 1970, 80 percent of the beds were in state or county hospitals; in 2002, only 27 percent were (Sharfstein and Dickerson 2009). This trend continued during the beginning of the current century. As a result, there were only 43,318 public psychiatric hospital beds left by 2010 (Torrey et al. 2012).

There was less of a consensus about what we should do to replace the psychiatric hospitals. I favored community health and mental health programming, including the establishment of supported living arrangements and supported work programs for people with developmental disabilities or mental illness, and respite services for caregivers. I also worked on passing an amendment to Connecticut's constitution giving equal rights to people with disabilities. But it was always much easier to cut funding from state hospitals than to add dollars to community programs. In 1981, the federal government repealed the Community Mental Health Centers Act of 1963, which ended the dedicated flow of federal dollars to the new community mental health centers that were supposed to help replace the hospital beds that were disappearing.

At the time, there were no loud voices in our communities clamoring for more mental health services. The families affected by serious mental illness often kept this information to themselves. I recall the time a successful Middletown attorney who served with me on our Democratic Town Committee quietly approached me after a meeting to express his sincere appreciation for my efforts in funding mental health services. His daughter had a serious mental illness, he explained. I had known him for years and had no idea that he even had a daughter. Now I know how he felt. Parents—too often unfairly shouldering blame or shame for the mental illness of their child—are often just as reluctant to speak up today.

There is a myth that a well-run government is like a well-run business and that the skill sets needed are the same for both. This isn't true. What I learned on the job about policy making was that well-run governments provide services that address the needs of their constituents, while well-run businesses provide products that respond to the demands of consumers. These are very different missions.

In the case of mental health treatment, we usually deal with a reluctant consumer. Just because people need services doesn't mean they are lining up to get them. If anything, the opposite is true. A 2005 study calculated that nearly half of us will have a behavioral health disorder at some point in our lives (Kessler et al. 2005). "Behavioral health disorders" is a term for which I don't care because it often implies to laypeople that bad behavior is the only problem. But these are all real diseases of the brain and include addiction disorders as well as all mental illnesses, including the so-called Big Three—depression, bipolar disorder, and schizophrenia—as well as PTSD, personality disorder, and others. Other surveys suggest that only 36 percent of those with a mental illness in any given year receive treatment (NIMH n.d.a).

Like many of my colleagues, I learned about mental health policy as I listened to advocates and made decisions about what to fund based on their presentations. Their perspectives were usually provider-focused. Connecticut's mental health commissioners explained the reasons for the department's budget requests. The unions representing mental health workers wanted better working conditions at hospitals and an expanded role for state employees in community treatment programs. Community mental health providers advocated for more funding for the services they provided. And the Vietnam veterans taught me about one of the greatest ironies in our mental health system at the time—our primary "treatment" program for addicted veterans at our state Veterans Home and Hospital was a basement bar called the Foxhole. The idea was to confine residents' drinking to the hospital grounds so that they wouldn't be getting drunk in nearby Rocky Hill. Only after this became public were more active forms of treatment added.

In building my policy expertise, I had an advantage over other citizen-legislators. I was content enough with the low pay to make the state legislature my full-time job. I used the time to attend as many

educational forums as I could, becoming a regular at policy workshops offered by the National Center for Health Services Research
(NCHSR), which is now the Agency for Healthcare Research and
Quality (AHRQ). At those workshops, government officials from
around the country gathered with health services researchers to explore
health policy topics in depth.

I learned in these workshops that many of my out-of-state peers
struggled just as much as I did with policy expertise. After listening to
one research presentation, a colleague requested, "You need to make
this simpler and clearer; I've got to be able to explain this to a plumber." "I get it," the researcher responded, "you mean you have to explain
your actions to people who aren't well versed in health policy." "No,"
my colleague replied, "I mean that the chair of my Health Committee
is a plumber!" At least we had some time to get up to speed; there were
no term limits in those days.

The one area with which NCHSR couldn't help us was mental
health, which was under the purview of NIMH. Many states also split
the responsibility for health and mental health services into different
agencies, promoting a nonintegrated approach to the delivery of health
and mental health services. This approach is changing slowly. In 2010
the Milbank Memorial Fund reported on two decades of efforts around
the country to integrate health and mental health services (Collins et al.
2010). These efforts and others resulted in some language in the Patient
Protection and Affordable Care Act of 2010 promoting services integration. But the concept remains an elusive one for many policy leaders.

During my time as a legislator, we never fully integrated mental
health services at the policy level with other health or educational
services. At least I learned to make some connections. For example,
I learned about the relationship between mental illness and substance abuse: people with mental illness sometimes use drugs to self-
medicate. By doing so, they may ease the symptoms of their mental illness, in some unfortunate cases at the cost of addiction.

When I was making policy, our mental health and substance abuse
services systems had recently been administratively separated. While

they were reconnected in Connecticut later on (and are commonly found within a single agency in most states today), community service providers still often specialize in either mental health or addiction services. And that's not all. Despite clear connections between mental illness and other chronic diseases, we have made little progress administratively connecting health and mental health services delivery in our states. And with the notable exception of school-based health centers, there is next to no connection among educational, health, and behavioral health services to school-aged children—which is what my son Tim so desperately needed.

When Tim was diagnosed with mental illness, he entered this fragmented world I helped to create.

Tim's clinical services would be managed under one set of rules; his educational services under another. Correctional services would have a third set of rules; social services yet another. For Tim, as for many people with serious mental illness, following all these rules was often overwhelming . He was never quite able to bend to them. And too often, the well-meaning adults who tried to educate, support, and serve him could not bend from them. Rules could not be broken. As a result, his young life was.

two

TIM GETS HIS START

TIM WAS SEVEN weeks old in May 1985 when my then-wife Linda and I adopted him. As we began the process, we had no idea that we were walking into such controversy. I had grown up with three siblings and around twelve first cousins and hoped to have several children of my own. Linda agreed. And as she worked in direct service to people with developmental disabilities, she thought she could handle a child with special needs. I thought so, too. We had discussed it at length over many months as Linda tried to get pregnant, and we finally decided to adopt a baby. We knew that this might take some time, because there were not many babies available for adoption. Those who were, were often children of color or children with special needs.

We discussed this, too, and it did not matter to us that we might be adopting transracially. Nor did we specify that we would only take a normal, healthy baby. A baby was a baby to us. But it turned out that race, especially, did matter to people at both ends of the political spectrum—so much so that our state Department of Children and Families was not doing any transracial placements at the time. I realized how deeply some people cared about this the first time I was accused of engaging in cultural genocide. All I wanted was a family, and Linda and I hoped that Tim would be the first of many children.

Fortunately, our diocese's Catholic Charities office was willing to make adoptive placements without regard to race. We went through a months-long home study, during which we talked through many of the scenarios that could arise for any parents, for any parents adopting a child with special needs, and for any parents adopting a child transracially. By the end of the process, we were as prepared as any prospective first-time parents can be. A few months later, our social worker called and told us that there was a seven-week old, eleven-pound baby boy waiting to meet his new parents. We raced to the Catholic Charities offices in Norwich, Connecticut, and as she brought Tim down the hall and into the room, all our social worker said was, "I want to introduce you to your son." He had bright brown eyes and dark-brown curly hair. When I held him, after months of training for the moment, my first thought was, "Am I prepared for this?" My second was, "He's heavy; please don't let me drop him."

Tim's development as an infant and toddler was normal. He snuggled comfortably with grown-ups. He relaxed while being held, cuddled, and touched. He liked picture books and games, and settled easily into my lap to watch television or listen to music or conversation. At rest, he was peaceful, patient, and contemplative.

At play, Tim put his abundant energy to work. He loved big, noisy playscapes, bright colors, and constant motion. He enjoyed racing around on a tricycle, scooter, or Rollerblades, and splashing the water in his nightly bath and in our small backyard pool. He loved racing back and forth with our dog, Peggy, and loved building houses and castles with his big cardboard blocks in the afternoon and tearing them down at the end of the day. He spent hours taking things apart to see how they worked and didn't seem to mind that he never could get them back together again. He loved running fast and climbing high, and crashing into the piles of leaves I raked each fall and the snow I shoveled in the winter. He was outgoing, energetic, and never afraid to take a risk.

Tim's bedtime always seemed to arrive before his day was through. He required a lengthy routine of quiet time, reading, and cuddling to settle down at night, and he stubbornly refused to go to sleep.

Because my work hours were flexible when the legislature was not in session, I divided day-to-day parenting responsibilities with Linda. On my days at home with Tim I got in a little work, but mostly enjoyed being a new parent—changing his diapers, playing with him, feeding him, bathing him, and reading to him. Tim was a popular visitor when I took him to work with me at the State Capitol. He loved the attention.

He was crawling by the time he was six months old and walked at ten months. We nicknamed him "Timber," as something always seemed to be falling around him as he scooted from place to place. Long before he talked, I awakened one night to find him standing next to our bed, grinning from ear to ear. He had climbed up and over the side of his crib and trotted into our bedroom.

Tim got his first sibling, Larissa, ten months after he had been placed with us. She was seven weeks old and was also in perfect health and of mixed race. Her eyes crinkled into beautiful half-moons when she smiled. Tim took one look at her and decided that he liked his new playmate very much.

As young children, Tim and Larissa were inseparable. Larissa took her cues from Tim. When he built something with blocks, she helped. When he went for a swim, she did, too. When he rode a tricycle, she rode alongside him. When he tried a new food, so did she.

Their relationship changed when both children entered their first day-care program, in the fall of 1987. Larissa, who was eighteen months old and beginning to establish her independence, fit right in. She made friends easily with the other children and enjoyed her time with them. Tim, who was two and a half, didn't adjust as well. Comfortable around adults, he was initially surprisingly shy around the other children. He had a tendency to ignore the rules, not distinguishing his "outdoor voice" from his "indoor voice." He also often had to be redirected from more rambunctious activities to calmer ones, especially during rest times. At the end of the day, I usually found Larissa playing in the middle of a group of other children, and Tim on the lap of an adult—mostly because he needed to have an adult keeping a close eye on him.

In late 1988, Tim aged out of the day-care program and entered the Yale Divinity Nursery School. His liked the activities there, but he could be a handful. One afternoon when I arrived to pick him up he was running around with a group of boys, terrorizing the girls. "We're the bad guys!" he exclaimed as he ran by. It seemed that Tim had become a leader in a boys-only Divinity Nursery School gang that day. I wondered how this would look on his future resume.

Tim challenged rules constantly as he turned four, but his behavior was still within the boundaries of "normal." He clearly needed and thrived on positive adult reinforcement, but he didn't always make the connection that positive reinforcement was tied to following the rules. And, conversely, negative reinforcement only seemed to make his bad behaviors worse. If he broke a toy by accident and got scolded for it, he might break another one on purpose. If he got a time-out for doing that, he might kick a wall or door and make a mark on it. What worked best for me when it came to de-escalating Tim's bad behavior was to break the progression as soon as possible. I could usually do this by redirecting him to something more positive and then reinforcing him for that before addressing the bad behavior with a consequence. The problem with this approach was that once he received his consequence, Tim was seldom able to internalize the lesson. He would repeat the same mistake.

I do not know whether these behavioral problems were the earliest symptoms of Tim's mental illness. I do know that his pediatrician, who was exceptionally skilled, never suggested they might be.

As the children got older, Larissa grew more distant from Tim. She sometimes liked sitting at a desk making drawings or pretending to write, when he wanted her to go outside to play. She made play-dates with other girls and didn't include Tim. This frustrated him. He responded by bothering her until she got upset, hoping she'd get in trouble and perhaps get her playdate canceled or cut short.

In early 1989, when Tim was four and Larissa three, I decided to leave the legislature to run for mayor of Middletown. I was in my sixth term, serving as deputy majority leader, and was weary of the legislative process. As I was busy gearing up for my mayoral campaign, we initiated the process of adopting another child. My mother raised an eyebrow when I told her. But she had raised four children, so there wasn't much she could say. And even though Tim was a handful sometimes, I told her tongue-in-cheek that another child could be a real help to us. With only two, everyone still expected that the parents were always in control. With three, they knew we would be outnumbered!

A month before the mayoral election, our social worker called informing me that in a few weeks we were going to be the proud parents of a new baby girl. On November 1, 1989, Lizzie—our third healthy, gorgeous baby of mixed race—came home to us at the age of almost five months. She had blue eyes, an easy smile, and beautiful long fingers and toes. She was with us in time to celebrate my election as mayor six days later.

The presence of Lizzie in our home took some pressure off Tim's relationship with Larissa, as he took to his new sister immediately. Six months later Lizzie was walking and beginning to talk. She was an easygoing, cuddly baby. Tim loved to hold her in his lap and "read" picture books to her, and she adored Tim. She also smiled all the time, which was very reinforcing for him. Lizzie soon assumed Larissa's previous role as Tim's primary playmate. She cheered him on as he climbed trees, settled in beside him as he watched TV, and admired him as he played video games.

My election as mayor elevated my profile—and the profile of our growing family—in the community. While my life was busier and somewhat more complicated than it had been when I was in the legislature, working at city hall meant I was close enough to home to check

in on the children during the day. I was also able to get home for dinner most nights, and on weekends when I needed to go to a community event, the children could usually go with me. As a father with
three young children, I tried to make city hall a little more kid-friendly
while I was mayor, even creating a policy that allowed city employees
to bring their children to work when they had day-care emergencies.
This turned out to be surprisingly controversial, attracting the attention
of the New York Times in an article titled "The Talk of Middletown:
1950s Town Battles 1990s Woes" (Ravo 1990). (Ironically, the article
juxtaposed downtown problems created by the release of people with
mental illness from Connecticut Valley Hospital with my child-care
policy, accompanied by a picture of our family.)

In August 1990, when he was five, Tim began kindergarten. Larissa,
at four, entered nursery school, and one-year-old Lizzie attended a
small day-care program at the home of a friend. Just as things seemed
to be settling down, we got a note from our adoption agency informing
us that Lizzie had a newborn biological sibling, and that the agency
hoped to place him with Lizzie. Would we like a fourth child? We did
not hesitate before saying yes because we understood that in order for
the agency to get to Lizzie as the nearest available blood relative on the
list, others had already said no.

In December, when he was five months old, Lizzie's biological
brother, Ben, arrived at our home. Tim was thrilled to have a new
brother. Just as he had with Larissa and Lizzie, he bonded with quiet,
easygoing Ben immediately. Our lives, however, became even more
hectic, as any might with four young children in the household.

On the one hand, we were a pretty typical middle class family. We
attended our local Catholic Church regularly, and as the children
grew older we became more involved in church activities and CYO
basketball. I eventually joined the Parish Council. Linda and I shared
parenting responsibilities, dividing up the diaper changes, the cooking,
and the cleaning. We kept to pretty straightforward routines, with regular mealtimes and bedtimes for the children. We took a lot of day trips
and enjoyed short overnight vacations. We read books together, played

together, went to our favorite family restaurants, and usually settled in on the weekends for TV watching or family movie nights.

But we were also different from most of the families we knew. We had four young children of mixed races, all under the age of six. I juggled my political life with my family life, and Linda juggled family, her growing work as a special education consultant, and her work on her Ph.D. We were busy, politically active antinuclear advocates (and even activists on occasion); we believed strongly in the inclusion of all people with developmental disabilities in the mainstream of society (a special passion of Linda's) and in expanding community-based care for elders (a special passion of mine after spending years volunteering as an accordion player in nursing homes). We were also not meat eaters—a little unusual among Middletown's ethnic families!

When all four children were young, the regular sitters we hired gave most of their attention to Lizzie and Ben. Larissa was a pretty independent four-year-old, but Tim was a challenge. He tested his caregivers by misbehaving and often needed almost constant supervision.

The problem was that nothing seemed to work very well or for very long to reverse his bad behavior. We tried rewards and consequences, gentle and not-so-gentle redirection, time-outs, and lots of one-on-one attention but had no consistent success with any of these. Just as any parents would, we kept coming back to what we might be doing wrong but were stymied because all of these strategies worked just fine with our other three children.

We were probably better prepared than most parents to recognize the potential for problems in our children. Because transracial adoption could present special challenges, during our home study we had been taken through a number of issues that could arise. How would we respond to adults and children wondering about our little "rainbow coalition?" How would we assure, as part of a healthy upbringing, that our children would be exposed to role models of all races? What would we do to encourage them to make friends of their own race? How would we handle discrimination and bigotry directed toward us or the children when we had never faced these before?

In addition, like almost all adoptions at that time, our adoptions were closed. This meant that we did not know who Tim's biological parents were and knew next to nothing about his family medical history. As a result, we were instructed to look out for inherited conditions and to be sure we had a regular pediatrician whom we could trust to do comprehensive well-child exams. Tim's size was another concern. Early on, his pediatrician told us that it was likely Tim would be well over six feet tall—far taller than I am. This might be an advantage later, but appearing to be older than his peers as a child could lead to unreasonable expectations about how he should behave.

In any event, we thought we were prepared for most anything. But no one is ever really prepared for mental illness. And Tim's behavioral challenges soon made every theoretical concern moot.

Still, Tim had a special charm about him when he was five. One time, we were invited by a city council member to a backyard picnic. We arrived there to find a typical Italian family celebration under way. Tim immediately focused his attention on a group of older men who were standing around a large metal pot full of clams on ice. He watched them take the clams out, slice them open, squeeze lemon and Tabasco sauce on them, and then slurp them off their shells. He edged closer.

"You want one?" one man asked, sizing Tim up. Tim nodded.

The man laughed, pulled a clam out of the icy water, opened it, and handed it to Tim.

Tim examined it for a moment, then asked, "Can I have some of those?" pointing to a lemon wedge and the Tabasco.

"It's hot," the man replied, pointing to the Tabasco.

"That's okay. I like hot." Tim squeezed a little lemon and poured a few drops of Tabasco on the clam, then slurped it all off the shell just as he had seen the men do it. He chewed a couple of times and then gulped it down.

For a moment, everyone waited for Tim's gag reflex to set in. It didn't. He just looked up and said, "Can I have more?"

The man laughed and shouted to everyone, "Look at this little boy, eating raw clams!"

"Raw?" Tim said, his gag reflex finally setting in. "You didn't tell me these were raw!"

Tim certainly appeared to be ready for kindergarten in 1990. He had looked forward to school for months. He knew his colors, numbers, and letters; he expressed himself well verbally; he usually played well with other children; and he was charming around adults. He had good reasoning skills, could put together simple puzzles, and was quite good at constructing things out of his Lego blocks.

Tim was also four feet tall and lean, making him one of the tallest children in his class. In play, he was full of energy and somewhat precocious, and other children looked up to him, figuratively as well as literally. He rode a bicycle and was a good swimmer, a swift runner, and a competent climber. Though shy, he had begun to make friends with his peers. At the beginning of the school year he went to school eagerly each day and came home happy and animated.

Most of the time he was a good big brother at home. But he could also swing from easygoing and friendly to contrary and argumentative in no time. He sometimes pushed his considerable weight around to get his way with his younger siblings.

Within a few weeks, however, there was also trouble at school. His teacher began to notice some things that concerned her. Tim was good at hands-on activities, but he struggled to keep up with his classmates in writing and drawing. He also had trouble following directions, staying focused, and completing assigned tasks. In November, in one of the first written evaluations we received, his teacher gave us an unsettling description of Tim in the classroom: "Timothy is very distractible," she wrote. "He has a hard time staying on task. He also has a difficult time following directions and often seems confused or disoriented." She added that while his gross motor skills were fine, his fine motor skills, which he needed for writing and drawing, were weak.

At first I was skeptical, and had to see for myself. I took some time off from work to visit Tim's class and read to the students. Tim sat next to me as I read, attentive and proud to be hosting his father in school. He was as focused and absorbed in the story as any of the other children, and I did not see much difference between him and them. I shared my observation with his teacher. She listened to me but gently persisted, saying that she would continue to document her concerns. In early December she wrote that Tim's "off task times [were] more likely to occur in large group situations requiring small motor skills." She also noted that "copying printed matter is very hard work for Tim," that his cutting skills were weak, and that he had a hard time getting materials together for projects. He was unusually disorganized, slow to act, and did not seem interested in much of his work. She observed again that he often seemed distracted. Also, she said, Tim seemed unhappy much of the time and was something of a loner. "At first, he didn't interact at all, but it's a little better now. He will play with one child at a time, but if another joins, then Timothy turns away. He's not sought out by others—and sometimes he curls into a fetal position and rocks."

If we had the behavioral health-screening tools for children available then that we have now, I know we would have used them. And they would have given us some more clues about what was going on with Tim—even at the age of five. As it was, we talked about Tim's behaviors at every exam with his pediatrician, but in every check-up all of Tim's physical and developmental signs were normal. His heart was strong, his teeth were good, his coordination was excellent, his eating was normal, and his energy level was high. His mental health was not systematically evaluated. And while Tim's kindergarten teacher observed those behaviors, they were at first only a small part of the whole picture. Tim was not the only child who had some difficulty adjusting to kindergarten, and this alone was not enough to trigger any immediate action by the school.

This is probably still true today. What looks serious in hindsight often disappears into the activities of the day. We could do mental health screening in schools to help tease out early manifestations of mental illness, but there are plenty of educators and parents who object to mental health (i.e., "brain") screening—because of stigma—when they would never object to school-based vision or hearing screening. But there is also another problem. If Tim had been screened and we did discover an emerging problem, at the time it would have been weeks or months before we could get appointments with the right specialists. And, even today, what good is screening if we aren't funding the services needed to treat whatever conditions are diagnosed?

I became convinced that Tim needed services a few weeks later, when it was clear that he was struggling with his work, unhappy about school, and felt he was failing to make friends. Tim's teacher offered to try some classroom strategies that she thought might help. She moved Tim closer to the front of the room, started giving him gentle reminders to listen, and helped him assemble his materials. She also thought that we should reinforce good classroom behavior at home, so we offered little rewards to Tim, such as special meals, some extra "alone" time with mom or dad, or simple praise when she reported to us that he had had a good day.

She also created some informal instructional objectives for Tim. These included improving his fine motor skills, his ability to follow directions and his ability to comply with classroom routines. She also requested that a case manager be assigned by the school district to help her evaluate Tim's progress. Her request was approved, and at the beginning of February the case manager reported: "Tim is making steady progress. He is fitting in better and following routines in class. [He] seems happier."

I was relieved that Tim seemed to be on track again. But over the next eight weeks, his progress slowed. In March and early April, his teacher reported that he seemed tired, sullen, and even less able to focus. He was increasingly distracted in his work. Although he was getting along better with the other children, his teacher summed up the quarter by writing: "Timothy is still disorganized and forgetful. [His] fine motor [skills] still [need] improvement."

She told us that she considered a referral for so-called Chapter 1 services, which were commonly used with students who were not yet ready for school. In our district, they helped with reading readiness, colors, and simple math concepts. But these services did not seem quite the right fit for Tim because he had appeared ready at the start of the year. Special education services were another possibility, but the school wanted more time to evaluate him first and also to see whether his problems might correct themselves by the start of the next school year.

By the end of the school year, Tim was unable to comply with even basic routines unless he was given constant reminders. Tim's teacher was worried and asked that his first-grade teacher be briefed fully in advance of the new school year. She also asked that the case manager continue to formally monitor Tim's progress during the next school year.

That summer, Tim seemed to grow more comfortable and at ease around his peers, reducing some of my anxiety. He played T-ball, enjoyed a family vacation to Lake Ontario, and bonded with a boy who lived nearby. The new friend was three years older than Tim. He was a good role model and treated Tim like a younger brother.

But my anxiety increased on other fronts. Tim often rode his bike between his friend's house and ours. One day he came home without his bike and couldn't remember where he had left it. We walked the neighborhood and found the bike leaning up against the side of a stranger's house. Tim could not say why it was there. That summer, he often misplaced his playthings.

His risk taking also became a more serious problem. He climbed to the top of the thirty-foot maple tree in our front yard. One day I looked outside and saw Tim lying in the middle of the street. I thought he had fallen and raced to him. As I got closer, he lifted his head to see what the commotion was. "I'm okay," he said, waving me off. "I just wanted to see if a car would run me over." This was a wake-up call to me that even more serious issues might be emerging, and I was fearful about what those might be.

Tim's pediatrician tried to reassure us that this could still be considered within the boundaries of normal behavior. Tim did not seem depressed or suicidal, and he claimed he was just playing and knew that few cars actually came down our street. But we began to monitor him much more closely.

By the time the new school year began, Tim needed our constant supervision. I thought it might help that Larissa, who was beginning kindergarten, would have the same morning routine as Tim; perhaps he would imitate her as she prepared for school, and at least his organizational skills might improve. It took me about a week to figure out that this was not going to happen. Larissa managed everything she was supposed to—snacks, lunch money, homework, and simple chores. Tim, on the other hand, managed next to nothing on his own.

We signed Tim up for youth soccer that fall, hoping it would give him a chance to make some new friends and hone his teamwork skills while running off some excess energy. He was very athletic and taller, stronger, and faster than most of the other children. But he couldn't integrate his play with that of his teammates. Much of the time, he seemed to be drifting in his own world while all the action took place around him. He was much better alone, playing his video games. While he was often distracted while playing team sports like soccer, he could attend to video games for hours if we let him.

Tim's first-grade teacher was aware of his kindergarten teacher's concerns. About a month into the school year, she also began to document Tim's difficulties, reporting that she still observed fine-motor weakness and distractibility. But she did not see mental illness, perhaps because she was not trained to look for this.

She also described Tim as sluggish in class, and she was uncertain how well he was processing information. Then one day she called on him to give an oral report to the class. She said he "kind of shuffled" to the front of the classroom, turned and faced the class, and then was surprisingly animated and enthusiastic in his presentation, recalling much of what he had been taught. She recognized that he was an auditory learner, and that his verbal processing skills might be strong enough to offset some of his weaknesses in writing.

My term as mayor ended that November, and I put to bed thirteen years in elective office to begin work as a public policy consultant. I chose consulting partially so that I could focus again on health-policy training, and partially so that I could work from home. I wanted more time with the children, and Tim especially needed it. The downside of consulting was that I also had to travel a great deal, and so I wasn't always certain that I was getting a clear picture of Tim's school performance and behavior.

By midyear, Tim was not doing well. His mind seemed to wander in class, and he struggled with arithmetic, spelling, and reading.

We moved to a new house in January, a couple of miles away from our old one. There were fewer children in the new neighborhood, and the houses were set farther back from the street, which was also much busier. Fortunately, our long driveway kept Tim from riding his scooter or bicycle out into the traffic. We had an above-ground pool with a deck in the backyard, and our four acres of woods beyond the pool abutted a three-hundred- acre nature preserve, which created endless opportunities for safe play.

The first year we lived there, I cleared a path through the woods to our back property line. This gave Tim and his siblings plenty of room to get "lost" in without ever leaving our property. Tim thoroughly enjoyed exploring the woods, hauling around small logs and old pieces of wood to make himself little shelters to play in. We helped him build a tree house so that he had a place to escape to when he didn't want his siblings too close. Tim also found a new friend in the neighborhood who was a couple of years older than he was. They played together often. Tim looked up to him and tried to emulate him as much as he could.

Meanwhile, Tim's list of academic difficulties lengthened. "His report card grades are satisfactory," his teacher reported during a January meeting, "but he tends to try to avoid written work." Most noteworthy, she added, "He stands out in terms of his distractibility."

Later she wrote: "Tim is inconsistent. Sometimes he reads beautifully, other times not at all well. He still dislikes written work but is getting it done (even though it's sloppy). He often seems oblivious to what is going on."

She tried some new cuing and positive reinforcement strategies with Tim and also began exchanging regular notes with Linda and me to keep us updated on his progress. In April, her report was more positive. But as the school year neared its conclusion, she warned that he was not out of the woods yet and said that his second-grade teacher should continue the strategies she had developed. She and the principal also sought advice about Tim's inattentiveness from the school psychologist, who agreed.

When Tim began second grade, he was still heavier and taller than nearly every other student in his grade and the grade above him. He played youth soccer again, but I never knew what to expect from him. When he played well, he was one of the better members of the team. But when his head wasn't in the game, watching him could be painful. Sometimes he would lie down on the field and pretend to take a nap. Once, when he was playing defense, Tim lay down and his goaltender yelled at him to get back up. This was a mistake; Tim didn't like being scolded. The next time the ball came near Tim, he was on his feet. He fielded it cleanly, turned around, and kicked it past his own surprised goaltender, scoring a goal for the other team. The goaltender left him alone after that.

In school, Tim continued to exhibit many of the same worrying traits. He had problems mastering all of his academic subjects except science, where much of the work was hands-on. He was unfocused, disorganized, and unable to follow basic classroom rules and daily routines. He didn't remain in his seat during lessons and would often talk out of turn.

He also developed a quirky eating routine: he skipped breakfast and then ate both his snack and lunch at snack time. When he then didn't have anything to eat at lunch, he sat and fidgeted, which bothered the other children. The cafeteria monitors told him to stop, which only made his behavior worse.

By now, Linda and I were pushing the school to consider him for special education services. In our view, plenty of evidence had accumulated over the past three years that would qualify Tim for special education, but the school personnel were dragging their heels. I believe that they felt that we wanted more services than they were equipped to provide and that Tim may only have required a little help with organization and academics to succeed. On the other hand, we were thinking, at the very least, about services to address possible learning disabilities and attention deficit disorder, and we were certain that whatever conditions Tim had were clearly affecting his ability to learn. His second-grade teacher sealed the deal for us where she wrote: "Timothy has difficulty focusing on daily academic tasks. He lacks organizational skills (setting up papers, keeping [his] work area organized, remembering assignments, remembering [his] lunch ticket and personal belongings needed at home and recess). His lack of focus causes him to only complete 2–3 of the daily assignments."

She also wrote that he "mixes up many letters and has great difficulty copying from the board or book." She was using the cuing strategies, but without success. She did note some positive things: "Timothy is able to follow class routines (when reminded). He reads fluently and with expression. His fine motor [skills are] average and he has a high interest in science."

She believed that Tim needed more support than she could give him, so in late October she made a formal request for additional assistance. This resulted in a "Plan for Alternative Strategy (PAS) for Tim. At the time, this was one step short of a special-education referral and created a record that certain formal changes to Tim's program were being made to help him be more successful in school.

These changes would sometimes be called modifications and sometimes be called accommodations. I would soon hear both of these frequently. For special education purists and experts, they mean two different things. Modifications are those changes in a child's program that alter educational standards. Accommodations are those changes that alter the instructional environment. But at the local level, the terms are often intertwined. Giving a child five spelling words to learn each week instead of ten is an accommodation if the child ultimately still must learn how to spell two hundred words by the end of the year to be considered proficient. But it can be thought of as a modification if it changes the standard of proficiency for that child to one hundred words by the end of the year. Many of the school personnel I encountered used the terms almost interchangeably.

Tim's PAS changes were modest and—as I learned later—not mandatory for the school. One was the use of a special check sheet to ensure that Tim completed his classroom tasks. Tim was also to be given "consumable" textbooks, in which he could write directly, which would eliminate the need to manage a separate answer sheet. This was a help to Tim, who had difficulty copying his work.

A case manager was also assigned again to monitor Tim's progress and determine if additional modifications were needed. She reported after a month: "Timothy has shown improvement by using the checklist to assist himself in organizing his daily morning jobs. By week four he was completing an average of four jobs with minimal assistance."

We also agreed to an evaluation by an educational consultant with a background in child development, Dr. R, who underscored many of the observations already made by Tim's teachers. She wrote: "Throughout the testing Timothy was restless. Although his restlessness was not extreme it appeared intermittently. At times he was unable to remain seated. His legs rocked or shaked occasionally. These manifestations appear to be similar to observations reported by Timothy's teachers." Dr. R also reported that throughout the testing, Tim had tried very hard to succeed but was often driven to frustration. She thought that he showed ingenuity in compensating for deficits in his math skills. "His score on the calculations test is on the positive side of average. Timothy was quick to respond to additions of numerals whose sum did not exceed 5. Beyond that point his computations slowed down. He uses his fingers for all computations. At one point he explained that he can't continue because he did not have enough fingers. He quickly resolved this problem by lining up pumpkin seeds and manipulating them."

Her conclusion unnerved me: "His lack of endurance in the face of complex demands and vague verbal justifications suggest very real difficulty with driving his processing to an explicit, fully conscious and fully analyzed level. His mild fidgetiness, early feeling of frustration and the rapidity with which he fatigued as well as teacher concerns suggest the possibility of attention deficit disorder with hyperactivity as a component of his processing difficulties. The two areas, phonological processing and attention dysfunction aggravate each other. "Timothy has a learning disability. His disability is manifested in reading and writing and appears to be undermining math performance as well." On the basis of Tim's history and this evaluation, I thought that Tim should be referred to special education at once. But the consultant recommended that the school do more testing, including a language evaluation, occupational therapy consultation, and psychological evaluation. In the meantime, she made some suggestions for modifying his program by providing Tim with books on tape, oral testing, and external prompts at all times, and advised that he should have someone read to him from his textbooks.

After this evaluation, Tim was clearly headed in the direction of the special-education system. We all understood this, and Linda and I approved of it for reasons I will explain in the next chapter. For reasons I did not understand, however, the school didn't respond very quickly. It took a full and frustrating year before school officials would implement a plan of action.

three

OUR INTRODUCTION
TO SPECIAL EDUCATION

W HEN THE Education for All Handicapped Children Act (EHA) was enacted in 1975, two of its key
provisions were that all children were entitled to a "free
appropriate public education" in the "least restrictive environment" possible. The EHA was renamed the Individuals
with Disabilities Education Act (IDEA) in 1990, and this
federal law governs special education services to this day. In
addition to requiring that each student with special needs
receive an Individualized Education Program, the IDEA
requires schools to take into consideration a student's disability before imposing disciplinary measures, including
suspensions and expulsions. It also gives parents the right
to participate in the drafting of their children's IEPs and
take school districts to administrative hearings if the two
sides cannot come to an agreement.

The law applies to children with any disability. But
when the regulations implementing it were being drafted

in the late 1970s, policy makers and regulators had a specific picture in mind of the students these regulations would affect. "Paul," a colleague who had been involved in the effort in Washington once told me, "we were thinking of kids in wheelchairs." That was a problem for children like Tim. Children with all kinds of chronic conditions form a pretty big picture, but the policy makers who design services often have only a narrow piece of the painting in mind.

It was one thing to make buildings accessible to children with physical disabilities—and even that took years—but quite another to make regular instructional programs available to children with developmental disabilities or emotional disturbances. Those of us in public office focused a great deal of attention on both of those things. But, like the regulators who wrote the rules, most of us did not even think about what it meant that children with emotional disturbances had the right to a "free appropriate public education." If a child brings a gun to school as a result of a mental illness, does he have the right to remain in his school?

And education in the "least restrictive environment" means what it says. On a continuum, that first means education in regular schools and classrooms among peers without disabilities. If that is inappropriate for the child, then services in regular classrooms with additional supports (such as an aide) might be considered next. If that doesn't work, then the child might be taken out of a regular classroom and educated in a special classroom for part of the day. Next, if the school has one, it might try a special classroom all day. Later on in the continuum, there might be special schools in the mix. But no matter what, the less restrictive environments must be considered first, and the least restrictive environment for that child must be chosen.

Given that children with emotional disturbances—the catch-all term the special educational system uses to describe children with a variety of mental illnesses—are sometimes disruptive in the classroom on account of their illness, how do we protect their right to education in the least restrictive environment, among peers without disabilities, without interfering with the instruction of other students in the classroom? This is not an easy question to answer, especially when the people who wrote the law didn't really have it mind and were not really thinking about the supports and resources these children might need to succeed in school.

After passage of the EHA, many of the "Special School Districts" in which children with disabilities had been receiving their education disappeared as students returned to their community schools. The IDEA requires that students be classified in a category of disability. Some are more specific than others. The categories are autism, blindness, deafness, emotional disturbance, hearing impairment, intellectual disability, multiple disabilities, orthopedic impairment, other health impaired, specific learning disability, speech or language impairment, traumatic brain injury, and visual impairment. When Tim became eligible for special education, more than 12 percent of children in the United States were in special education programs (NCES 2012). More than 40 percent of these children were categorized as having learning disabilities, and nearly two-thirds had either learning disabilities or speech or language impairments. The percentages are similar today. Just over 13 percent of children are in special education; just under 60 percent of them are categorized as having learning disabilities or speech or language impairments.

Most children with mental illness are put in the category "Emotional Disturbance." The number of children in this category who received special education services under IDEA grew from 283,000 in 1976 to 437,000 in 1995, around the time Tim entered special education. It fell back to 389,000—the lowest number in twenty years—by 2011 (NCES 2012). These children made up 1 percent of the school population in 1995, and make up only 0.8 percent today. Yet SAMHSA and NIMH both report that up to one in five children has a mental disorder in any given year, and NIMH reports that as many as 21.4 percent of teenagers have a severe mental disorder (Merikangas et al. 2010). In other words, for every child with an emotional disturbance who is in special education for that reason, roughly twenty more are not. And the discrepancy appears to worsen as children age.

Many parents are reluctant for their children to receive special education services because of what they perceive as a stigma, but I did not feel this way. I believed that Tim needed additional educational supports. I thought that he could benefit if his teachers focused less on his lack of organizational skills and more on mitigating his difficulties with attention, for example, more oral instead of written instruction and evaluation and targeted strategies—such as the possible use of a computer—to accommodate his writing challenges in particular. I also thought his instructional program might be revised to be more hands-on and that he would benefit from guided and supervised teamwork with his peers because of his difficulties in relating to other children.

I also felt that there was some urgency. Whatever services we decided on, the sooner he got them, the better off he would be. I was not worried about the cost; I knew that our school district had to provide appropriate services to Tim at no cost to us. By law, we as parents had to be invited to work with Tim's teachers and the rest of the team to develop his IEP, and because Linda was a special education consultant, we had access to the best advocates and practitioners in the region to help us—an advantage most parents navigating this complex system do not enjoy. Finally, I was knowledgeable about the policy theory behind special education and felt comfortable in my ability to navigate the system. Not only had I served in the legislature, but in the 1990s I also taught special education policy as part of a graduate-level public policy course I developed.

Because they know their child best, parents are equal partners—at least in theory—with teachers, administrators, and other school professionals on the IEP team that drafts the education plan for their child (U.S. Code 2014). To facilitate parent involvement, the federal law requires that every state have at least one "Parent Training and Information Center" (PTI). But the truth is that educators have a tremendous home-court advantage when the team sits down to meet. The team schedules the meetings, chooses the location, prepares the agendas, and conducts the evaluations that define the issues to be discussed.

They know the teaching environment, the jargon, and what resources they have at their disposal. And they usually outnumber the parents.

In Connecticut, the IEP team meeting was called the Planning and Placement Team (PPT) meeting. I attended my first PPT meeting for Tim in February 1993. I attended dozens more in the years that followed, and I learned from my own experiences many things about the practical limitations of PPTs that policy leaders did not anticipate. (I am sure others could add to this list.)

First, our PPT meetings were never long enough—especially if parents brought any of their own ideas to the table. The meetings were often shoehorned into the beginning or end of the school day to minimize intrusions into classroom time. They were also sometimes slotted into time periods of only fifteen or thirty minutes. Participants would often hurry through the meetings, with little time for discussion and debate. This invariably led to problems with plan implementation later on, which in turn required more hurried PPT meetings.

Second, every one of our meetings began with a review of our son's educational progress. These status reports could take up most of the time allotted. Then we would have to reconvene to discuss the goals, objectives, and modifications to be included in his IEP. This was especially frustrating for me, because whenever we reconvened we would have to start again with the progress reports.

Third, because of the way the law was written and interpreted, the plans always spelled out goals and objectives for the child but never for the teachers or parents. For example, an objective might state: "Tim will complete 70 percent of his work on time." This made Tim the only person accountable for meeting the objective. If he completed only 50 percent of his work on time, then Tim alone was responsible for the failure. I always thought it would be better to restate objectives to shift the burden. For example: "Tim's parents will monitor his homework to assure that he completes 70 percent of his homework on time." But when I asked for this kind of statement, I was told it wasn't done that way; goals were for the children. That may be the law, but this lack of adult accountability for the achievement of IEP goals and objectives was my greatest frustration with the process when Tim fell short of his goals.

Fourth, in most cases, the school officials already knew what modifications they wanted to make before the PPT meeting began. Discussion was superfluous. Whenever I suggested a modification to Tim's IEP, I found that if it fit into the framework the school personnel already had in mind, it was accepted at once. If it did not, I usually got back a blank stare or at best an offer to look into it later.

Fifth, money mattered. In theory, the federal government reimburses school districts for the costs of special education based on the assumption that it costs 40 percent more to educate a special education student. But the program isn't fully funded. The federal government budgeted $12.6 billion for IDEA in fiscal year 2012—about half of what advocates claim is needed, according to the Federal Education Budget Project (2013). The balance is picked up by the states and the local school districts. So while decisions about special education services are supposed to be made without regard to local funding constraints, the opposite is often true. The greater the cost of the service, the more likely a decision about it will be deferred. This means that another PPT meeting has to be scheduled, which in turn means more delay in developing an IEP.

Our first PPT meeting should have resulted in some action. After all, Tim's teachers had been documenting their concerns for over two years. We already had Dr. R's recommendations and could have acted on some or all of those. But this is not what happened.

First, we reviewed Tim's progress reports. Then the PPT formally accepted Dr. R's report. Next we agreed to have the school's reading consultant, occupational therapist, and psychologist conduct additional evaluations.

When Linda and I also requested an assistive technology evaluation to determine whether using a computer or other technology might help Tim, the principal said that the school could not make a decision about this until after the other three evaluations were completed. Then

she adjourned the meeting before we could ask for a behavioral evaluation, too—something else that had been on our list.

So despite having teacher observations spanning more than two
years, our experiences in parenting, and a formal evaluation from Dr.
R to guide us, all we had accomplished was delay. It was the first of
many delays to come.

And we still had some unanswered questions. Tim had what appeared to be learning disabilities, but which ones, and how significant
were they? According to Dr. R's evaluation, Tim had "attention dysfunction," but how much did this contribute to his poor mastery of
subject matter? He also had some behavioral issues. Were these related
to a bigger behavioral health problem or not?

The school's three consultants were supposed to help us find answers. They took about a month to do their work. The reading consultant weighed in first, informing us that, surprisingly, "Timothy is
in the average range for all the standardized tests he has been given."
In fact, Tim always tested in the average range in ability, although his
scores on oral IQ testing were considerably higher than his scores on
written tests. The discrepancy helped to identify him as having a learning disability, but that was a double-edged sword. Because it seemed
to account for so much of his poor academic performance, it diverted
attention away from his illness.

The school psychologist's report came next, confirming Dr. R's observation that Tim's attention issues were significant. "Timothy was on
task less than 15% of the time, in short spans of 1 to 30 seconds," she
wrote.

However, she also found, somewhat paradoxically, that Tim engaged
easily in classroom discussion. "The teacher then encouraged the class
to generate a list of many varied and unusual things one could be an
expert at. Tim's facial expression showed more interest in this, as he
turned to watch the children who were speaking. Near the end of this
discussion, he raised his hand and offered the suggestion that he could
be an expert at making people laugh. The children did in fact laugh
at this and the teacher remarked good-naturedly that it must be true."

The occupational therapist weighed in last. She wrote that some of Tim's fine-motor problems would resolve themselves: "I feel that cursive handwriting will help Tim to gain speed in his writing. At this point, I do not see the need for me to do anything further with him." But then she also recommended that Tim have the assistive technology evaluation we requested to help the school devise "a game approach to keyboarding" as part of Tim's educational program modification.

What made me unhappy about these evaluations is that they did not really go far enough to justify waiting for educational modifications. They did not offer any evaluation of Tim's behavioral issues, even though these seemed to be contributing to most of his difficulties. So Linda and I asked for an evaluation by a pediatric neurologist to rule out any physical causes for Tim's problems. Our thinking was that we might seek a psychiatric evaluation after that.

The principal put us off for a couple of weeks. We repeated our request in writing and pushed for an April deadline to complete the evaluations. Two more weeks went by, and then the principal notified us that instead of asking for the additional evaluations she was scheduling another PPT meeting in May to review the evaluation findings to date.

At this meeting, I once again sat through the mandatory reports of Tim's progress in the classroom. His reading, math computation, and "modified" spelling (his phonetic spelling was acceptable for the time being) were all satisfactory. His word decoding, mastery of math facts, and written expression, however, were not. His teacher also confirmed the observations of the consultants: "He is friendly with one boy in class, but is a loner much of the time."

We formally accepted the reports of the three school consultants, adding them to Dr. R's report, and then officially concluded that Tim had "one or more" learning disabilities. The record described him as having "great difficulty expressing ideas in writing, trouble staying focused," "being 'inattentive," and requiring "a lot of extra prompting."

We finally got around to setting educational goals for Tim. These included increasing positive participation in social and academic activities, increasing self-reliant behavior, and increasing self-esteem. I was a little surprised by these, because they seemed generic and did not have much to do with the evaluations we had just accepted. We then approved ten educational objectives, among them "Tim will advocate appropriately for himself," "Tim will volunteer information when appropriate," and "Tim will increase self-esteem." These did not seem to have anything to do with the four evaluations in our possession.

Other objectives were at least targeted to Tim's education, if not to the specific points in the evaluations. These included "Tim will complete modified math assignments," "Tim will use an independent work organizer," and "Tim will ask when he needs an extra copy of an assignment."

Given the problems the school had documented, I asked whether these were the most relevant objectives for Tim and whether his progress in meeting them could even be measured. They were the first objectives I had ever seen, and the first thing I noticed was that they were worded in a way that put the burden on eight-year-old Tim, not on his educators or parents. So I brought this up, and I was informed that I did not know how to write objectives.

Perhaps as a concession, everyone finally agreed to something for the adults. We added a requirement for a "consistent system for homework between home and school," and a "daily notebook between home and school."

Finally, we agreed unanimously on a specific set of modifications and instructional accommodations. These included consumable textbooks, modifications in the amount of homework, and classroom seating near the teacher. Tim was also to be given fifteen minutes of unspecified direct special education services per day in the classroom.

There were still a couple of missing pieces: the assistive technology evaluation and the evaluation by a pediatric neurologist. Because of Dr. R's finding of "attention dysfunction," Tim's pediatrician had also recommended that we not wait for the pediatric neurologist's evaluation to try auditory integration training with Tim, a technique that seemed promising at the time, which involved using filtered music to mitigate the effects of ADD and improve concentration in children without the use of drugs. Linda and I asked the team to recommend all three. The principal replied that the PPT was not authorized to incur these expenditures without the prior consent of the school district. So we decided to move forward with the evaluation by the pediatric neurologist and pay for it ourselves.

Although we signed off on Tim's IEP in May, none of the modifications or accommodations required by it was put in place that school year. Meanwhile, Tim was paying the price. His academic performance, which the school's teachers and evaluators had reported to be satisfactory as recently as March, had fallen off so dramatically during the spring that he was no longer testing at grade level in reading, language arts, or math. Linda and I wrote to the principal in June expressing our concern about this and asking that the PPT be reconvened to address the inaction.

Despite his difficulties at school, Tim was still a generally happy and delightful boy toward the end of second grade. He completed a project titled "Tim's Times," for which he created a poster of pictures and narration to describe his life and aspirations. This was what he dictated:

> Allow me to introduce myself. I am very proud to be a second grade student. I have a dog named Peggy. I am a boy and I have black hair and brown skin. My name is Timothy James Gionfriddo.
>
> The most important person in my life is my dad. My dad is my best friend. My dad is a good worker. He is a consultant. My dad is very special to me.
>
> I am an expert at making people laugh. I can look at them and make a funny face. Sometimes I just look at people and they laugh. It is easy to make friends laugh. I am very good at making people laugh.
>
> Let's look into my crystal ball. In my future I will be a basketball star. I will be very famous. I will be very good at making shots. Now you know about my future as a basketball star.

Tim's self-esteem was about to change when he advanced to the third grade. After what would become another year without an IEP in place, his only aspiration would be to be the "school bully."

That summer Tim had his appointment with the pediatric neurolo
gist. She agreed that Tim had a language-based learning disability and
also suggested a trial of Ritalin to manage his attention dysfunction,
which she diagnosed as attention deficit disorder (now, ADHD). She
recommended that she conduct a follow-up examination of Tim in the
fall — something that we very much wanted the school district and PPT
to endorse.

Linda and I had mixed feelings about the use of Ritalin. I knew that
while it might help him focus, he had more problems than just lack of
concentration. We still hadn't sorted out the reasons for Tim's behavioral problems, and I wasn't sure that I wanted him on any medication
before we did. Finally, we really wanted to try the auditory integration
training Tim's pediatrician had suggested to see if we could avoid medication entirely. So we decided to put off the Ritalin for a while.

According to the National Center for Health Statistics (NCHS
2012), the reported prevalence of ADD/ADHD around the time Tim
was diagnosed was 7 percent; it has grown to 9 percent in recent years.
In the late 1980s less than 1 percent of children used drugs like Ritalin
to manage ADD/ADHD, a proportion that grew to 3 percent in the
late 1990s and almost 4 percent by 2010. These rates create controversy
today, and they created controversy then. It boils down to this: Are children overdiagnosed? Are children overmedicated? And can the side
effects from treatment mask or mimic the symptoms of mental illness?

The principal eventually denied our June request for a PPT meeting
during the summer but made a commitment to convene a "program
review" with Tim's third-grade teacher in late August.

But when the school year started, the principal had not yet scheduled the meeting with Tim's teacher. More troubling, Tim's IEP was
also not being implemented. There were no consumable textbooks;
instead, he was sent home with an assignment requiring him to copy
math problems from a textbook. There was also no daily notebook from
school to home. I started my own the next day. I wrote in it that copying was a problem for Tim and it hindered his ability to work on actual skills. When his teacher replied the next day, it was clear that she
missed the point. "At this point of the year, copying numbers would

have been good practice for him. I never know just how much someone forgets over the summer."

Her response, although seemingly innocuous, suggested that she
had not read Tim's IEP. In her defense, she was only doing what most
of Tim's well-intentioned new teachers would do. At the beginning of
the year, they tried not to be biased by what might have happened the
year before, but sought to form their own impressions of their new students. "I'm just getting to know him" and "I'm treating him like every
other student" were comments I often heard. The problem was that the
new teacher's impression was supposed to be biased by Tim's IEP and
by what had happened in the past. Neglecting Tim's plan invariably
undermined his opportunity for success.

Tim generally did pretty well at the start of the year. He had two
strengths—an excellent memory for what he had learned the previous
year and a desire to please adults. As his fifth-grade teacher would later
comment: "Tim is my best auditory learner. He remembers nearly everything read to him down to the merest trivial details." Reviewing old
material came fairly easily to him. New material did not. So the first
days and weeks went well. But as soon as teachers began introducing
new material, his performance would fall off. Teachers often attributed
this to a lack of effort on his part. By the time they figured out that
he was doing the best he could (some never did figure this out), we
were well into the fall, he was behind academically, his motivation was
gone, his IEP was out-of-date, and he was pretty much lost for the year.
Tim's third-grade teacher just lost him sooner than most.

Three days after the math-copying assignment, Tim failed to bring
home his homework folder. His IEP included a requirement that he be
reminded to do this every day, and the teacher acknowledged that she
hadn't given him the reminder. She said she didn't think she should
have to remind a normal eight-year-old about this. That might be true,
but Tim was not a normal eight-year-old.

I went to the principal and urged her to schedule the promised
program-review meeting as soon as possible. The principal seemed a
little put off by my insistence. She scheduled the meeting for two days

later, on a date she knew I would be out of town. Linda attended, but I had to put my thoughts in writing. I expressed my concerns about the delays in developing and implementing Tim's IEP.

The principal wrote back to me after the meeting, offering a brand-new interpretation of Tim's IEP. She told me that the school's position was that Tim's goals and objectives were in place from the prior year but not the modifications and accommodations to which they had agreed at the same time. This meant no consumable textbooks, no homework modifications, no small-group reading, and no reminders about his assignments. It got worse. Tim's third-grade teacher didn't like the idea of Tim eating his snack and lunch at snack time, so she wanted that issue back on the table, too.

As upset as I was about what the principal's reply would mean for Tim, I realized that it made the situation worse for her and the school, too. It suggested that she considered Tim's IEP to be incomplete months after Tim was legally entitled to special education services. In other words, he was not yet receiving the individualized services he needed in order to succeed.

To appease me, the principal assured me that within a week Linda and I would receive a copy of a new set of instructional modifications that were being implemented in the classroom. The fact that the PPT hadn't developed or agreed to these didn't seem to bother her. She also promised to schedule another program-review meeting and to "look into" an assistive technology evaluation. Then she added that Tim appeared happy in school. He was not. Within a few weeks, Tim's teacher, playground and cafeteria monitors, and principal were all complaining about his disagreeable behavior. I wasn't surprised; his siblings were complaining about his behavior all the time, too.

I received the list of new "modifications" a week later. They were written on a plain white sheet of paper and appeared to be in draft form. It wasn't clear who had written them or whether they had been approved by anyone. Contrary to what the principal had told me, it also wasn't clear that they were being implemented in the classroom. The list included giving Tim fewer spelling words each week, fewer examples in

English, and fewer examples in math. It also included allowing him to use a calculator for math and provided for him to use a homework folder, task sheet, and extra paper. One modification called for him to sit "in the mainstream of the class," whatever that meant. On the other hand, consumable texts (which, I learned, the school had apparently forgotten to order), the lunch period modifications, and the teacher's responsibility to check Tim's homework folder, all of which were in his May IEP, had disappeared. So, too, had the requirement that Tim's teacher have daily journal communication with us, his parents.

To give us a chance to respond, the principal scheduled another PPT meeting in October. As usual, it began with progress reports. Tim's special education teacher, who according to Tim's IEP spent fifteen minutes per day in the classroom with him, reported that "although Tim appears to be doing well he is still having some organizational difficulties." His regular teacher's contribution was in part to wonder why Tim was using a Trapper Keeper binder to keep his papers organized as opposed to a regular loose-leaf binder.

Then Linda asked for the school district to pay for the second appointment with the pediatric neurologist so she could observe Tim in school. The principal said that she did not have the authority to agree to this and that Linda should make the request directly to the district's central office. Incredibly, the principal and teachers then announced that they were out of time and adjourned the meeting. As we left, the principal told us off the record that although the modifications and accommodations—which we didn't get a chance to discuss at the meeting—were still officially only in draft form, she intended to implement them immediately.

Two weeks later, I learned that even this had not happened. Tim's teacher graded him on a full set of spelling words the class received that week, not the "short list" in the school's modification to Tim's plan. Linda wrote to Tim's teacher asking that she either adhere to the modifications as they were drafted or request that the PPT be reconvened to come up with new ones.

Meanwhile, the school district agreed to our request to have the pediatric neurologist observe Tim in the classroom. She observed that "Tim always appears to be a step behind the other children."

While we were trying to use the pediatric neurologist's evaluation to understand whether Tim's behavioral difficulties were related to a potentially serious mental illness, I was surprised to learn that Tim's teacher had thought it was important to ask the pediatric neurologist to weigh in on the lunch controversy. The principal reported to us that the neurologist "suggested that Tim bring two bags to school in the morning. One for snack and one for lunch. Tim is a vegetarian so does not eat many of the school lunches." As if we did not know that Tim was a vegetarian—our whole family was!

But I began to understand why the teacher was focused on something as trivial as lunch. It was because the rules were much clearer at lunch than they were during the rest of the school day. Lunch period was brief and incorporated a single task. Presumably, anyone could master these rules there if he tried. And if Tim could not, then it wasn't because of the rules; it was because of the changes we made to the rules. If only Tim would follow the rules, then all of his problems would disappear.

In mid-December, I also received a detention notice for Tim in the mail. I was surprised by this because neither the principal nor the teacher had said anything about it in all of our recent conversations. The notice informed me that Tim's detention was because of an unspecified "third" conduct violation. I contacted both his teacher and the principal to figure out what this third violation was, as well as what numbers one and two were.

I learned that Tim was bothering other children in the cafeteria and that the disturbances had spilled over into the recess period after lunch. The cafeteria and playground monitors wrote up Tim's conduct violations. His first had been for teasing a girl, but I couldn't get the details of the second and third, other than that it appeared he had started to bully other children. Tim's bullying behavior was a problem at home, too. Linda and I began to wonder if a formal behavior modification plan might need to be a part of Tim's IEP.

Not that Tim had an IEP yet. We were halfway through third grade and the process was stalled. Applying various deadlines under the law, even allowing for adjustments for evaluations on top of other evaluations, it should have taken no more than three or four months at the most, not counting summer months, for a referral to special education to result in special education services. But every new evaluation could also trigger a new sixty-day clock for updating a program. But in our case, the initial program had not yet been implemented. So while our experience was theoretically unusual, it probably was not as uncommon as it felt.

In Tim's case, the educational evaluations the school had commissioned in the spring were unused and outdated. The assistive technology consultation requested by the occupational therapist had not been ordered. Except for the "two bags for lunch" recommendation, the pediatric neurologist's report was also already beginning to gather dust. It was thirteen months after Dr. R's evaluation, and we still had no formal modifications in place. So we asked the school to hire an independent consultant, which was our right under the law, to help implement Tim's IEP.

It was only after Tim's attention, academic, and behavior problems took another turn for the worse that we even got a response to this request. In the first week of January, Tim's teacher reported that Tim was not paying attention to her anymore. He "was sprawled on his desk" during class and "was fidgety during group." She also expressed her concerns about Tim's difficulty in reading. She said point-blank that she disagreed with the evaluations suggesting that Tim's difficulties were related to a possible learning disability; she felt that Tim's problem was rooted simply in inattention. We sat with her at a meeting completely on the defensive, despite the fact that we were two concerned and involved parents with a great deal of expertise in special education policy and services and armed with multiple expert evaluations. We left confused, having resolved nothing.

That month went poorly for Tim. One day his recorder didn't come home with him, and he was unable to do his music homework. He had forgotten it in school and no one had noticed. Another day he came home without his coat, something that also might have been noticed as it was the middle of winter. He stopped bringing his homework home, although his teacher was still supposed to be checking for this each day before he left school. He got a low grade on a science test, the one subject in which he had been doing well.

Tim also became more aggressive with his siblings. He took toys from them and insisted that they do whatever he wanted to do. While eight-year-old Larissa pushed back, four-year-old Lizzie and three-year-old Ben either steered clear of Tim or did whatever he asked. To help him burn off some steam, we started Tim in a judo program at the local YMCA. He was very engaged at first and quickly advanced. But when he had to focus on technique and discipline, he began to tune out. The praise he had been receiving from his instructor became critique and then criticism, and after a few months Tim dropped out.

In late January, Tim really got his teacher's attention. He was playing with a Game Boy in class, and she confiscated it. We were surprised to hear this, because Tim didn't own a Game Boy. When we confronted him, he admitted that he had stolen it from another boy in school. We scolded him and told him that we expected him to tell the teacher so she could return it to the boy. A couple of days later, we found the Game Boy in Tim's book bag. He admitted that he had taken it back from the teacher's desk that day. He acknowledged that this was wrong but didn't seem to care. The idea that Tim was stealing things from other children and the teacher was especially unnerving to me. I was worried that this and his newfound aggressiveness meant that his behavioral issues were getting lost in the arguments over his academic and organizational problems. And I still desperately wanted to know what was causing all of this, because I had no idea at the time and was tired of guessing.

The principal finally scheduled a meeting in early February, but just to discuss the pediatric neurologist's evaluation and recommendations.

It was too little, too late. The neurologist's full report had been available to the school for almost two months. She had again found Tim to have learning disabilities, "severe problems with executive functions," and a component of ADHD contributing to his distractibility. She wrote in her report to the school district: "Timothy is not intentionally poorly motivated. In any child with school difficulties, maintaining good self-esteem is essential. This should be accomplished by highlighting those skills that he excels at. Timothy's strengths should be stressed to him (and to the rest of the class)."

This is where we were. It was over fourteen months since Dr. R had conducted her evaluation. Tim had an unimplemented IEP, from which all the original modifications and accommodations had been removed. He had a set of informal "modifications" that were sometimes followed and sometime not. In addition to his academic, organizational, and attention problems, he had developed new aggressive and antisocial behaviors. But help did not appear to be on the way.

We decided that it was time for a due process hearing.

Policy makers intended the special education process to be responsive to a child's needs and a parent's perspective. For those times when a parent believes it is not, he or she can request mediation—a less formal step—or a due process hearing (called an impartial hearing in the IDEA) —a formal administrative procedure to resolve conflicts between parents and school districts over special education programs and services. Parents can request a due process hearing, for example, if they believe that the district is not implementing their child's IEP, not providing educational services in the least restrictive environment, or not providing the services—even clinical services—the parents believe are necessary to meet their child's educational needs.

What constitutes an "adequate education," the "least restrictive environment," and an "appropriate" service, for example, is open to interpretation. So it is not surprising that parents and school districts sometimes end up in disputes.

A due process hearing is by its nature adversarial. A hearing officer listens to sworn testimony provided by both sides. Any documents either side brings to the hearing that are admitted are marked and labeled as exhibits. To protect everyone's legal rights, lawyers are usually present. The process can be expensive and time-consuming, depending on the complexity of the case and the schedules of the hearing officer, parents, teachers, administrators, lawyers, and witnesses. The hearing officer issues a formal finding some time after the conclusion of the hearing, and it is binding on the parties. The parties then have to agree on how to implement the finding. Unless the hearing officer has been very specific, this agreement can be difficult to achieve, and even a "binding" agreement can fall apart.

I hate due process hearings and think they should be avoided if at all possible. One reason parents choose not to go to due process is that from the time they file their child's program is basically frozen in place. This is called "stay put." If, as the parents contend, the program isn't working, then it continues not to work until the hearing process is concluded. So they are far better off exhausting all other remedies first.

Due process hearings can also be expensive. Parents are entitled to hire and pay for their own independent consultants and their own lawyer to challenge the district. If the parents lose, they can be out thousands of dollars in consultant and legal fees. If the parents win, then the district has to pay the parents' legal and consultant fees as well as its own, plus whatever it costs to implement the new program and to provide compensatory educational services to make up for lost time. This makes due process hearings a high-stakes game for both sides—one that can interfere mightily with what should be from the start a cooperative and collaborative relationship between the parties.

We had three independent reasons for requesting a due process hearing when Tim was in the third grade. In our view, the school had failed to implement Tim's IEP, failed to provide supports adequate to his diagnosis, and failed to engage an independent consultant to help the school develop his program. We believed our case was strong. Fortunately, so did the district's lawyer; we were offered a settlement a week before the hearing. Without admitting that Tim's IEP was inadequate, the district agreed to pay for auditory integration training, an independent educational consultant to monitor the implementation of Tim's IEP, and an assistive technology consultation.

In essence, we had to request a hearing just to get the district to agree to do the evaluations we had been requesting for the past year. This still didn't guarantee that we would get an appropriate program in place afterward. And we did not.

The hearing officer entered an order in support of our position on February 16, in plenty of time to get the three new pieces completed, and a new IEP written and implemented, by the end of the school year. The school hired an independent educational consultant almost immediately and she observed Tim twice in March, as his bullying behavior in school escalated. He was written up twice that month, once for bothering another student at story time and once for intentionally bumping into another student.

The pediatric neurologist started Tim on Ritalin on March 19. Linda and I had resisted this recommendation for some time, hoping that the auditory integration training would result in the same outcome. It hadn't done any harm, but it hadn't seemed to do much good, either. We eventually agreed to try the medication because school staff together felt it might improve Tim's attention and performance, and we were trying to be cooperative in the aftermath of the hearing. It turned out that neither Tim's teacher nor we could see any difference in his behavior, attention, or focus when he was on Ritalin. The reason, as we would discover later, was that ADHD wasn't really his problem.

We emerged from yet another PPT meeting in March with a new set of goals for Tim that covered his full educational program: to improve language arts skills, reading skills, math skills, social skills, self-management skills, and self-esteem. These goals were heavily influenced by the independent consultant's work. We adjourned without any objectives or modifications in place, deferring these to yet another meeting, scheduled for the first week in April.

The April meeting resulted in some very complex and detailed objectives that we felt were unworkable. For example, to assist Tim with organizational and social integration skills, he was to follow a structured, monitored, and assisted routine in the morning and afternoon to pack and unpack his book bag. He was to have appropriate behavior on the playground 60 percent of the time. He was to invite or be invited to a friend's house. In the area of academics, he was to read two chapter books independently, spell five new words per week, participate in whole class decoding and spelling activities, and use a typing teaching program on the computer, among other things.

He had a new behavior modification plan that was equally complex. For example : "Tim will participate in a behavior modification program while on the playground. Recess will be divided into 2 parts. He will earn a good behavior coupon. If he has 1/2 good recess he can earn 1/2 a coupon or one coupon if the entire recess is good. The playground monitor will closely watch Tim, redirect him, give positive feedback, get him involved in structured activities as needed."

That was only the beginning: "The criteria for having a good week on the playground will change as time goes on. To begin, if Tim earns a total of 2 full coupons, he will spend his 20 minute extra Friday recess doing an appropriate activity of Tim's choice. Tim can invite 1 or 3 friends to join in his special time. Tim may save earned coupons to earn bonuses once he has reached the criteria for that week." I was certain that the school would not be able to implement this behavior modification plan.

His instructional modifications and accommodations were no less complex. For example, the following eight steps modified his spelling lesson each week. First, Tim would use words from linguistic word family lists, not the usual lists other students were using. Second, the list would be coordinated by the school with a tutor we had engaged.

Third, the list would be coordinated whenever possible with academic subject matter. Fourth, a pre-test would be given to determine the number of new words for Tim. Fifth, Tim would start with twenty words, ten of which would be simple, ten of which would be difficult. Sixth, there was a ceiling of no more than five misspelled words on the pre-test. Seventh, both the pre-test and the post-test would be given to Tim orally, and the teacher would type on the computer as Tim spelled. A second column would be created on the computer to show corrections. Eighth, and last, attending to task would be monitored during the spelling test.

There were seven more sets of instructional modifications after this one!

The school seemed committed to carrying out all of these, but Linda and I wrote to the independent consultant a week later to tell her that they needed to be simplified. In fact, the playground plan fell apart the morning after it was adopted.

A small group of boys was playing football, and they invited Tim to join them. He went happily, a major step for a young man who had been having trouble making friends throughout the year. Tim lined up on defense, the ball was hiked, and the quarterback threw a pass to the receiver. Tim and another of his teammates tackled the receiver to the ground. Tackling wasn't permitted, so the playground monitor called to the boys to stop. Whether or not they heard, the ball was hiked again and Tim tackled the quarterback a second time. The monitor told Tim he was writing him up because Tim had continued to play after being told to stop.

Tim realized instantly that, given the new playground plan, his first reward was pretty much up in smoke. With no incentive to be good, he continued to bother other children at lunch. A few days later, he was written up again for another playground incident, and two weeks after that he was written up a third time after being caught twisting another boy's arm in gym class. He received another detention, and that was when he told me that he just wanted to be the "school bully."

His behavior began to worsen in every setting. Even his Sunday School teacher reported that he was talking a lot and fooling around in class. She observed that "Tim likes to draw pictures of violence while the rest of the class is drawing more holy pictures." I could only imagine what his pictures looked like. After evaluations from multiple consultants and clinicians over the past couple of years, I found myself with lots of strategies to try, but no closer to understanding what was wrong with Tim.

During the remainder of the school year, Tim's IEP proved too complex for the school to implement, as we had known it would. In April, Tim's assistive technology evaluation resulted in a recommendation that Tim be provided with a classroom computer and the training to use it. Because his keyboarding skills were weak, the consultant also recommended software that would minimize his use of the keyboard. The district agreed to provide a computer for Tim, but not until the start of fourth grade.

We and the school spent the rest of the school year documenting what was and was not happening and whether what was happening was consistent with the IEP. As we and the school went back and forth, Tim was lost in the shuffle. Sometimes he had his homework at night, sometimes he didn't. Sometimes he played well with others in school, sometimes he didn't. Sometimes he was attentive in class, but most times he wasn't. I was frustrated, and my frustration reached a boiling point in late May, as we all shuffled along aimlessly toward the end of the school year. It was eighteen months after Dr. R's evaluation, an educational lifetime. It had taken four years for Tim to get an IEP, even one that did not work, during which time his achievement levels had declined, his attention problems had worsened, and some serious behavioral concerns had emerged. But I was worried that I hadn't seen the worst yet.

And so I was very pleased when I was informed at the end of the school year that we were being redistricted, and that Tim would be spending the next two years at a different elementary school. I looked forward to the summer's rest (if not for Tim then for myself), and a new start.

But Tim and I both still had plenty of cause for concern. In May, Tim had met with the school psychologist for an evaluation. "Are you worried about the test?" she asked him. "I worry all the time," he answered. So did I.

four

A NEW SCHOOL,
A NEW CRISIS

I STEELED MYSELF for a meeting with Tim's principal, special education teacher, and classroom teacher at his new elementary school in late August. But this principal was a special education expert, and the meeting could not have been more different from the ones to which I had become accustomed. Everyone from the school was knowledgeable about Tim's IEP and was on the same page. His IEP was in place. The computer was in his classroom, and someone would train Tim to use it. An aide was assigned to Tim's classroom to help meet his needs and the needs of other students in the class. The teachers had identified a classroom "buddy" for Tim to help with his peer relations and to check assignment sheets with Tim at the end of each day. The teachers had read Tim's evaluations and had a list of assignment modifications they believed would play to Tim's auditory strengths while helping him overcome or minimize his writing and spelling deficits.

Tim's behavioral issues were in apparent remission that fall. I thought this might be related to the change in environment. In any case, it gave the school time to focus on Tim's academic problems. He was especially weak in writing and spelling, and he had few organizational skills. The school staff implemented the modifications in his IEP, and after a few weeks he seemed better organized and his grades started to improve. He received plenty of well-earned positive reinforcement.

His classroom teacher skillfully picked up on the nuances of praise that were supposed to have been incorporated into Tim's IEP the previous year. In one instance, she wrote him a note praising him for "working hard on being organized." He beamed when he saw it, and the transformation in his attitude in general was striking. He set aside his ambition to be the "school bully" and wrote a paper on kindness. "There are many ways to be kind to people," he wrote. "One way would be to donate money to a homeless shelter. Another way that I would show kindness would be to read a story to a blind person. I would baby-sit for my little brother to be helpful to my mom and dad. I could help my brother or sister with their homework to show that I am thoughtful. One other way I could show that I am a caring person would be to rake leaves in my neighborhood. Those are just a few of the many ways to be kind to other people."

Tim's fourth-grade instructional program also played to his active imagination. In another paper, he described what it would be like if he could talk with animals. "If I am late for school my dog could wake me up. I could plan anything with animals. I could fly with a crow. I would feel like a king, because the animals would be my subjects. It could be a dream come true. I could play with an alligator without him eating me. If the animals could talk our language we would not have so much work, because they could do it for us. I could swim with a seal or jump with a kangaroo. It would be the funnest thing."

Throughout the fall, Tim went happily to school every day. He had no absences and no tardies, and nearly all of his grades were in the B range. In November, Tim's teacher reported that he was making good progress and that she enjoyed having him in her class.

Just as I thought that Tim might be out of the woods, things took a turn for the worse. The students had begun to switch rooms and teachers for certain classes, called "specials." One of the specials was science, Tim's favorite class. The science teacher had not been a part of our earlier meetings, and she did not pay attention to Tim's IEP. She was "old school" and expected her students to conform to her methods of instruction. I even felt there was a dose of cruelty in her approach. One day, in front of the class, she emptied Tim's desk onto the floor and told him to pick everything up and get it all organized again.

At first, I did not know about this incident. All I knew was that in mid-December, Tim was suddenly failing science. Linda and I contacted the teacher directly, but we were unsuccessful in getting her to understand Tim. She said that he should be able to do what was expected of him without a lot of support during the one class for which she had him.

We appealed to the principal, who set up a meeting for all of us. The science teacher reported that Tim was forgetting assignments and materials. It turned out that the "buddy system" was not in place in her classroom. She also noted that Tim's behavior had taken a turn for the worse after the desk-clearing incident; he was throwing spitballs and wandering around the room when he should have been in his seat. Tim's bad behavior was front and center again, but she saw no connection between her actions and his.

The principal worked hard to get things back on track. He encouraged the science teacher to follow Tim's IEP and made sure Tim's classroom aide accompanied him to his science class. With the aide there to run interference, Tim's attitude and grades improved almost immediately, and he did A-level work in science over the next couple of months. Tim also developed a strong interest in current events and did A-level work in social studies as well. The highlight of his year was a class trip to the State Capitol, which I chaperoned. Several people there remembered Tim as a toddler and treated him as a returning celebrity. The clerk of the House of Representatives invited him to serve as the official guest chaplain for that day's technical session of the House.

Tim started wrestling with his identity as a young black man that winter. He had never been terribly interested in his adoption, although we had always been open about it. Until fourth grade, he identified closely with me, and we often joked that we even looked just like each other, drawing incredulous looks from innocent bystanders who weren't in on the joke. For his school picture, he insisted on wearing a jacket and tie, "because that's what Dad wears when he has his picture taken."

As he entered pre-adolescence, however, he began to talk about who he imagined his biological father to be. "I think he was probably a drug dealer," he told me one day. "Not like you." Both Linda and I assured Tim that there was no reason to believe that this was the case. For a brief time, he used Linda's last name (which she had kept when we married) instead of mine on some of his schoolwork. He became a little more distant. None of this alarmed me because I understood that part of growing up was finding one's own identity, but something else did. He was becoming more challenging at home than ever. I thought he might be emulating a friend who was also wrestling with issues of self-identity. This friend was two years older than Tim and always seemed to be in the vicinity when Tim was getting into trouble for bullying his siblings. And whenever I confronted them, I never got a straight answer to a question. Something did not seem quite right with that relationship.

Tim couldn't say why, but his behavior and demeanor suddenly became much worse right around his tenth birthday. His teacher reported that he had stopped concentrating on his work, and his school performance was suffering. His Sunday School teacher expressed similar concerns. At home, he seemed anxious and worried and kept more to himself. We scheduled a meeting with the principal to talk things over and see if he had any insights, but he and Tim's teachers were just as puzzled as we were by this change in behavior.

His science teacher reported in early May that Tim had choked another child in class that day. His classroom teacher added that Tim and the other student "had lots of battles this year." Our brief respite seemed to be over.

At the end of that year Tim would reflect back on fourth grade, on balance, as having been a positive experience. "In fourth grade I had one favorite teacher," he dictated for an assignment. "She was kind of like a teacher's helper who switched from class to class. I think she helped me a lot in the fourth grade. On top of all that, she was nice to everybody. My teacher who I had all the time was nice, too. She worked us a little harder than I think we should have been worked but, other than that, fourth grade was fun."

Tim had come a long way in one year. I was sorry that he had only one more year in that school, with its helpful principal and staff. I thought the next year would be a successful one. When it did not turn out this way, I was at least grateful that he was among adults who clearly cared about him.

I sat at Tim's PPT meeting that August listening to school personnel praise him for his academic progress during the preceding year. Linda and I praised them for their efforts, too, and we agreed to keep his supports in place, including his aide, his daily assignment sheet, and his positive behavioral reinforcements.

Tim had suffered from unexplained episodes of aggressive, antisocial, and oppositional behavior in the spring. We thought he might need therapy, but these episodes disappeared during the family's summer vacations in Virginia and Utah. So we waited, wondering if the problem was in Tim or in his environment, uncertain about what we should do next other than keeping his pediatrician informed until he suggested a referral to a specialist. On some days, it didn't feel as if we were raising Tim so much as managing his growth while waiting for the next shoe to drop. He was a handful, but as I reminded myself constantly, he was also often delightful.

Tim returned to school with enthusiasm, happy that for the first and only time in his life, all three of his siblings would be in the same school as he was. He was growing into his five-foot frame, lean and strong, and he looked more like he belonged in seventh grade than in fifth. He also felt more grown up, and he especially wanted to be a mentor to his brother, Ben. Ben was entering kindergarten and had become Tim's near-constant companion.

Tim took some standardized tests at the beginning of the school year. We all wanted to see where he stood academically in comparison to his peers, so we agreed with his principal and teachers that he would take them like every other student. I didn't expect him to do well because they weren't modified in any way to account for his learning disabilities, but I was still surprised by his low score in math, where he placed in the third percentile. He was in the thirty-fifth percentile in reading and around the middle of the pack in writing. But his spelling was very poor. After getting the results, we met with his new classroom teacher and his special education teacher. We talked over some ideas they had to help Tim.

They proposed sending home some of Tim's spelling words every day instead of all of them once a week, so that we could work with him on spelling in small doses throughout the week. I thought this was a good idea, especially when they added that this would give them the chance to evaluate his spelling daily to look for patterns in his misspelled words. They thought that if they could find some especially problematic letter or sound patterns, they might be able to modify his spelling instruction to help him improve. They thought that this might help his reading as well.

To address his math needs, they offered him a calculator. From the testing, it appeared that he was mastering math concepts but getting wrong answers because he had trouble with simple addition and subtraction. They didn't want addition and subtraction to hold him back as they introduced new math concepts during the year.

Tim was working on the computer regularly but was not developing his keyboarding skills. The principal offered to purchase some new keyboarding software to see if that would help. Dictation software was not reliable enough at that time to be useful.

In my opinion, what distinguished this group of educators was that they were not bound by the rules. Instead, they adjusted their thinking when faced with new challenges. They worked as a team and were unusually skilled, creative, and collaborative in their approach. From my perspective, they did all that they could for Tim. But even their best efforts were not enough. Tim's mental illness was about to present itself dramatically. And we would all see the need to integrate outside clinical treatment with Tim's educational program.

Tim's teacher was still optimistic about his potential after the first marking period. "When Tim does contribute to the class discussion," he wrote on Tim's progress report, "his thoughts are very well-formed. He sounds more like a 7th grader in his reasoning." He added: "Tim has been a welcome student in all areas. He adds much to the class with his knowledge of many diverse topics. His advancement in all areas is continuing, with no real lapses in any area being evident."

But just after we received this report, Tim lost focus again. When redirected he became easily agitated, both at school and at home. He started fighting again with other children in school. He became even more forgetful and was increasingly impulsive, aggressive toward his siblings, depressed, and angry. He began stealing again. When he was caught, he was defiant. He also had trouble sleeping. I found him wandering around the house at all hours of the night, unable to settle down. We talked with his pediatrician, who decided to discontinue Tim's Ritalin for good because he thought it might be contributing to Tim's anxiety. But because we were not averse to trying other or newer medications with Tim, when Tim's focus and concentration worsened again, we looked into other medications and tried Adderall, which had at best a modest effect on his symptoms.

We could see the change in Tim's personality in his own words and deeds. In September, Tim had written about cruelty to animals. His empathy was apparent: "Cruelty to animals is against the law. Because the animals fear pain just [like] you and me. So if you don't feed cows there will be no food. And if you put toxins in the water fish will die. Sometime in the circus they whip lions and they might bite you in the cage. And if a little kid is there he might be traumatized for life at the sight of a grown man getting eaten by a lion. Some animals can tell us about our past like how our ancestors were and stuff like that and if you abuse them they might die. I think abusing animals is bad and I hope you do, too."

Three months later, I was very worried that Tim was losing his empathy. He made a slingshot and aimed it at birds. He tied up our dog and wouldn't let her loose. He hit his siblings when they touched his toys. He continued taking things that didn't belong to him and sometimes damaged them. Small amounts of money went missing from the house and turned up among Tim's possessions.

Tim also began to put some distance between himself and his older neighborhood friend. He would not say why, other than that "he did some bad things." I wondered if this might be related to Tim's new behaviors, but Tim was mum. He just became agitated when Linda or I brought up the subject. When it was clear that Tim wouldn't talk to us, we started searching for a therapist.

We barely got through the holidays. By the time Tim went back to school after the Christmas break, our attention was devoted nearly entirely to his behavioral problems rather than his academic troubles.

In January, after a particularly rough day, Tim gulped down a few ounces of mouthwash. He said that he was trying to get drunk. We called the state poison control center in a panic and were told not to worry but to have him evaluated as soon as we could.

Then we got a call from Tim's teacher saying that he had been misbehaving at school. But when his teacher had tried gently to redirect him, Tim broke down in tears, wailing that he was a bad person and curling up into a fetal position on the floor. He was inconsolable for several minutes, and when he finally calmed down he was afraid to leave his teacher's side for the rest of the day.

We took action immediately. We talked over both incidents with the pediatrician, Tim's teacher, and the principal. We also made an appointment for Tim to have a psychiatric evaluation at a nearby children's hospital. The principal agreed that Tim's mental health problems were affecting his educational performance, and so at the principal's urging the school district agreed to pay for this evaluation and to incorporate the results into his IEP. We also found a psychologist, Dr. D, who agreed to treat Tim.

On the day in mid-February that we took Tim to the hospital for his evaluation, he was especially distressed and unhappy. The specialist who did the evaluation wrote that Tim had "a number of neurobehavioral problems including inattention and impulsivity. In addition, I feel there is also an element of depression and also anger." The specialist decided to put Tim on desipramine, an antidepressant that is also sometimes used to manage symptoms of ADHD. Tim began his therapy with Dr. D right away.

A little more than a week later, Ben accidentally broke Tim's cherished old scooter. The scooter was aged and worn, and barely held together. It broke in two when Ben stepped on it. Tim erupted in uncontrolled anger when he heard the news and yelled that he was going to kill Ben. He stormed into the kitchen and grabbed a knife from the drawer. Linda and I both immediately blocked the door, whereupon he threatened to kill us or himself. It took us several minutes to calm him down and get the knife away from him. For the rest of the night, we kept Ben—who had no idea Tim was after him—away from Tim, and at least one of us stayed close to Tim at all times. After we put Tim to bed, we quietly took all the sharp knives out of our kitchen drawers and locked them away. I was not afraid of Tim, and I did not think that he would use the knives, but I also did not want to take any chances. And I wanted to be sure that our other children were safe in our house.

A few days later, there was an incident on the school bus. Tim started to fight with some other children, and when the driver tried to break it up, Tim was defiant, shouting "You can't make me stop!" The driver reported the incident to the principal, who reported it to us. The next day, Tim accosted Larissa, blasting his boom box in her face to annoy her. She screamed loudly for help, and when Linda and I responded by taking the boom box away from Tim, he tried to hurl himself over the second-floor banister of our house. When we blocked his way, he grabbed a hockey stick from his room and threatened Linda with it. When I took the stick away from him, he started screaming and punching us. We pulled him down to the floor and restrained him for several minutes. At first, he spit on us and threatened to kill us, but finally he calmed down. We helped him back to his feet and cleaned ourselves up. By now, I couldn't wait to get him to his next therapy session and for the promised effects of his new medication to kick in.

As bad as things had become, they were about to get worse. Over the next two weeks, we were in regular contact with a psychiatrist to whom we had been referred and Dr. D. The school scheduled a PPT meeting so we could discuss the psychiatrist's report and decide what we should do next. No one knew what was happening to Tim, but we all agreed that for the time being he needed to be monitored constantly at school and at home. The next day he got into a fight during his after-school program.

I was keeping notes for Dr. D about Tim's behavior. One day we had to keep Tim home from school because he was threatening to cut his sister with one of the dull knives that were still in the kitchen drawer. We took that knife away from him and later locked up all of the dull knives, too. Then Tim pulled a switchblade out of his pocket. We didn't know where he had gotten it, and we locked it up as well. We were exhausted from worry, from trying to anticipate Tim's next move, and from trying to protect our other children. We did our best to hold things together from appointment to appointment, to do our full-time jobs, and to maintain a semblance of normalcy in our household. As our situation worsened, we did not have any respite; we didn't trust Tim with any of our usual sitters.

Our appointment with Dr. D provided no illumination about Tim's condition. Tim was apparently disclosing very little to his therapist. A snow day followed, and Tim and his siblings spent the day in the house. He was testy all day, and none of them would play with him. He finally declared that he was going to run away and charged out of the house into the snow. He then apparently decided it was too cold to run away and came sullenly back in, then headed to his room to listen to music.

The next day we took him to an indoor play space so he could run off some steam. That night at around ten, as I was putting the last of the day's dishes away, Tim came racing through the kitchen on his Rollerblades wearing only underwear and burst out the door into the below-freezing weather to skate down the center of the busy state road on which we lived. I had to call 911 for help. The police found him, unharmed, nearly a mile from home. When they brought him back home, they suggested that we seek therapy for him. I told them we already had.

Tim was clearly out of control. We called the hospital-based specialist who had evaluated Tim three weeks earlier, and he agreed to see Tim immediately. As Linda and I drove up Interstate 91 toward the hospital, Tim tried to jump out of the car. We were barely able to keep him under control and drove straight to the nearest hospital emergency room. He was evaluated there. His desipramine dose was tripled, and he was admitted to the children's unit at a local psychiatric hospital.

Tim's first hospitalization for mental illness lasted from March 10 to March 15, 1996—one week shy of his eleventh birthday. This was the first of what were to be many hospitalizations. I hoped that we would get a handle on his diagnosis and some better clues as to how to manage and treat what we now clearly recognized was a mental illness. It had taken us five years to get to this point—five years caught in a spiral of fits and starts with school IEPs aimed at learning disabilities, five years of family life turning on a dime from calm to chaotic, five years of worry that Tim was getting into way too much trouble for a normal child, five years of increasing concern for the safety and well-being of our other children. Now we would have an answer—and as frightened as I was about what we might be facing with a potentially serious disease, I thought I would now have at least some strategies for how we could all stop spinning in place and move forward again. I also thought that he would leave the hospital with a treatment plan with some clear next steps. I was naive. We may have had a generic diagnosis, "mental illness," but that was a little like coming home from the hospital knowing only that you have "cancer." Which one makes all the difference in your treatment. For us, arriving at a precise diagnosis would take six more years, not six days.

Tim felt deserted by us during his stay in the hospital. And putting him there made me feel as if I had failed him—at least a little—as a parent. Shouldn't I have been able to manage things better, I wondered, and willed him to happiness? Instead, I was confronted by an angry and contrary child during his first day there and went home relieved that he was safe but wondering if our relationship would survive. Fortunately, Tim felt better after a good night's sleep, and so did I. He was taken off the desipramine on the second day, and his condition seemed to improve. He seemed a little more like himself again, and I was hoping that everything would be back to normal in a few days. He attended group therapy sessions the next two days, and on the fifth day he learned that if he signed a behavior contract with us, the hospital would discharge him. So he signed it. The next day, he was deemed stable and was discharged.

As it turned out, the six days of hospitalization for which our insurance company agreed to pay, though generous by the standards of the day, did not give us time even to scratch the surface of his illness. Tim's medication dosage was adjusted, and he was stabilized and sent home. That was pretty much it. The rest we would have to figure out later.

At the hospital, Tim was diagnosed with depression. This was added to the learning disability, ADHD, and executive dysfunction disorder diagnoses he had received in his earlier assessments. His "label list" was starting to grow.

I worried about the use of the behavior contract with Tim. It was one thing to have such a contract if Tim could control his behavior, but he did not seem capable of that in those times of crisis. If his mental illness meant that he couldn't, then a behavior contract was the last thing he needed, since it would only guarantee failure. In hindsight, my worries were unfounded. Tim's mental illness was already so advanced that the contract was simply irrelevant.

Tim left the hospital with a referral to a child psychiatrist and a plan to see Dr. D twice weekly. On our morning trips to Dr. D's office, Tim and I listened to *Imus in the Morning*. Tim found the show hilarious, and the laughter generally put him in a good frame of mind as he started his therapy. Tim never wanted to talk about his sessions afterward, so I didn't pressure him.

One day, Dr. D invited me in after Tim's appointment and told me that Tim had reported hearing voices during the night. The voices were not telling him to do bad things, but they did bother him. While I knew that hearing voices could be a sign of serious mental illness, Dr. D suggested that Tim might be experiencing auditory hallucinations because he was not getting enough sleep. He had spoken with Tim's psychiatrist, and they wanted to start Tim on trazodone, an antidepressant also used off-label to treat sleep disorders. Linda and I agreed to this. Tim began to sleep better at night, and the voices seemed to abate.

At the same time, Tim's principal suggested that we have a once-a-week informal PPT meeting at the school. These meetings generally lasted only fifteen minutes, but they gave us a chance to report on any weekend problems we had had at home, and gave teachers an opportunity to share any concerns they had about the coming week.

Linda and I had only a vague notion of what the underlying cause of Tim's depression might be. His stay in the hospital had yielded no useful information on that front. So we muddled through the best we could. We made a long list of possibilities and shared it with Dr. D: Tim's adoption, his race, having white parents, having parents with strong values (vegetarian, pacifist, environmentally conscious), his cognitive dissonance over being better informed in some ways than his peers but having a difficult time with academics that came easily to them, his learning disability, his ADHD, his social reticence, his sensory hypersensitivity, his craving for intense stimulation, his poor sleep patterns, and his inconsistent eating patterns. In other words, we were searching for anything—no matter how unlikely—that would give us a clue as to what was the matter with Tim.

Tim's principal then asked the school district to commission three more evaluations of Tim. The first was a neurological evaluation by the pediatric neurologist who had examined Tim in the third grade. The second was an educational evaluation by a consultant who was experienced in developing educational plans for children with emotional disturbances. The third was a psychological evaluation by Dr. D.

The education consultant completed her evaluation in May, with recommendations for the staff to implement in late August in the sixth-grade-only school Tim would be attending. She addressed both Tim's educational and his clinical needs. She recommended that the informal weekly Monday meeting be continued. She explained that Tim's combination of learning, emotional, and psychological needs was complex and required ongoing collaboration among educators, therapists, and parents in developing his sixth-grade program. She also recommended the continued use of assistive technology, recognizing that Tim was not yet proficient in using the computer for schoolwork.

She specified several modifications that she believed Tim would need in his educational program for the next year. These included specific, brief assignments on which he could focus; modified homework; the choice of taking tests orally or in writing; and some freedom to move about the classroom during instructional periods. She recommended that Tim continue to have an aide in the classroom and that an informal "circle of friends" be organized to help Tim improve his ability to relate positively to his peers.

She also recommended a program of self-management-skills training for Tim. Because of his poor understanding of cause and effect and his poor response to negative consequences, she advised that he be given a formal method for processing behaviors and their natural consequences. She also recommended that he continue his therapy with Dr. D and that Dr. D's feedback and suggestions be incorporated into Tim's educational plan.

I was grateful that Tim's principal had taken the initiative to commission this evaluation, but he went even further to make it part of Tim's formal plan of instruction by arranging two more meetings before the end of the school year. The first was a meeting for him and us with the principal of the sixth-grade school to talk informally about Tim's needs, to review the recommendations, and to introduce us to the school's program. After the meeting, the new principal was positive and upbeat, and he assured us that Tim would have a smooth transition to his school. However, he also candidly acknowledged that by the rules of his school, some of Tim's behaviors could lead to suspensions. We talked at length about whether suspensions were in Tim's best interest and agreed that they were not because of Tim's significant academic needs and because he did not respond well to negative consequences. We agreed to take this subject up at the meeting scheduled for the following day—a formal PPT meeting to adopt the education consultant's recommendations and develop Tim's IEP for the following year.

Toward the end of the meeting, Linda and I brought up a sensitive subject. We had learned that sixth-, seventh-, and eighth-grade students rode the same bus to school, even though the seventh- and eighth-grade students attended a different school. This meant that Tim would be riding the same bus as an older boy of whom he was afraid. Dr. D was working with Tim on getting him to articulate why he was afraid of this boy, but at the moment we only knew that he was genuinely afraid of being near this boy, so we asked whether the bus routes could be divided up so that the two of them would be on different buses. The principal assured us that he would look into this.

We met the next day for a PPT meeting that included the principals and staff from both schools. Tim's IEP documented his academic progress and spelled out his strengths and weaknesses in detail: "Tim has done satisfactory work in all areas. He does an especially good job when a project interests him. Tim is very well informed in all areas of current events and has much interest in this area. His organization skills are very weak. He needs a lot of structure and assistance in the area. Tim's learning style is through the auditory channel. He has good long-term memory skills."

The IEP also clearly referenced Tim's mental illness, so that there could be no misunderstanding about its effect on his ability to learn. It recorded that "Tim is presently on medication to treat clinical depression and ADD. He attends therapy sessions twice weekly."

It also addressed the issue of suspensions. After everyone agreed that suspensions should not be used for Tim, the phrase "suspension of Tim is not an option" was written into the IEP. The principal agreed to convene another PPT meeting in the fall to develop a behavior support plan.

Though fifth grade had been full of unexplained illnesses and unexpected crises for Tim, he had surprisingly good memories of that year. He wrote the following in June:

> In fifth grade I had two favorite teachers. One was Mr. N and one was Mrs. C. I like Mrs. C because she told me to put away my toys when Mr. N came around so I didn't get in trouble. But, there was always time when I was tempted to take them out again. Mrs. C also was good because she gave us ice cream parties and most of us didn't deserve it. (But not me!) Mr. N I like for a lot of reasons. He helps me on a lot of things and I like how he reads his stories, how he kind of is the character he is reading about. He's a sweet old guy.
>
> Some other people that are pretty good is the secretary and the principal. They don't help me as much but they help me on things that I don't even realize. I think this school is good even though I'm a new kid.

I understood two things as Tim left fifth grade behind. One was that for Tim to succeed in sixth grade, we were likely to need the same level of commitment to his IEP from the sixth-grade staff that we had gotten from the fifth-grade staff. The other was that when problems arose, as it seemed almost inevitable they would, we would need to be creative in developing new strategies to manage both his mental health needs and his educational program. As it turned out, we got neither commitment nor creativity in sixth grade. In fact, the day in June when we agreed on Tim's IEP, two months before he started school, would prove to be the high-water mark of Tim's sixth-grade experience.

And largely because of this, after fifth grade Tim would never have another normal year in school again.

five
SUSPENDED ANIMATION

TIM'S BEHAVIOR IN the summer between fifth and
sixth grades was distracted, disagreeable, and disturbing. His organizational problems were almost comical. He
attended a couple of two-week summer day-camp sessions.
He would leave home in the morning wearing shorts, a
shirt, socks, sneakers, and sometimes a sweatshirt, carrying
a backpack with a bathing suit and towel, and he would
return home in the late afternoon with any combination
of these things missing. He might have on his bathing suit
and a borrowed shirt but be missing his shorts, sweatshirt,
socks, towel, and sometimes even his shoes. The backpack
would also be gone. We recovered some of his belongings
from the lost and found at the end of camp but never saw
most of them again.

Tim's distractibility was a daily problem, but his frequent
disagreeableness was a bigger issue for his counselors. He
refused to follow their rules and directions, stubbornly

ignoring every effort they made—from gentle reminders to denying him privileges to participate in reward activities—to get him to comply.

Most disturbing was his bullying. The Sunday before school began, Tim threatened to hurt Larissa while she was on the phone with a friend. The friend's mother heard Tim make the threat. After the girls hung up, the mother called us back to make sure Larissa was okay. We made Tim apologize to Larissa, her friend, and her friend's mother. Tim apologized as directed but then threatened to hurt me, screaming that he hated me because I made him lie about saying he was sorry. A couple of days later, Linda's mother was babysitting while Linda and I were at work. The children had been swimming in our pool. When Lizzie got out, she found a twenty-dollar bill on the ground. Tim jumped out and tried to get it away from her, but she immediately gave it to Linda's mother to hold. Tim then threatened to hurt Ben if he wasn't given the bill and jumped back in and attempted to hold Ben's head underwater. Linda's mother separated Ben from Tim, but she was still shaking when we arrived home.

The next day was Tim's first day of sixth grade. As he entered that year—especially in light of what had happened during the previous school year and over the summer—I never doubted that Tim needed the significant changes to his IEP that had been approved in June in order to be successful. And I never understood why the principal and staff did not immediately implement that IEP, which had been drafted with their input and agreement and which spelled out his strengths and weaknesses clearly and in detail.

Our first indication that the June meetings might have been forgotten by the start of the year occurred when we examined the bus routes. The principal had said he would try to keep Tim off of the bus with the older boy whom Tim feared. But when the bus routes were published a few days before school began we learned that this had not happened. It was too late to alter the routes, so the principal suggested having all the sixth graders sit at the front of the bus and the older children at the rear. I wasn't happy, but I agreed that this seemed to be the most reasonable accommodation under the circumstances.

Then I asked the principal when he planned to convene the PPT meeting to complete Tim's behavior support plan. The principal had acknowledged in June that Tim's mental illness made regular discipline problematic and had readily agreed to develop such a plan. But now he deflected my questions. He said that if Tim just followed the school rules like everyone else, then everything would be okay. A red flag went up, and I asked him to please schedule the PPT meeting as soon as possible.

Tim's first day of sixth grade was a harbinger of the difficult year to come. Fresh on the heels of the incident in the pool, and worried about the bus rides, he was rattled from the start. The morning was chaotic, but we got him out the door. Then he misplaced his backpack at school and couldn't find it. He made it to his classes but didn't eat lunch because he forgot he had lunch money in his pocket.

To top it off, he arrived home seething because of an incident on the bus. Instead of dividing all the sixth graders from the older students, the bus driver had singled out Tim and directed him to sit behind the driver's seat. Even worse, the bus driver told Tim that his parents had asked him to do this. The other children teased Tim and he was embarrassed. When he got home he charged into his room, emerging a minute later with a drumstick and a belt, and threatened Linda with them if she did not get out of his way. When she got him back into his room she discovered that he had ripped the screen off the window and broken a switch plate. We had no idea what had precipitated this behavior until we finally calmed him down and got the story about the bus out of him.

The next morning, I waited for the bus with Tim and explained to the bus driver that we had not asked for Tim to be singled out; rather, the principal had promised that all of the sixth graders were to be separated from the older students on the bus. The bus driver complained that he could not be expected to do this on his own without the help of an aide. So Linda and I made a formal request that one be assigned. The school district turned us down.

Tim did not have his behavior support plan in place when the school year began, and he also did not have an IEP that the school thought it needed to follow. Tim's instructional modifications and classroom supports were once again put on hold as his teachers "got to know" him. Linda and I made repeated requests to the school to implement Tim's IEP and to create a behavior support plan to add to it, but we got nowhere. Several weeks passed before the principal finally scheduled a PPT meeting, in early October.

As usual, the PPT began with reports on Tim's progress. We heard mostly complaints from his teachers—no wonder to us, in the absence of the modifications and accommodations for which his IEP called. After making these reports, the teachers had to leave to get back to their classes, so the meeting was adjourned before we even got to the IEP modifications or behavior plan.

The principal reconvened the meeting the following week. I took some more time off from work. I listened to the same progress updates. Once again, these took so much time that we hadn't made any headway on instructional or behavior modifications when it was time to adjourn. We were given a date in November for yet another meeting.

Impatient with the lack of progress, we asked to meet informally with Tim's teachers to try to get some of the pieces of the IEP and a draft behavior support plan in place. In the meantime, everything that cost time or money, such as the classroom aide, was on hold. In addition, Dr. D had been willing since June to offer his expertise to the staff and had said so, but no one from the school had even tried to get in touch with him. On the instructional side, the computer that Tim needed was sitting idle in one of his classrooms. I mentioned this to his teacher. "He doesn't use it," she commented. "Are you showing him how to do the lessons on it?" I asked. "I don't know how to turn it on," she replied.

Throughout these weeks, the principal held to his view that if Tim just followed the rules, everything would be fine. Meanwhile, the few teachers who did take the time to make suggestions were often simply uninformed about Tim's needs and deficits. Two of them suggested that Tim try an AlphaSmart Pro keyboarding device because he wasn't using the computer in his classroom. I pointed out that Tim didn't yet know how to use a keyboard properly; he was still at the point and click level. The school ordered the AlphaSmart Pro anyway. Tim never used it, but the teachers seemed to enjoy it when they gave me a demonstration the next week.

Maybe the teachers thought we should teach Tim to type at home. But this was impossible because on any given night we had our hands full just managing his behavior. We also had three other children who had activities and schoolwork of their own. They were often confused and overwhelmed by all the attention we gave to Tim. They needed whatever time we could spare for them and whatever sense of normalcy we could create for them. If we did have a few quiet moments each night, the other children were entitled to them.

But most of the time we were also fighting battles on behalf of Tim that we should not have had to fight. For example, my health insurance company was not paying for Tim's therapy, even though it had pre-authorized Dr. D's services the previous March. It turned out that the address Dr. D was submitting his invoices to—the one on the insurance form—was incorrect. Then the company representative told me that only two visits had been approved, even though Tim had been seeing Dr. D regularly for more than six months.

Dr. D was told he needed to submit a "continuation therapy" plan along with copies of all his invoices. He did this. The company still did not pay him.

In the dark days of November, the school finally started implementing parts of Tim's IEP. The classroom aide who was supposed to have been in place at the start of the year was finally hired. She was very nice. She liked Tim, and he liked her. This should have been a good thing. It turned out to lead to the worst thing that could have happened to Tim that year.

The incident with the gun took place a couple of weeks later. The morning after, when I was at home getting ready for work after the kids had taken the buses to school, I had my telephone call with the principal, and he explained the next step: Tim was entitled to a "manifestation" review to determine if his having brought the gun at school was a result of his disability. The meeting was scheduled for the following Tuesday.

I tried to set aside the frightening image I had of the police arriving at school and leading my eleven-year-old boy away in handcuffs. I told the principal that he did not have the authority to suspend Tim; he insisted that notwithstanding the IEP, he could suspend Tim for reasons of safety. At that point I decided that I needed legal advice.

I spoke on the phone with Tim, who told me matter-of-factly about the boy who had sold Tim the gun and why he had brought it to school. I told him that he was in serious trouble and that the police might be on their way. I also told him to comply with any directive he was given at school but otherwise to say nothing, including to the police. He said okay, wondering what the fuss was all about.

On another call with the principal, he made it clear that the police were only going to question Tim and not take him from school, and I made it clear that I wasn't going to pick up Tim either because he was legally entitled to remain at school. I actually wasn't sure about this, but I was worried that if I brought Tim home I might be seen as agreeing to the suspension in spite of his IEP. I called the lawyer who had handled our due process complaint three years earlier. He said he would do some research and call me back. He also suggested that I call the chairman of the board of education, who happened to be my personal attorney and a close political associate, to see if we might be able to negotiate a way to keep Tim in school.

After hearing the story, the chairman suggested that I call the superintendent of schools and explain my position to him. I called and left a message.

I spoke to an associate of Tim's lawyer next. She advised me about a similar case in another town and said that Tim appeared to have a right to a manifestation determination before—not after—any discipline was imposed. The principal had apparently gotten this backward, and she told me that he could not even consider suspending Tim until after the manifestation determination. She also said that she suspected that the

school district's attorney would be advising the principal of this sometime during the day.

I next called Dr. D to find out whether the principal had gotten any
advice from him before proposing a disciplinary action for Tim as the
IEP seemed to require. He assured me that no one from the school had
tried to reach him at any time during the school year.

Just as I was hanging up the phone, the superintendent called me
back. He said that he wanted to assure me that Tim was being treated
just like any other student. That was the problem, I thought; Tim was
supposed to be treated differently. The superintendent also told me
that the school district's attorneys had advised him that under the possession of firearms statutes, he could suspend Tim for up to ten days
without a manifestation hearing.

I was a little shaken by this, but I argued that Tim's IEP overrode
the firearms statutes, and it stated explicitly that Tim would not be
suspended under any circumstances and that no discipline would be
imposed before Dr. D had been consulted. The superintendent hesitated when I told him that the district was acting in violation of Tim's
IEP (which was a violation of law), and I suspected that he had not
been made aware of the no-suspension provision in Tim's IEP before
he talked with the school district's attorney. He replied that he would
have somebody get back to me. I then asked him to clarify his understanding of Tim's current status. He said that Tim was serving an "in-
house suspension" until further notice and that his classroom aide was
supervising him. It was ten-thirty in the morning when we wrapped up
our conversation, but it felt much later to me.

I couldn't believe that as a parent I was forced to become an instant
expert on federal and state special education and criminal law just to
keep my mentally ill son in school. And I had political connections at
my disposal as well. I couldn't imagine what parents with fewer tools at
their disposal would have been able to do in the same situation.

Tim's lawyer confirmed that the IEP overrode the state law the superintendent referenced and also that the district could not use the

threat of an in-school suspension to force us to waive our right to a five-day notice for the manifestation determination. He predicted that the superintendent would decide that the school had to release Tim from the in-house suspension as soon as they reviewed Tim's IEP. We discussed filing for an emergency due process hearing if it did not.

When Tim arrived home from school, he reported that he had spent a most pleasant day freed from classroom work and in a day-long conversation with his aide. I grilled him for details about when he had gotten the gun (the day before, when his friend's father had driven the friend to our house), how he had paid for it (with twenty dollars he had taken from my wallet), where he had hidden it (in a bush by the street), and why he had brought it to school (because it didn't work and he wanted to get his money back).

It was getting near the end of the business day and I still hadn't heard back from the superintendent, so I called his office again. I was put in touch with the director of pupil services, who informed me that she was now handling Tim's case personally. She had been in meetings about Tim most of the afternoon and had also been reviewing his IEP, which she had helped to write. She concluded that the IEP clearly said that Tim could not be suspended; he should return to school the next day to attend his regular classes. Tim went back to school the next day as if nothing had happened; when I dropped him off in the morning after a therapy session the principal greeted me as if I were an old friend.

The director of pupil services wanted to schedule the manifestation determination as soon as possible, but because of the Thanksgiving school vacation she had to delay it for ten days. In the meantime, she volunteered that she was putting an aide on the bus immediately. This was the request the district had turned down three months earlier. I supposed that the district was agreeing now to protect itself more than to protect Tim.

On the Monday before Thanksgiving, Linda and I met informally at the school with Tim's teachers and Dr. D. It was the first time the school had invited Dr. D to advise the teachers—another concession to "gun day." Dr. D came all the way from West Hartford to Middletown, but the school had only allotted fifteen minutes for the meeting before classes began. The teachers portrayed Tim as a generally typical sixth grader. He was doing fine in school, they said, and except for the gun incident, his behavior was not unusual. "Tim may push and shove, but so do other kids; Tim may be forgetful, but so are other kids," one of them said. I wondered why they were downplaying the seriousness of his behavior. I suspected that the attorneys for the district had advised the teachers to say this because they had failed to implement his IEP. In fact, Tim's teacher would make these same points in a due process hearing three months later. If Tim was typical, then he did not need special ed services.

Tim's manifestation determination took place the following week. The meeting, which was a PPT meeting, seemed scripted and the outcome predetermined. The director of pupil services chaired the meeting, and the district's lawyer was present. The director opened by making a "finding" that Tim's disability had led to his behavior. But instead of offering a behavior support plan, she moved to revise Tim's IEP to allow the school to suspend him for possession of weapons or drugs. That was it; there were to be no other changes to Tim's IEP. I asked for the development of a behavior support plan with input from Dr. D. She denied my request. I asked for a vote. The district's attorney, who was ostensibly there just to give advice, cast the deciding vote against us. I asked him if he was at the meeting as counsel for the district or as a participant. He replied—incredibly—both, and the meeting was adjourned.

We huddled with Tim's lawyer and an advocate from our State Advocacy Office whom we had invited to the meeting to decipher what had just happened. On the upside, the school had realized that it could not suspend Tim. The downside, however, was bigger. After the district had failed to implement most of Tim's IEP for almost six months, the only thing it wanted to do was to add suspension to the list of consequences it could give Tim in the future. We decided that we had no recourse but to request another due process hearing. We hoped to get to this before we had to confront the suspension issue again, but Tim did not cooperate. In fact, it took him less than a day to face suspension again.

Tim left school early with us that afternoon for a family dentist appointment. We were the only ones in the dentist's office suite, so he allowed the children to go in and out of the exam rooms while Linda and I had our teeth cleaned. While walking about, Tim discovered vials of Novocain and put several of them in his book bag to take home.

Tim did not know what Novocain was, but he wanted to give the vials to his aide. She had been using cologne as a reward for Tim when he did something good. He liked the smell, so she let him dab a little on himself as reinforcement. To Tim, the Novocain vials looked just like the cologne vials, and he wanted to return the favor. The next day, Tim brought all of the vials with him to school and presented one to his aide.

She reported it to the principal and then, feeling she may have gotten Tim in trouble, called to tell me. Linda and I immediately contacted the dentist's office to verify that the Novocain was missing, to tell him where it was, and to make sure we could account for all of it. We made arrangements to return the vials immediately. The next day, the principal asked to see Tim when he went to school. I suspected that a suspension was coming, just thirty-six hours after Tim's IEP had been revised. Because we hadn't had time yet to file for the due process hearing, and I didn't want Tim to be suspended when we did, I made the decision to bring Tim home from school that day before the principal could see him.

The next day the principal, frustrated that he couldn't suspend Tim in person, wrote me a letter:

> It has been reported to me that Tim was in possession of eleven (11) vials of novocaine [sic]. I have been told that novocaine can only be dispensed by a doctor and is considered a controlled substance. In view of the fact that on December 4th, 1996 you removed Tim from school before allowing me to talk to him, I can only tell you that this report being true, I would have suspended Tim from school on the grounds of

being a danger to himself and others, as well as being in possession of a
controlled substance. This matter has been turned over to the Middletown Police Department for their investigations. My understanding . . .
is that you have removed Tim from [school] at this time. This letter
then serves as a statement of what the course of action would have been
subsequent to an investigation.

So much for innocent until proven guilty, I thought.

Tim's due process hearing was supposed to take place three weeks
later, but the district's lawyer asked that it be postponed because the
principal and teachers were on vacation. In the meantime, no one was
certain of Tim's current educational placement. Was he suspended or
not? As a compromise we agreed that Tim would go on homebound
instruction, with a teacher coming to the house for an hour or so a day.
It fell to us to arrange for the tutoring, to bring Tim to his psychiatric
evaluation and counseling appointments, to make sure Tim was supervised, and to tend to the needs of our other children. We also had
to deal with Tim's arrests for bringing the gun and the Novocain to
school. He was referred to a juvenile pretrial diversion program run by
a local social services agency. He had an informal hearing in December, at which he was "sentenced" to keep a behavior and consequence
journal for one month and write a letter of apology to his school.

He was minimally penitent. "Dear school," he wrote, "I am very sorry
for what I did. I have gone to the Diversion Board. They said to write a
letter to you so that's what I am doing . . . Sorry again. Sincerely, Tim."

Tim's behavior and consequence journal during the following
month offered a window into the mind of a boy who had little insight
into the reasons for his troubles. One day he wrote, "I ran around outside." His consequence was "I got in trouble." Another day, he recorded: "I helped my grandmother. It felt good. I was bad to my sister. I
got in trouble." Another day he offered: "I was bad to my brother. He
would not play with me. I yelled at my sister. She hit me."

While it was not evident from his journal, the underlying cause of
Tim's depression was finally bubbling to the surface after a full year of

therapy. His breakthrough came in mid-February, when he disclosed to Dr. D that he had been involved in incidents of sexual abuse with an older boy a year earlier. We were not surprised because we had suspected for some time that something like this might have happened—and had tried to communicate this to school teachers and administrators in general terms. Tim had been feeling shame, guilt, and trauma about this for a year. (For legal reasons, I cannot disclose more about the boy or what happened to the case after we reported it.)

We were distressed but also relieved that we finally had what seemed to be a concrete diagnosis—post–traumatic stress disorder (PTSD)—on which to build Tim's recovery. Dr. D assured us that there were more powerful and pointed therapeutic techniques he could use to help Tim cope with his PTSD.

It had taken a year of therapy for Tim to get to this point. Dr. D had worked patiently, tenaciously, and effectively with Tim. However, Dr. D had still not been paid by my insurance company. The company asked him to submit all of his invoices a third time then said he would not be paid at the preferred rate because he had not received prior authorization (which had been provided a year earlier). I finally wrote to the company and the Connecticut Insurance Commissioner asking for a formal case review. Only then was Dr. D paid for his work, fourteen months after he had started treating Tim.

As I fought with the insurance company, we were also fighting with the school district, which was not honoring its agreement to tutor Tim at home. The tutor came to the house a few times but wasn't always on time and didn't always come ready to tutor Tim. We were blamed for this because, although we had juggled our work schedules to accommodate Tim's being at home (including bringing him to work with us when we could), we were sometimes still unable to be home when the tutor arrived, and, for the protection of Tim and the tutor, tutoring could not take place without another adult present at all times.

The director of pupil services offered several options—such as arranging to have Tim tutored at the public library—but all meant that either Linda or I would have to leave work even earlier to get him there and pick him up—and other adults, who knew nothing about our case, would be the ones "watching" him. We suggested as an alternative that Tim be tutored at the district's central office, which was attached to a school and had plenty of space, but the director turned that down. When we could not reach an agreement, she simply unilaterally put an end to Tim's tutoring and offered him no educational program at all.

Meanwhile, the date for Tim's due process hearing kept slipping because hearing officers, lawyers, and school personnel could not find dates convenient for them to meet. I thought it was absurd and unconscionable that Tim would have no education program for months. So after Tim had his therapeutic breakthrough, I proposed having him return to school. Dr. D cautioned that the school would still need to make some additional accommodations for Tim for this to be successful. The district flatly refused to do so while we were in due process, so Tim continued to receive none of his legally mandated educational services.

The hearing finally began on March 6, and ran though March 12 without concluding. Working around the schedules of the lawyers and the district, it was reconvened at the end of March and then again at the beginning of May. It finally concluded on May 2—effectively wiping out Tim's entire school year.

One of the reasons the hearing took so long was because there were scores of exhibits—papers, memos, notes, correspondence, and IEPs stretching back to the beginning of Tim's time in kindergarten— presented by both sides, all of which had to be entered tediously into the record.

I was the first one to take the stand, and Tim's lawyer presented our case mostly through my testimony over multiple days. I spoke about Tim's disabilities, psychological difficulties, and history in special education. I reviewed the provisions in the June IEP, most of which had never been implemented. Finally, I testified about Tim's recent therapeutic breakthrough. I argued that we all knew what supports Tim needed to be successful and that he should return to school with these in place as soon as possible.

Dr. D was Tim's next witness. His advice was that Tim be returned gradually to school, beginning as soon as possible. He confirmed that Tim had learning disabilities, behavioral issues, sleep problems, suicidal tendencies, and PTSD and that Tim's IEP (to which we had agreed in June), in combination with a behavior support plan, reflected the supports he would need to help him cope with these problems.

The district put on most of its case nearly a month later, through the testimony of one of the special education teachers at Tim's school. When asked what he thought Tim's primary diagnosis was, he responded, "overprotective parents." I just shook my head, unable to comprehend how he could say this under oath after we had entered so much clinical data about Tim's mental illness into the record of the hearing. His message was simple. The school was fully capable of meeting Tim's needs, he argued, but his parents expected far too many supports.

When the hearing reconvened in May, the district presented the remainder of its case through the testimony of its director of pupil services. She surprised us all by contradicting the special education teacher. When asked if she thought the district was capable of meeting Tim's educational needs, she flatly answered "no."

I knew that we had won the hearing at that point because the school was going to be required to implement an IEP with significant supports for Tim after all. But I suspected we might have lost the war to get a decent IEP implemented. It didn't seem likely to me that the director of pupil services and the school's teachers were on the same page. And we still had to await the hearing officer's decision.

To this day, I still dream about what should have happened instead of a six-month due process hearing. Tim's IEP should have been reviewed. We should have had a discussion with the school about what additional supports he needed to stay in school. Because the state had an interest in the outcome, it should have been included as a third party. A mediator should have been engaged. Tim's pediatrician, psychiatrist, and psychologist should have been asked to weigh in with their recommendations about how to integrate his clinical care with his educational instruction. All of their recommendations and services should have been proposed for his IEP. And only then—if we still disagreed—should we have had to go to a due process hearing.

Mandating changes this comprehensive would involve changes to public policies and procedures because they would involve broadening the definition of what constitutes an educational support for all children. Integrating clinical services into educational services would also carry a cost, one that the current law would require local school districts to bear. Such changes would not be inexpensive to implement. It might not be fair to burden the local school district with the full cost, so perhaps the state—or even the federal government—should pick up part of it.

In our case, such changes would have been much less expensive than the due process hearing proved to be. They also would have changed the trajectory of those few months and might have even changed the trajectory of Tim's life. But even today, when students are about to be removed from school for behavioral reasons the law doesn't bring in the state, doesn't mandate mediation, doesn't divide the costs fairly between state and local governments, and at a time of impasse doesn't really give parents many options other than going to a due process hearing or home instruction.

Our lengthy due process hearing cost both sides more than $100,000 combined, much of it in legal fees eventually paid by the district. This was far more than it would have cost the district to implement an appropriate IEP for Tim and many other special education students that year. Nothing ended here, however. The hearing officer's decision did not come until June. All of those dollars might just as well have been thrown directly into the Dumpster with the BB gun.

I agreed with the school district about one thing during the due process hearing: Tim's current school was unable to provide him with an appropriate education. So of course the district sent Tim back to the same school that fall.

The chain of counterproductive decisions and negotiations that led to this perverse result began with the hearing officer's ruling in June. After listening to the testimony of the director of pupil services, the hearing officer decided that Tim should be placed out-of-district. But he did not say where. He left it up to the district and us to decide because the district—arguing mostly that Tim would do fine with minimal supports and less protective parents—had never defined during the hearing what an appropriate placement might look like for a child like him.

I was surprised by this, but should not have been. According to the U.S. Department of Education (NCES 2012), 95 percent of special education students are educated in regular schools. Only 3 percent are in special schools for children with disabilities, and none of them are there simply because of "overprotective parents." In 1997–1998, the percentage of students in special schools was similar—around 4 percent. So there weren't going to be many options. At the time, Tim didn't fit the profile of someone needing a residential or hospital program. His "homebound program" in the spring had already failed. Linda and I thought a private school was the only viable option. But the district had another idea.

The director of pupil services wanted to find partial-day treatment program that would accept Tim. We argued that neither Dr. D nor any other therapist treating Tim at the time thought such a program would be appropriate for him, but that did not deter her.

We had a PPT meeting in mid-August that lasted for an entire day to try to come to some resolution. From the moment the meeting began, there was no hope for compromise. We wanted a private school and had identified one nearby, but she rejected it. She wanted any day treatment program at all, but we rejected that. We finally thought we had reached a compromise—that Tim would continue in regular education but have a community-based therapeutic component, including counseling, wrapped around it. But then she refused either to consider Dr. D's input or to have Dr. D serve as the community-based therapist. What frustrated me most about her response wasn't even that she ignored that Dr. D, as Tim's regular psychologist, had already established a strong therapeutic relationship with Tim that I didn't want to undo. It was that she never even tried to identify some other therapist whom the district thought would be better for Tim.

And when she suggested day treatment programs, she brought with her a list of service providers in Connecticut that accepted out-of-district placements. Neither she nor others from the district could say whether they provided a therapeutic or educational environment that was even relevant to Tim's needs. It seemed that we were supposed to choose one on the basis of name, reputation, or location.

Toward the end of the day, the director of pupil services suggested that we default to Tim's stay-put placement until we could agree on a placement. We agreed reluctantly. We then had to figure out what stay-put meant for Tim because he had not spent a day in school after December and had not received any instruction at all after January.

We finally decided that Tim's stay-put plan was the IEP that had been drafted at the end of fifth grade with the updated suspension language added by the district. This meant that Tim would go back into a regular classroom for the time being. We also agreed that the district would identify an alternative placement for Tim and that we would approve or disapprove it.

This battle dragged on for many weeks and was discussed widely in Connecticut special education circles that year, though we and Tim were not identified. In late August, I hosted a meeting of some district superintendents and public officials in Connecticut to plan for a policy workshop I was developing on the topic of special education. When I asked the superintendents what frustrated them most about the special education process, they agreed that it was the lawyers, advocates, and consultants who worked with parents to take districts to due process hearings. They went on to name Tim's lawyer, Tim's advocate, and Linda (who used her own last name and so was not immediately identifiable as my wife) as their three biggest threats. Needless to say, I kept my mouth shut.

Linda and I were in the process of divorcing that summer. We reassured all our children that it had nothing to do with them and that we both loved them and planned to continue to be involved fully in their lives. But it would be a difficult adjustment for them getting used to living in two homes and dividing their time between us. We negotiated a shared-custody arrangement under which the children would live half of the time with me and half with Linda. This meant that on Tim's bad days, we always had the option of separating him from the other children. She began looking at houses in nearby Middlefield, which was part of another school district, Regional District 13. She made overtures to educators from that district and found that they might be more amenable to devising an in-district program there for Tim. We kept that to ourselves, knowing that if things didn't work out in Middletown, District 13 might be another option for us.

This strategy seemed like a good one when the director of pupil services informed us that instead of advancing Tim to seventh grade and a new school with his peers, the district had decided that his stay-put placement was sixth grade at his old school. She offered no substantive reason for this. But she knew how we felt about that school, and I believe she thought this would pressure us to agree to any out-of-district placement to avoid it. We did not. Tim started the year with the same principal, the same teachers, and the same IEP as the year before.

The district soon paid an unexpected price for its decision. Tim was a year older and bored with repeating the same material. He was also almost five and a half feet tall and was six months shy of being a teenager. He neither looked nor felt like a sixth grader anymore.

His favorite social activity now was engaging other sixth graders to bother and bully his new classmate, his sister Larissa. She had no idea how to handle this, having been given a mixed message—on the one hand, to stand up for herself, and on the other, to advocate for her brother.

But the schoolwork was easy for him. And so, just as the director of pupil services was trying to persuade us that the district couldn't educate Tim in a regular classroom setting, Tim was having some of his greatest academic successes. He received a B+ in language arts, a B in math, an A− in science, and a B+ in geography for the first quarter. She had lost her educational rationale for removing him from the classroom. And because the district did not want to accept Dr. D's increasingly positive psychological evaluations or pay for its own, it had no clinical rationale for removing him either.

Tim probably could have ridden out the year like that, but his attitude toward school had soured. His good grades were earned in spite of his increasingly poor effort. He rarely completed his class work, and he constantly challenged his teachers and the administrators.

In late October, the school finally contacted Dr. D for advice: Was Tim's growing attitude problem a symptom of a mental illness, and was it serious enough to support an out-of-district placement? In his response, he wrote that Tim's diagnoses were PTSD, major depressive disorder, ADHD, learning disabilities, and dyssomnia. He then wrote, "As [Tim] has progressed in treatment his clinical symptoms have improved consistently," and concluded, "At this point, Tim's clinical profile no longer supports the out-of-district placement indicated by the Hearing Officer. Tim should be able to be maintained within district as long as appropriate modifications are made and as long as he continues in outpatient treatment of his PTSD."

Despite this, Tim's principal continued to lobby for an out-of-district placement. Knowing that Linda and I were breaking up—but not that we had already pretty much decided to transfer Tim to the adjoining district—he asked me informally one day if I would support this. I told him that I would not go along with him. As I saw it, if he was unhappy with the district's decision to put Tim back in his school, he had three choices: to transfer Tim to seventh grade, to convene a PPT meeting and write a new IEP, or to make the current situation work.

Tim was not helping matters. He began using his IEP as a weapon against his teachers. He would say, "I don't have to do homework. It's in my IEP." (He was referring to a provision saying that he wouldn't be graded on his homework.) On another occasion, he refused to do an assignment in class because the students were told that what they didn't finish was homework. Since homework didn't matter, he said, what was the point of even starting the assignment?

In spite of his bad attitude, Tim did just enough to avoid suspensions. He technically followed the rules, just as the principal had asked the year before. He received only one detention between August and December.

In December, Linda closed on her house in Middlefield, and she and I agreed that in Tim's best interests, we would transfer him to District 13. The Middletown district finally got its wish. It had an out-of-district placement after all.

And as the District 13 folks welcomed Tim to his new school in January 1998, I still clung to the notion that the people, not the policies, were the problem. I was to learn differently over the next few years.

six

ROCKETING THROUGH
MIDDLE SCHOOL

T IM WAS ALMOST thirteen years old when he transferred to the sixth grade in Middlefield, Connecticut
in January 1998. Middlefield was a small, rural community
with a less socioeconomically and racially diverse population than Middletown. The transition was difficult for all
of our children. There were few children of color in their
schools, and our children tested the racial sensitivities of
the district. Regarding Tim, a teacher wrote to me: "He is
blending in very well" and "making some eye contact with
teachers now." I thought these were odd ways to describe
the only African American male student in the class but let
it go. Several years later, when Larissa was in high school,
students planned a "ghetto day" with the blessing of the
administration. They asked Larissa for advice about how
they should dress. She laughed about it but was clearly of-
fended. So was I.

Tim took some standardized tests when he started at his new school, and the results suggested how little academic progress he had made during the past two years. He was below grade level in math and spelling. Only in reading comprehension was he at grade level.

The school scheduled a PPT meeting for late January to update Tim's IEP. At that meeting, his new teachers expressed concerns about both his academic and his organizational skills. They proposed removing Tim from the classroom for extra math help five days a week and for writing support two or three times a week. Linda and I agreed to this; otherwise, his new IEP looked pretty much like his old one.

Tim's new teachers made mistakes in implementing his IEP. In one instance, a teacher noticed that he hadn't been organizing his binder. Tim was given the assignment of writing out "I will pass the binder check next week" fifty times as a reminder. It was not an approved IEP strategy and did not work; he still didn't pass his binder check. The course work was also different from what he had been working on in Middletown, and Tim struggled with the new material. His April report card was distressing. He failed English, math, and science.

The comments of his teachers showed their frustration with Tim. They thought it was all about effort, not mental illness. One wrote: "Tim, your math grade could have been a 'C' if you put in the required effort." Another wrote: "When Tim chooses to put effort into his assignments, his work improves dramatically. Tim's effort and attitude toward schoolwork and homework needs a great deal of improvement." His attitude was a problem, I knew, but his academic weaknesses were related to his mental illness and learning disabilities. If anything, the effort he put into just getting through the day was nothing short of extraordinary.

Tim still did good work sometimes, and I think this confused some of his teachers who did not understand how his mental illness affected his academic performance. For example, in February he wrote a paper on capital punishment for his social studies class. "Let me tell you what I mean when I say it is not right to play God," he wrote. "Our whole system of beliefs is based on the belief that it is wrong to kill.

Just because a criminal killed someone, two wrongs don't make a right. Also, we sometimes make mistakes. Nobody's perfect, [and] if we impose capital punishment on the wrong person, then we will be guilty of taking an innocent life." His teacher must have thought, "If he could reason so well, how mentally ill could he be?" What his teachers didn't realize was how much extra help Tim needed in order to express these thoughts. His thinking was his own, but we were spending considerable time at home helping him with his spelling, punctuation, and presentation.

In the spring, the teachers made some additional concessions to Tim's learning disabilities but not to his mental illness. For example, they reduced and simplified his spelling lists. When he still failed his assignments, they reduced and simplified them some more. It took cutting his list down to six simple words before he lifted his grade from an F to a D–. Of course, learning only six simple words per week was not going to improve Tim's spelling proficiency.

In early May, we met with school officials to review Tim's progress as measured against his IEP goals. Tim was behind in many of the objectives, yet the school summarized Tim's level of performance in the following way: "Tim is a very capable student who lacks the motivation and determination to progress in school with success. His math, spelling and written expression skills are weaknesses, while comprehension of concepts, understanding of vocabulary, and verbal expression are areas of strength. Tim has a difficult time organizing himself, as well as attending in school. He is extremely pleasant and has not been a behavior problem in school. However, when he makes up his mind not to do something he quietly stops."

Tim got the message that his failings were his fault, the result of his poor choices. He was a teenager now and acted like one. He felt different from other children and believed he was singled out and picked on by authority figures who thought he was lazy. There was a lot going on in Tim's head, and precious little of it was comforting.

When Tim moved on to seventh grade at yet another school he was a boy in a young man's body. He was over five feet, eight inches tall, and he felt and looked out of place. Moving to middle school required more adjustments on his part at a time when he was just beginning to deal with worsening symptoms of his mental illness—symptoms that suggested that PTSD might not be his primary diagnosis after all.

Those occasional voices in his head seemed to reemerge, and his sleep medication no longer seemed to be helping him to clear them away. His thoughts may have been disordered by those voices—or by the fact that he had entered puberty. He also did not always distinguish right from wrong. He impulsively took things that did not belong to him, refused to do what he was told, bothered his siblings, and broke things, sometimes on purpose. He took Lizzie's new bike out for a ride without her permission and lost it. I also found evidence that Tim was engaging in new risky behaviors. He was using marijuana and occasionally smoking cigarettes, and one day I found an empty liquor bottle in a downstairs closet. I locked up all the remaining liquor in my house.

In our separate homes, he tested both Linda and me to see how far he could push us. When he confronted Linda, she often confronted him back, and they would both dig in their heels. He had grown taller than she was, and sometimes he "bodied up" to her, daring her to move him if she could.

Tim would not confront me physically. Instead, he damaged property when he was angry, starting with pots and pans in the kitchen and progressing over time to my car, his bedroom wall, and his bedroom windows.

When school began in the fall, he literally made a game out of forcing me to drag him from his room to get him ready for school or one of his appointments.

I wasn't naive about what it took to manage Tim. I went to the expense of renovating my house, moving my bedroom next door to Tim's so I could keep better track of him at night. I put Ben and the girls in new rooms at the other end of the upstairs landing, so that they could escape to private, locked rooms when they needed to get away from Tim. They often had no idea why Tim was causing trouble, but they learned to retreat to their rooms without asking too many questions whenever he was.

Tim had a burst of academic achievement at the start of seventh grade. I wasn't surprised because it was his third review of sixth-grade material. After the first week, his science teacher commented that Tim had "wonderful oral participation" and was "prepared for class." His English teacher was "pleased with his reservoir of knowledge" and described Tim as "pleasant." His math teacher praised his behavior.

After his second week, the reports were not so glowing. His math teacher reported that his work was "messy"; his English teacher, that he couldn't find his paper in his notebook; and his Latin teacher, that he wasn't prepared for class. He had also written with Wite-Out on another student's notebook. He was reported to the principal and received a stern lecture about respecting other people's property. In September the school convened a PPT meeting to consider a solution. Everyone agreed that Tim was maturing physically very rapidly and would likely fit in better with his age peers in the eighth grade.

Tim embraced the idea. He wanted to be back with his peers, and he was itching to get to high school. He had begun to take a keen interest in cooking and was already setting his sights on an area high school with a culinary arts program.

Tim was an above-average cook. Cooking, like the hands-on science projects of his younger days, played to his strengths. It held his attention, allowed him to experiment with intense smells and flavors without risk, and helped him organize his thinking. It also gave him an immediate reward. He did not have to follow recipes exactly or measure ingredients precisely. His experimentation led to some spectacular failures, but he soon figured out what combinations of flavors worked and produced some very palatable dishes.

His disabilities did not disappear when he cooked, however. He was far from neat and clean in the kitchen and was never very well organized. After he finished, every countertop was messy, the stovetop was often caked with burnt-on spills, and every pot and pan he used had remnants of food in them. I decided to focus on the result, figuring that this was more important than the process.

Tim advanced to eighth grade in October. His IEP goals and objectives were kept in place, but he was not given any additional supports to make the abrupt transition. Educationally, this was a huge but thrifty mistake. Not surprisingly, he didn't do very well academically in the beginning. Tim clearly needed some extra help to get caught up, so Linda found a high school student to tutor him. Although his teachers wanted Tim to have the tutoring, the school district would not make it a part of his IEP. So Linda paid for it out of her own pocket.

In the next month, Tim did not make much academic progress. His teachers continued to blame this on his attitude toward school and his lack of effort, not on his learning disabilities or his admittedly weak academic foundation. Even when Tim did well, the praise was muted. "Tim had a science test on Thursday and managed to get a good grade," his teacher wrote. "He does manage to participate in class discussions."

But despite what his teachers thought, I was beginning to come to the difficult conclusion that schools with regular academic programs simply did not have the resources or training needed to teach children like Tim. Yet there seemed to be no alternative. With little help from his teachers or IEP, I did not see how Tim was going to make it to graduation unless somehow he was able to motivate himself. I knew that Tim's diagnoses were the primary reasons for his lack of success, but I could not understand why these well-documented clinical issues did not resonate as reasons for failure with educators in the classroom and cause them to write some mental health services into his IEP. If only Tim could have appeared to be making more of an effort, then perhaps they would have seen through to his real needs.

The problem was that the teachers at his middle schools were all trying to treat Tim normally. But this minimized the importance of his IEP and held him accountable for all of his failures.

And Tim failed more often than not toward the end of that school year, at home as well as at school. Every calm moment was prelude to a new crisis. He'd snuggle with Ben while watching television, but then go out to find people with whom he would use alcohol or marijuana—which were becoming a bigger part of his life at the time. He'd quietly read a book or magazine before going to bed but refuse to do his schoolwork the next day. He was caring and compassionate with his siblings one day but cruel and bullying the next.

His teachers complained about many things, but there was little talk of revising his IEP to create new objectives and no desire to have Dr. D update Tim's clinical profile for them. The bottom line seemed to be that the school had no idea what to do with him. To be honest, neither did I, and I was becoming exhausted.

Tim began to give up on school that year—almost three years after schools had seemed to begin to give up on him. He served suspensions for fighting with another student and for kicking in a bathroom partition during a school dance. And still no one suggested making any changes to his IEP.

Then one spring day, Tim asked Linda if he could Rollerblade through the park after school. I was picking him up that night, so she let me know where to find him.

As we were to find out later, in the park Tim came upon some high school students who were drinking alcohol and asked if he could join them. Soon he became very drunk and began to stagger about. They abandoned him as he was falling to the ground, losing consciousness.

I arrived at the park and a young teenager came running toward me. He told me that Tim was passed out on a path. I found Tim on the ground, covered in vomit but still conscious. I tried for several minutes to keep him awake and get him upright, finally hoisting him to his feet and helping him toward my car.

An ambulance arrived and raced Tim several miles to Middlesex Hospital. I followed closely behind in my car, running every red light they did.

When Tim arrived at the emergency room, his blood alcohol content was over 0.20. The ER staff pumped out his stomach and watched him closely over the next several hours until he was out of danger. As I sat there, I wondered how many more times this scene would be repeated in the future.

A few days later, I spoke with Dr. D. "The good news," he said, "is that Tim got scared by what happened. Often, after younger teenagers have an experience like this with alcohol they stay away from it." For the most part, Tim did shy away from alcohol after that.

What Dr. D didn't want to tell me was that Tim might turn more heavily to marijuana and other drugs instead.

In a conversation with the school superintendent after the park incident I offered to help the district enhance its drug awareness program if he would help identify the high school students who had given Tim the alcohol and get them into an alcohol awareness program. He politely declined. Then he disclosed, sincerely: "This drug problem is even hitting suburban and rural school districts such as ours. Just last year, for the first time, we had marijuana in our high school." For the first time? I supposed that we all sometimes deny obvious but unpleasant truths.

Tim had passed through seventh and eighth grades more than he had passed them. It was time to try something different. I hoped that the culinary arts program at our vocational high school would be the right fit for Tim. It was not.

seven

HIGH SCHOOL COOKS UP TROUBLE

C OOKING AND FOOTBALL—those were the two things in which I placed my hopes as fourteen-year-old Tim entered high school. I had many reasons to be concerned about the high school years. Academically, Tim was significantly below grade level. He had low self-esteem, rebelled against rules and authority, and made poor choices in friends and acquaintances. During the past year, as a result of his more emergent bullying behaviors and his inability to conform to rules, he had received two new diagnoses: a personality disorder and oppositional defiant disorder. This was in addition to his previous diagnoses of ADD, depression, and PTSD. He had been in therapy for over three years and was on trazodone to treat his sleep disorder and Adderall for his ADD. He only reluctantly took the drugs prescribed for him because he said they made him tired. Instead, he used marijuana to self-medicate.

But at least he looked forward to cooking and football.

Tim's first high school—I'll call it High School 1 to distinguish it from the ones that followed—was a vocational-technical school that was part of a statewide school district. Its principal was a friend of mine. When I visited the school in the summer, he took me aside and assured me that he would do all he could to make Tim's time there successful. The school had a new culinary arts program, and I was hoping that Tim, who still loved cooking and wanted to be a chef, would have a chance to enroll in it.

The school also had a new football team. When we visited the coach noticed Tim—tall and with an excellent build for his age—and invited him to try out for the team. Tim—who was a good athlete but had never liked team sports—decided to give it a try. Practice began late that summer.

In late August we had a PPT meeting, where we were introduced to the school's assistant principal—who would oversee much of Tim's academic program—and other school administrators. They were all cordial as we went to work on his IEP. They crafted an overall education goal for Tim to "develop the necessary work skills and behaviors to maintain competitive employment" and an academic goal "to succeed in mainstream academics with grades of 'C' or better in all classes."

However, there was no explicit mention of the effect of his mental illness on his academic performance. Predictably, our discussion bogged down when we began talking about the supplementary services Tim would need. Linda and I suggested immediate behavioral and academic supports, but the school wanted to do an academic performance assessment during the first three weeks of school before considering these. We agreed reluctantly but requested a peer tutor. The school deferred a response to this until after the assessment was completed. They did, however, assign him to receive two and a half hours per week of special education instruction in the resource room and an hour and three-quarters per week of counseling with the school psychologist.

From the start, Linda and I were concerned about how frequently detentions and suspensions were used for discipline. We explained that Tim needed to spend as much time in class as possible to succeed academically. He was beginning to look at suspensions as a way of avoiding class, and toward the end of eighth grade he sometimes tried to get suspended on purpose. We suggested drafting a behavior support plan that would create alternatives to suspension if Tim broke school rules.

But when we talked about what such a plan might look like, we might as well have been speaking in different tongues. Linda and I knew all about Tim but had only a surface understanding of the school rules. The school knew all about its rules but had only a surface understanding of Tim. We left the meeting without a behavior support plan in place. The school psychologist agreed to contact Dr. D for help in developing one. In the meantime, the school said it would issue Tim a "time-out pass" to allow him to leave a classroom whenever he was upset about something.

Unfortunately, Tim's fledgling football career ended abruptly. The coach was initially happy to have him on the team. I talked with him about Tim's illness, and he told me that he thought football might be just what Tim needed. Within a couple of weeks Tim emerged as the backup defensive end and offensive end — one of just a couple of freshmen who had advanced that high on the depth chart. He worked hard in practice, responding well whenever he was praised.

But he did not take well to criticism. When the coaches yelled at him, he refused to practice. When he refused to practice, he was assigned to run laps. When he refused to run laps, he was dropped down the depth chart. By the second scrimmage of the season he was a backbencher, suspended from the game for disciplinary reasons. A week later, the coach declared that "some kids need football more than football needs them" and dismissed Tim from the team.

Tim made it through the first couple of vocational rotations without incident, but his academic rotations did not go as well. I never heard the results of the performance assessment the school conducted, and no peer tutor was ever assigned to Tim. He was cited for failure to pay attention, swearing, and tossing pencils at other students, and all of these transgressions led to detentions. As the detentions added up, they led to lost class time — exactly what we wanted to avoid. As he lost class time, Tim fell behind in his work.

It took a month of pushing before the school psychologist finally spoke with Dr. D. That conversation resulted in confusion. The school psychologist expected Dr. D to offer a behavior plan for Tim, but Dr. D expected the school to draft a plan to which he could react.

After that conversation, the school psychologist finally crafted the goal that "Tim will improve self-esteem, anger control, and problem solving skills." He created six objectives for Tim: to discuss his personal strengths and to develop strategies to use them to succeed; to discuss situations that caused him to become angry; to develop problem-solving and stress-reduction strategies; to "describe his disabilities independently and accurately to people;" to follow school rules, "including leaving peer situations that are likely to result in rule breakage"; and to "seek the support of staff, teachers, or other responsible parties to process it out" whenever Tim had "a day . . . in which he believes a behavioral incident to be likely."

I thought these objectives were unrealistic. How, for example, was Tim supposed to acquire the skills to do any of these things, or to identify through the haze of depression, oppositional defiance disorder, ADD, learning disabilities, and a personality disorder "a day . . . in which he believes a behavioral incident to be likely"?

And the objectives came at least a month too late. In the first week of October, school officials discovered a small bag of marijuana, a pipe, a lighter, and a burned pencil in Tim's pocket. They called the police and suspended him for ten days. Tim entered the juvenile justice system for a second time. The pretrial process took almost two months, during which he was ordered to undergo a drug use assessment. When he was determined to be only a casual drug user, he was placed on probation for six months, ordered to attend group counseling (in addition to his individual counseling with Dr. D), and required to submit to periodic drug testing, a curfew, and possible house arrest if he violated the terms of his probation.

Tim served his ten-day suspension from school in late October. When he returned, he was even more behind academically, so the school assigned two tutors to him. One provided twenty hours of tutoring to help him make up the work he had missed while on suspension. The other—his algebra teacher—was supposed to help him with his general academic needs as part of his IEP.

After Tim's suspension, Linda and I requested a PPT meeting to develop more classroom-work modifications and to flesh out Tim's behavior support plan to improve the connection between his educational supports and his clinical care. Our goal was to prevent future suspensions. Our requests were denied. The school believed that the tutoring was sufficient to address Tim's academic needs and that the school's rule book was sufficient to guide his disciplinary needs. They were treating Tim as they would any other student, they argued. We replied yet again that the purpose of special education was to treat qualifying students differently from other students. And we believed that the rule book could not substitute for a behavior support plan.

The urgency I felt about this increased as Tim continued to violate school rules and the school continued to suspend him for a day or two at a time. His academics declined as he missed more classes. He was in danger of failing several of his courses. While tutoring was technically available to him, he was expected to make use of it voluntarily after school, when the algebra teacher had some free time. But that was also when Tim had to attend his court-ordered group counseling.

He became increasingly pressured, tired, and frustrated. He would often erupt in anger at home and threaten family members. It wasn't that these outbursts were unpredictable; Tim was like a gathering storm over days and weeks. He might start out somewhat innocuously by refusing to pick up his things, then escalate by taking his siblings' things without permission, and then further escalate by physically bullying his siblings into doing what he wanted. By the end of the progression, his siblings were afraid of him, and he refused any redirection. Linda had it worse than I did; at one point she even contacted the Department of Children and Families for help, including requesting a wilderness program for Tim and respite services for the family.

When Tim's academic progress reports arrived in early December, they were bleak. He failed science, phys. ed., algebra, life skills, and geography. He was barely passing English. In the one class in which he got a good grade—reading—his teacher asked that he be removed because of his bad behavior.

We had another PPT meeting to revisit Tim's IEP. For the first time, Tim attended. He had a single request—to end his sessions with the school psychologist. Three court-mandated group sessions per week and therapy with Dr. D were all he could handle. The school psychologist supported the request. So the school counseling was dropped from his IEP, and Tim left the meeting happy.

We then discussed Tim's academic issues. The school proposed moving Tim into easier classes to lift his grades. Linda strongly opposed this, arguing that Tim needed adequate supports in more challenging classes, not easier classes without any supports. The school disagreed, with the worst possible result. They decided that Tim would remain in the more challenging classes but without any additional supports or the after-school tutoring, which was discontinued because it conflicted with Tim's court-ordered group counseling.

We then discussed Tim's suspensions. Everyone agreed that Tim was being suspended too frequently and needed every available minute in class. The team agreed to the following language:

> Tim will not receive any out-of-school suspensions. If his behaviors involve drugs, weapons, severe assault, or any behaviors which violate criminal statutes Tim will be placed in an interim alternative educational placement for up to 45 days. If an interim alternative educational placement is necessary Mr. Gionfriddo agreed for up to five school days for the placement to be implemented. During these five days Tim will be home schooled. Work will be provided by the school.

That seemed pretty clear to me. But just four days later Tim was given an out-of-school suspension for a reason that did not involve drugs, weapons, severe assault, or any criminal behaviors.

The events began when someone called in a bomb threat that resulted in the evacuation of his school. In all the confusion, Tim left the school and asked for a ride home from a student he knew. The student agreed, but the car was overcrowded. An emergency services worker approached the car and asked Tim—the last one in—to get out. Tim did just as he was told but then left school on foot. An administrator called after him to return, but he did not.

When Tim arrived at school the next day, he was given a six-day out-of-school suspension for refusing to follow directions. Linda and I spent the entire day arguing that the suspension wasn't permitted by the IEP to which the school had agreed just four days earlier. Despite that, the school's vice principal refused to budge. So Tim happily sat at home for six days.

I was keeping count. Tim had already been suspended for a total of nineteen days, and it was not even the end of December.

When school reconvened after the Christmas vacation a manifestation determination meeting was held to decide if Tim's behavior was the result of his disability. This time, Linda refused to go, feeling that she would only be wasting her time. I requested that Tim not be given any more out-of-school suspensions because they were making it impossible for him to succeed in school. The members of the team agreed, and the agreement was recorded in the minutes of the meeting. Four weeks later, Tim was suspended again, this time for swearing. Tim's suspension was to be served in school but outside of the classroom. He was placed in a room with another student. Bored, the boys started tossing pencils at each other. For this Tim received two additional days of suspension, in further violation of his IEP.

His suspension count for the year was now up to twenty-two days, nine of them after the adoption of IEP provisions that explicitly prohibited them.

Tim's next progress report reflected the results. He failed geography, science, and phys. ed. His reading teacher again asked that he be removed from her classroom. The only class he passed—nominally—was English. The school psychologist and Dr. D exchanged communications during this time. While the school psychologist still blamed Tim's failing grades on bad behavior, Dr. D tried to steer his academic problems back to the symptoms of the underlying disease: "Tim has little interest in academic issues or his future in general. At this point he is very short sighted and is primarily focused on reducing current psychological and emotional discomfort at any cost. He does this by avoiding any focus on his behavior and by avoiding difficult situations and tasks. The usual consequences of detention and suspension will predictably either have no effect for Tim or will actually worsen his behavior. Detention just gives him more time with the peer group that abhors school and suspension allows him to avoid school altogether."

During the same period, Tim provided some further insight into his darkening mood with these lines from a poem:

> As the calm pack runs through the star lit sky
> Their silver fur catches my eye
> I get a chill as the deer give a cry
> And the hungry pack moves in for the kill.

On the last day of February, the school scheduled a PPT meeting to request a "manifestation determination, functional behavioral analysis and a review of his behavioral intervention plan." I was told that a behavioral consultant was being engaged to conduct an evaluation of Tim. The school agreed that it would not suspend Tim while the evaluation was being done. Already twice burned on the matter of suspensions, I did not believe them.

To add insult to injury, when Tim finally rotated to the culinary arts program, he was disappointed. The introductory lessons focused on the mechanics of organizing a kitchen. His hopes of being turned loose to create new recipes were dashed. His educational program was a mess. His progress in counseling with Dr. D had stalled. He was becoming more defiant at home. And after he had an altercation with Linda in her home where they came close to blows, she called the Middlefield Resident State Trooper's Office to intervene.

Tim's probation officer was well aware of all of Tim's troubles. At this point, he decided it would be best to send Tim to an inpatient program. After talking with both Linda and me, he notified Tim that he had violated his probation and that because of his drug offense from October, he would have to cooperate with an inpatient admission to a substance abuse treatment program.

Tim was sent to a program an hour away from Middletown. The program described its mission as being "to provide an innovative, high-energy environment within which adolescents can develop new social and behavioral skills helping them to harden their resolve, reinforce their strengths, and refocus their lives." The only resolve the program hardened for Tim was to disobey rules and chart his own course. There was a reason for this—the program was designed for people who accepted that they had an addiction disorder and were ready for treatment. Because of this, the residential facilities were not locked. Tim did not have an addiction disorder at the time—he was a casual user—and he was not ready for treatment. And an unlocked door to him was an invitation to explore the outside world.

Tim was expected to be in the program for three to six weeks. He stayed ten days. He left his supervised group home one night to go bar hopping. When he returned, he was immediately discharged from the program.

Under the terms of his probation, he was now put under house arrest. He was fitted with an electronic ankle bracelet and was not permitted to leave my house except to go to therapy. It was a three-week vacation for Tim, but I felt imprisoned. At certain times of the day, a commanding computerized voice would interrupt my telephone conversations, ordering me off the phone so that the bracelet's signal could be tested. This did not deter Tim. One day when I was running some errands, he arranged for a delivery of marijuana through a downstairs window.

A week later, Tim's high school provided a grade report for the year. Tim had failed every subject. Only his science teacher made a positive comment, indicating that Tim "actively contributes."

High School 1 wasn't working, so Linda searched for an alternative. She wanted something closer but eventually settled on an "emotional growth" boarding school in the northwestern part of the United States as the best option for Tim. I did not want him so far away but did not have an alternative to suggest, so I went along. The school—I'll call it High School 2 —agreed to admit Tim. The court ordered the placement, and the school district agreed to pay part of the cost. And so, when he was released from his house arrest, Tim headed west.

eight

WEST TO THE
NORTHWEST

M Y CURRENT WIFE, Pam, and I met in October 1999 at a Kids Count conference in Baltimore sponsored by the Annie E. Casey Foundation. Pam was from Austin, Texas, and ran the Kids Count project in that state. I was working for the Connecticut Association for Human Services, the Kids Count grantee in Connecticut. We sat next to each other at dinner on the first night, and I paid attention as she shared stories with another woman at the table about her teenage daughter, Verena. Verena was coming out of a rebellious, blue-haired phase of teen life, and many of her recent experiences were similar to Tim's.

Pam was a single parent. She recounted in a matter-of-fact way a few scary anecdotes about drug use and threats of violence that had been made against Verena. It was as if these things were a normal part of her everyday life. The person to whom Pam was speaking seemed at a loss as to how to respond to her. But Pam was describing my life, too. I waited for an opportunity and then joined the conversation. We hit it off and spent as much time together as we could for the remainder of the two-day conference. When it ended, we exchanged phone numbers and e-mail addresses. We launched a long-distance relationship, e-mailing and talking on the phone nearly every day. I visited her and Verena in Austin in December, and she came to Connecticut the following April to meet my children. When Pam met Tim for the first time, he was sleeping on the couch in the family room. He was wrapped tightly in a blanket in front of the television, and he barely opened his dull, listless eyes when she said hello. He curled back up again as soon as we left the room. "He seems nice," Pam commented sweetly as we headed back upstairs to play Monopoly with Ben.

A few days later, Tim flew with Linda to the northwest, arriving at his "emotional growth" boarding school. He was emotionally and physically drained. He told the social worker who was conducting his intake evaluation, "I'm in a tired, tired state all day" and reported that he had difficulty falling and staying asleep. He added, "I worry about stuff a lot. I don't like having friends; it's hard to find people who are like me. When I'm really, really sad, I cry. When I'm a little sad, I sit and stare."

His wish, he said, was that he could "turn invisible."

Emotional-growth, or therapeutic, schools grew in popularity beginning in the 1970s. They offer an alternative educational experience for students who are typically identified as troubled teens. These schools include specialized outpatient programs, residential treatment programs, boarding schools, and wilderness programs, and offer a variety of therapeutic services and approaches to the mostly teenaged population they serve. There are scores of programs around the country, and in 2013 the National Association of Therapeutic Schools and Programs estimated that its members were serving over 4,600 clients. So it was not unreasonable at the time for us to consider such a school for Tim, or for the court and the school district to approve the placement.

According to its brochure, Tim's new school focused on "the academic, emotional, social and physical needs of students," with a thirty-month program leading to a high school diploma. I didn't think that Tim would stay for the full thirty months. I anticipated that if all went well, he might spend six months or a year there getting back on track academically and emotionally and then return to Connecticut to finish high school. For one thing, the program was very expensive, and the school district was paying just a portion of the total cost. For another, I didn't like him being so far from home. In addition, I wasn't fully sold on the program or convinced that the school was prepared to teach and care for a young man whose mental illness was becoming increasingly serious.

What ultimately persuaded me to give the program a try was that its staff said they would work with Tim's clinicians and educators in Connecticut to develop the most appropriate services for him. To me, integration of educational and clinical services was appearing more and more likely to be the key to Tim's success.

And if the first set of services didn't work, then the school's parent entity offered a backup option, a nearby six-week wilderness program. The wilderness program appealed both to Linda, who had been searching for such a program for Tim, and to Tim, who loved the idea of spending more time outdoors.

The school district agreed to reimburse us for the educational share of Tim's program—around 60 percent of the roughly $60,000 annual cost of the program. Linda and I split the rest. I built my share into my budget, grateful for my generous home equity line of credit and the part-time teaching position I held at Trinity College. If Tim were to need the wilderness program, it was going to cost even more.

Tim wasn't allowed to talk with me on the phone when he first arrived at the school because school rules dictated that he had to "earn" that privilege. Officials explained that in many instances parent-child relationships were part of the problem for their students, so the rule was also intended to reduce parent-child tension and drama. I thought that this came dangerously close to blaming the parents for a child's mental illness, but I let it go and waited for the letters he could write whenever he wanted.

My regular communications with Tim took place through an inter-
mediary, a parent liaison named Rachel. Once a week, Rachel called
to relay messages between Tim and me. The first time we talked, she
told me that she was also the parent of a child who had attended the
school. She was very reassuring. "Just last night," she reported in one
early conversation, "I walked into the library and found Tim snuggled
up in a blanket quietly reading a book." She also told me that he was
fitting in with the other students and working on building a fence to
keep deer out of a vegetable garden they had started.

She assured me that Tim would start classes soon. The school was
getting to know him and evaluating him first. She explained that the
school didn't put too much emphasis on academics at the beginning,
when new students were adapting to the school's routines and structure. He had started group counseling sessions, called "raps," and she
said that he would earn high school credits for these because they were
also considered an elective course in the school.

Tim's first letter home in late April suggested that he was having
some difficulty adjusting to life in his new school. "I think you guys
are making a mistake in sending me here," he wrote. "I have not gone
on one hike yet and if I do want to go on a hike then I have to get in
trouble, because here going on a hike means going to [the wilderness
program] for about seven weeks."

I chalked up his comments to hyperbole, especially when his first
postscript read: "Send food and candy." His second postscript, however,
worried me just a little, as I wondered if my now drug-free, insightful
son knew something I didn't: "I still can't see what your money's paying for."

I sent Tim a letter counseling patience. "You've got to try to give this
program a chance. It'll probably get better in a while. I talked with Rachel today, and she told me that you should be patient about the hikes;
while some kids are assigned to the wilderness program, you don't have
to misbehave to go on hikes."

But we did not have time for patience. In just a couple of weeks,
Rachel reported that Tim was not sleeping well and that his anxiety

levels were increasing. He became increasingly agitated and adversarial during the first two weeks in May and refused to follow the rules and routines of the school. I learned that the school's staff psychiatrist had discontinued Tim's trazodone when Tim arrived. I thought this was a terrible idea—Tim needed the trazodone to sleep properly, and a sleep-deprived Tim usually spelled trouble.

I spoke with the program's psychiatrist about this and learned about many other aspects of Tim's treatment that troubled me. Neither Dr. D nor Tim's psychiatrist in Connecticut had been consulted before Tim's trazodone was discontinued. I also learned that the program's psychiatrist believed that teenagers like Tim should be given a choice as to whether they took their medications, writing to me later on that this was "an effort on my part to help give him a sense of choice in such matters."

I responded that Tim's history was chock full of bad choices, and going off his medication cold turkey seemed like another one.

The psychiatrist agreed to reassess Tim but also wanted to consider a trial of a new antidepressant, Serzone, to help Tim with his sleep and anxiety.

I told him I preferred the trazodone, which I knew did some good, but would agree to try Serzone. (The drug would be withdrawn from the market four years later because it carried a rare but serious risk of liver damage.) But there was still the problem of getting Tim to take it. "I am uncertain whether he will utilize it, but I have made it available to him," the psychiatrist wrote to me. "I have also given him a reasonable range of 50 or 100 mg to try."

I couldn't help shaking my head. At the age of fifteen, Tim was being asked not only to decide which medications he would take, but also to determine his dosage. He was expected to make this choice without talking with his parents, without any input from the clinical professionals who had been treating him for years, and after a brief visit with a psychiatrist with whom he had no prior relationship. I understood the rationale behind giving an adult with mental illness a choice in his treatment. But a fifteen-year-old? The psychiatrist's view about this also added to my confusion about how serious Tim's illness was. After all, if he—a professional—thought that Tim had the judgment to know whether he should take his medication, then, I concluded, he must also believe that Tim wasn't very sick. And this conclusion affected how I responded to all of his treatment recommendations over the next few months.

Predictably, Tim did not take either the Serzone or the trazodone. And by the end of May, Rachel called to tell me that the school was "considering" moving Tim to the wilderness program.

Two days later, the wilderness program admissions office asked me where to fax the admission forms for my signature. I was surprised to find out that Tim was already in the program. Rachel called later to report that there had been an "incident" at school that precipitated the move. Apparently, Tim decided that after waiting six weeks to go hiking, he would go on his own. He left the campus and was missing for several hours.

The wilderness program did not send Tim directly into the wilderness as he had hoped, either. Its six-week program was divided into three phases. In the first phase, Orientation, Tim was to process the thinking and behaviors that created barriers to trust and success for him. During this phase, we still could not talk to him directly but were asked to write "issues letters" to tell him what behaviors had led to his being placed in the wilderness program. He had to formulate his responses through intense group-counseling sessions. The second phase, Pre-Course, would take him through survival-skill building exercises to prepare him and his group for the wilderness experience. The third phase, Course, was the actual wilderness experience, which happened over the last several days of the program.

With the wilderness experience as his incentive, Tim at first made an effort to comply with the program. He created a "dart board," putting his core issues in the bull's eye, his core feelings in the next circle, his behaviors in the next, and his coping tools in the outer circle. The first three circles were very detailed. Tim identified his core issues as low self-esteem, being out of place, and inconsistency; his core feelings as "mad, stupid, inadequate, hurt, unsafe, guilty, scared, upset, and depressed"; and his behaviors as "smoking pot, breaking things, not listening, threatening people, being alone, running away, letting people use me, being lazy, passive aggressive, stealing, and pushing people away." The outer circle, for his coping tools, was blank.

I also wrote Tim my issues letter. The issues I identified were that he had been failing his classes, using drugs, stealing money, damaging property, and not following rules at home or at school. I did not want to write only negative comments, so I closed on an upbeat note. "Don't be afraid to be the best Tim that you can be. Just as you're big in height and weight, you've got a huge heart, too. When you do finally decide to live a clean, safe life, I think you will be amazed by how much courage and power you have to make it happen."

Tim's response letter was brief and clear. "I don't like it here. I don't think it will make a big difference in my recent behavior, but I will try to be positive in my stay. I am sorry for the things I did and said to you and Ben, Lizzie, and Larissa. I am sorry for my behavior as well. I want to get better just as much as you want me to, maybe even more so." The last two sentences didn't sound much like Tim.

During the Orientation phase, Tim was caught filing a broken pen down to a sharp point. As a consequence he was "timed-out" of the program for a few days and dropped from his group into one beginning the program later. The wilderness school's parent liaison later explained to me that they dropped Tim two groups instead of one because they wanted "to be unpredictable and to send the message that he cannot find an easy way out." Of course, we had already learned through years of clinical care that structure and predictability worked better with Tim.

After Tim joined his new group, the parent liaison wrote: "Over the last couple of days, Tim has done very well—after a rough beginning to the week. Wednesday night we did find another piece of sharp plastic from the broken pen in his sleeping bag. We separated him from the group for the night and put him in a tent under constant night staff supervision. He has definitely been in an upswing since then."

With that minor crisis abating, I tried to be helpful. I wrote back that Tim was not capable of deferred gratification and that he might start acting out as he got closer to the wilderness experience. This was, in fact, exactly what happened.

Tim wrote to me: "I am unhappy but I think it will get better. We sleep in tents and learn about a medicine wheel. Tell Ben I said hi and I love him and miss him. Happy Father's Day!" He had a calm week, so I thought it would be a good time to pass along some news: Pam and I were getting married, and I was going to move to Texas afterward. Because I was still not allowed to talk to Tim directly, I sought the parent liaison's advice about how to tell him about these big changes in our lives. She suggested that I write Tim a letter and promised me that a seasoned counselor would help Tim process the news in a safe environment. I mailed her the letter on June 27.

I didn't hear back from Tim over the next couple of weeks, as he advanced to the Pre-Course phase of the wilderness program. He finally wrote to me on July 11, telling me, "My goal for Course is to open up to my group so they can get to know me better and we can build trust together and to stop trying to defend myself when I get confronted on my behaviors." Tim also reported wanting to "level out" himself so that people would know what to expect of him. I was surprised that he didn't mention my engagement to Pam. I later found out that because of an administrative error the letter had never been delivered to him.

But before I could follow up, Tim had a major breakdown. It was during a group rap, when he was being "confronted" by his peers. The school never told me exactly what happened, citing the need "to protect the confidentiality of all the students," but Tim shut down completely, going into a near-catatonic state. He sat down in the teepee and did not move for twenty-four hours, refusing even to eat or use the restroom.

The parent liaison convened a conference call with me and Linda and staff members, and reported that the psychiatrist recommended hospitalizing Tim for an evaluation. But Tim had ended his sit-down by the time of the call, so there was no rush. The staff felt that Tim could complete the wilderness program by having a modified wilderness experience for a day or two with a member of the staff. After this, he could go directly to a hospital that was about an hour's drive south of the campus.

I was skeptical about this approach for three reasons. First, I didn't think that our insurance company would fund a hospital stay that didn't have an immediate "danger to oneself or another" component to it. Second, Tim was still not taking trazodone or Serzone, so I questioned the urgency of the need to hospitalize him before insisting that he take his medication. Third, the school had still not communicated with Tim's Connecticut clinicians to discuss Tim's current state. I urged that there be a "clinical professionals only" conference call before any decision was made. This never happened.

At least there was some good news that day. The liaison reported via e-mail: "Tim climbed the Alpine Tower yesterday (50-foot high ropes course). He was glowing afterwards! He felt great about it." That may have been the extent of his modified wilderness experience. Tim "graduated" from the program on July 22 and went back to the boarding school instead of going to the hospital. He was taking no medications, and there was no more talk of hospitalizing him. I learned later that the reason was that my insurance company had turned down the admission request, as I had foreseen.

While in the wilderness program, Tim had been asked to write about what was in his head versus what was in his heart. His "head," he said, told him to "smoke pot, blow off boundaries, be mean, eat food all the time, lie, get violent, run away, stay clear of confrontation, stay alone, argue." His "heart" told him to "love people, smile, make friends, be nice, try new things, trust people, make people proud, and be healthy." But he hadn't learned any strategies for helping his heart prevail over his head.

Rachel reported during the last week in July: "Tim returned successfully to [the school] on Saturday afternoon at 1 p.m. He was welcomed back to the campus and is now settling down. He has talked a bit about some of the behavior that led him to [the wilderness program] and has acknowledged that, because of it, he is probably rightfully not a candidate to go on a camping expedition in a couple of weeks. Rest assured that Tim is doing ok. We're glad to have him back. Talk to you soon."

Tim was already being denied his next hike, and I imagined this had not gone over well with him. I decided that I needed to see for myself how he was doing. A parent weekend was scheduled in a couple of weeks, and I decided to go to it.

Three days later, there was a new crisis. It began with another bad rap, or group-counseling session. Tim, still unmedicated, had been "indicted" for not showering enough and was confronted about several other behaviors, including bullying. When the session was over he was fuming, but he continued with his daily routine. He did some afternoon chores and then went to dinner. After dinner, he hung out with a girl he had begun to think of as a special friend. This was not the first time they had been together, but "pairing off" violated school rules. She and Tim were told that they could only spend time together as part of a larger group. Tim headed back to his dormitory unhappy.

He found a group of young men who were talking together and joined in the conversation. His mind was still on his girlfriend. He was surprised to hear about a friend who had cut himself with a razor and needed medical attention. A staff member who was present later reported to me that Tim kept turning the conversation to the cutting episode and talking about how bad it made him feel. Finally he got up, announcing that he was going to the bathroom to write a good-bye letter to the girl.

The staff person on duty was not sure how to interpret Tim's comment, so he conferred with a supervisor. The good-bye letter sounded like a suicidal red flag to the supervisor, who did not know its context, which was that Tim thought he couldn't see his girlfriend alone anymore. The supervisor decided to call for an ambulance to take Tim to the hospital and had Rachel call me for my permission. In the meantime, Tim came back out of the bathroom and rejoined the group, unaware of the flurry of adult activity around him.

My phone rang at three-fifteen in the morning, awakening me from a sound sleep.

It was Rachel telling me that there was an emergency. Fearing the worst, I held my breath and asked what had happened. She told me that Tim didn't "feel safe" because of stress and was "threatening to harm himself" and that another, unnamed student didn't feel safe around Tim. She wanted me to authorize the school to hospitalize Tim immediately.

I was relieved that it wasn't worse and, groggy, was not sure that I understood what the emergency was, so I asked for more details. She told me about Tim's bad "rap" and trip to the bathroom but left out the part about Tim and the girl. "You woke me because he went to the bathroom?" I murmured. "That was the emergency?" Now she acknowledged that he was back with a supervisor and other students, apparently still participating in the late-night conversation. But it was after midnight, she said, and Tim was not settling down for the night.

"You could give him his trazodone," I told her, attempting to get us both some sleep. She persisted, however, saying that Tim had to go to the hospital at once. But because she had not actually seen Tim, I thought I should at least talk to him first or to the members of the night staff who were with him.

She agreed and then hurried off the phone because the ambulance was already on its way. She had to contact them, she said, to tell them that Tim might not be going to the hospital after all. She said that someone would call me right back.

No one did. I got up, got dressed, and waited for thirty minutes, worrying that the situation may have worsened. I called the school on its main number, but no one answered the phone. If they believed there was a suicidal student in crisis, I wondered, shouldn't someone be fielding calls? I checked my caller ID, found Rachel's number, and called it back. She answered right away.

"How did you get this number?" she asked as soon as she answered. I explained about the caller ID and said that no one had called me back.

She said that was because they were all still talking. She said she had to go, hanging up before giving me any updates about Tim.

With nothing to do but worry and wait, I sat and literally stared at the clock. My phone finally rang almost an hour later. It was a supervisor telling me that she had spoken to Tim and that he was "disoriented and asking for help." After reviewing the chronology of events with her, I suggested that Tim might be agreeable to taking some trazodone so he could get some sleep. She did not know that he had not been taking it. Then she volunteered that she was surprised when Tim returned to school from the wilderness program without any medications, but she had not thought to follow up.

I finally got to speak directly with Tim, and he didn't seem disoriented to me. Despite the late hour, he was calm and lucid. He was also very tired. Tim didn't tell me everything that had happened, only that he had "said something" and that he was "in a bad place" emotionally and needed a little time off. He had gone into the bathroom to think about whether he should go to bed or to a supervised "safe room" they sometimes made available to students. When I asked him what had put him in this "bad place," he put his "big brother"—a student mentor—on the phone.

The "big brother" told me about Tim's bad rap session. He also told me about the student who was afraid of Tim—apparently he and Tim had "a thing." I asked if he thought Tim needed to go to the hospital. He said no.

Then another student talked to me and repeated much of what Tim's "big brother" had said: Tim was having trouble dealing with his emotions and too easily got down on himself. I thought it odd that I was getting briefed so thoroughly about Tim from other students, getting more information from them in a few minutes than I had gotten from the staff over the past three months. This student also did not feel that Tim needed hospitalization; he thought that Tim should go to the safe room for a day or two to calm down.

Finally, I talked to the night supervisor. He believed that Tim needed a psychiatric evaluation but noted that his contact with Tim had been very limited. I shared Tim's medical history with him. He was unaware of much of it, including the conversations I had been having for more than three months with the school's staff and psychiatrist about Tim's medications. He did not feel that Tim was in any immediate danger, and also didn't think Tim needed to be hospitalized that night. He then added cryptically that Tim's behavior made the dorm "unsafe." He suggested that he would put Tim in a different room for the night, and that Tim could be evaluated further the next day.

It was after 5:15 in the morning, and I was trying to decide whether to go back to bed when the phone rang again. It was the supervisor, asking how my conversations had gone. I told her that there seemed to be a consensus that what Tim needed was rest, not hospitalization.

She shifted gears, telling me that she was pleased that Tim had asked for help before escalating his behavior. She also reported that he had started individual counseling a week earlier and that she would arrange to have Tim see his counselor later on in the day. The psychiatrist would also be on campus that day, and she was going to try to have him see Tim, too.

I sent an e-mail to Linda—who had missed all the excitement—to fill her in, and concluded with my impressions of Tim: "It was good to hear his voice tonight. It was good to hear him express himself, clearly and calmly and under control. He needs to process his emotions, though, and isn't quite there yet. He tells the 'what I did' part of the story accurately, but he can't yet talk about the 'why I did it,' leaving out any detail that would get into the specific emotions he was feeling."

Several hours later, the supervisor called again. She told me that Tim had not slept in over twenty-four hours and had not taken his trazodone. She also had a psychologist on the line. He told me that Tim had seen the psychiatrist, who reported that Tim was having auditory hallucinations. Rather than giving Tim the trazodone, the psychiatrist was recommending an immediate inpatient admission to the hospital where he had privileges.

I was tired, frustrated, and upset by this news. They still had not made clear the nature of the emergency. In the absence of other symptoms, auditory hallucinations in a sleep-deprived child should not have been enough to require immediate hospitalization. I told them that I still believed Tim should be given his trazodone, which was what his Connecticut psychiatrist and Dr. D recommended, and given a chance to sleep. But I also said that I would defer to their judgment.

The following day I had a forty-five-minute conversation with Dr. D. He had finally spoken with the school psychiatrist. After their conversation, Dr. D had agreed that an inpatient stay was appropriate because the voices Tim reported to be hearing might be an indication of another, more serious mental illness.

As Tim's hospitalization began, I took stock. Tim had not yet received any traditional educational services at his new school. He was not happy, and his wilderness experience had been a failure. He was not taking his medications and was showing signs of a serious mental illness. Dr. D advised me that we might want to consider withdrawing Tim from the boarding school and bringing him home. He suggested that I start thinking about alternatives.

nine

HOSPITALIZATION FROM THE NORTHWEST TO MIDDLETOWN

❝ TIM HAS BEEN having auditory hallucinations including command voices which direct him to hurt others," was the key statement that got Tim admitted to the small community psychiatric hospital about an hour away from the boarding school.

The psychiatrist there—who was also the staff psychiatrist at the school—wrote that Tim's "most recent intense hallucination was when he was in a conflict with staff and when another peer was restrained on the unit. He indicated that he heard voices indicating that he should jump in and stop the restraint." When I first read that passage, I didn't doubt that Tim was hearing voices. I just wondered if they were commanding Tim to hurt others or to help them.

On admission, the psychiatrist observed that Tim's symptoms could be related either to bipolar disorder or schizoaffective disorder. His recommendation was that Tim be started on Zyprexa, an "atypical," or second-generation, antipsychotic used to treat both of these.

A psychologist also assessed Tim. He wrote that Tim "was willing to answer factual questions about himself and his circumstances but was unable or unwilling to discuss his current thinking and feelings. Also, he was vague in describing his reasons for hospitalizations and would not talk about his reported hallucinations."

He reported that during the interview, Tim attempted "image management" and a "facade of control," which the psychologist interpreted to mean that Tim was hiding symptoms of his illness. He indicated, however, that he believed that he had enough information from Tim to summarize Tim's psychological state.

The psychologist did not find Tim to be suicidal. Instead, he wrote, Tim was "under considerable situational stress," which compounded a "capacity for suicide." He also found Tim to be depressed and despondent, calling him "apathetic" and "pessimistic regarding his ability to control his situation."

He observed that "Tim's reality testing is poor" and that this resulted "in Tim's frequent failure to anticipate the consequences of his actions." He added that Tim reported "feeling lonely, misunderstood, and mistreated," and that "there is some evidence from testing that the auditory hallucinations reported by staff are present."

Finally, he observed that Tim "is in a nearly chronic state of pique that extends beyond an aversion to authority and encompasses most of his life space. . . . He may even choose to make those mistakes if it means frustrating those in positions of authority."

The psychologist recommended an antidepressant, an antipsychotic if the antidepressant did not work, psychotherapy, and a return to the boarding school. He cautioned that illicit substances "are particularly dangerous for him and they would almost certainly cause irreversible psychological damage."

I had mixed feelings about the psychologist's evaluation. On the one hand, his conclusion that Tim was unable to anticipate the consequences of his actions was consistent with everything I had experienced with him. Also, the determination that Tim felt lonely, misunderstood, and mistreated was consistent with how Tim had described himself on more than one occasion. On the other hand, his seemingly carefully chosen words of "a capacity for suicide" fell short of describing Tim as suicidal, and the "situational stress" that "compounded" the "capacity" for suicide might only be compounded further if Tim returned to the emotional-growth boarding school.

Also, his and the psychiatrist's reports seemed to disagree on an important point of treatment. The psychiatrist seemed convinced that Tim's behaviors were signs of serious mental illness requiring an antipsychotic drug, but the psychologist seemed to be recommending the use of an antidepressant first. I did not know which one to believe.

Tim settled into the hospital routine, and his symptoms seemed to diminish almost immediately. The environment was less stressful for him than the school. There were no more "raps," just regular group and individual counseling sessions, and a much simpler routine consisting of meals, counseling, quiet time, and recreation. But, as best I could tell, there was still no educational component.

After being apart from Tim for four months, I was looking forward to seeing him so I could form my own judgments about how he was doing.

Before I left I asked both the school and the hospital to consider allowing Tim to have a day pass to go back to the school with me when I visited. I explained that allowing him to be my guide would give Tim an opportunity to take some ownership and control of his space there. They both denied my request, each blaming the other. So I never actually got to see the inside of the buildings where Tim was living and being educated. Rachel e-mailed me that the hospital would not approve this. The supervisor "believes that it would not be appropriate for Tim to come back on campus to show you around this weekend because he has not yet been cleared for a campus pass," she wrote. And my contact at the hospital e-mailed me that the school didn't think Tim should be back on campus so soon. Neither one seemed aware of the other's response.

I knew that I wanted to bring Tim home as soon as I could. Over the past four months, he had been bounced between the school, the wilderness program, and the hospital, and the school had not delivered on the promise it made to me when he was admitted that it would work closely with Tim's Connecticut clinicians and educators to develop a meaningful plan for him. His educational program was nonexistent, he wasn't making friends, the rap session approach was causing him enormous stress, and he was exhibiting symptoms of serious mental illness. And it was costing us a small fortune. I also didn't think the school or the hospital was being entirely truthful with me about why Tim was there. On a day-to-day basis, the hospital was being as tight-lipped about Tim's condition and treatment as the school had been. Although the hospital knew that I had traveled across the country to come there, nearly everyone, including the psychiatrist, declined to meet with me. I had never before experienced clinicians who were unwilling to talk with me about my son's treatment. It seemed clear that they did not trust me, and I knew that I did not trust them.

There were risks associated with Tim's returning to Connecticut without a program in place. The most significant one was that he might refuse treatment and begin self-medicating again. So I wanted to determine if there was a program we might use as a transition to living at home with Linda or me. This could be followed, I hoped, by regular community-based mental health and substance abuse counseling.

But Linda was not yet ready to throw in the towel on the boarding school, which told her it would willing to take Tim back after his discharge from the hospital. Even so, I doubted that the school could manage someone with Tim's clinical profile. And I suspected they felt the same way. Tim's "situational depression" was a huge potential liability for the school should anything major go wrong after he returned.

As of mid-August, there was still time to decide. The hospital was in no hurry to discharge Tim. It kept asking for additional inpatient treatment days from my insurance company and talked only about moving Tim to an intermediate care unit if and when the insurer determined that he no longer needed his current level of care.

When I finally arrived at the hospital after an all-night trip, a social worker was the only one who made herself available to meet with me. Even that meeting almost didn't happen. Just before I left Hartford, I received a fax telling me that "protocol allows for parent/patient contact during therapy sessions only, except under 'extenuating' circumstances." The inference was that I might not be allowed to see Tim when I arrived because this had not been approved in advance. The psychiatrist also wanted me to "allow" the social worker to inform Tim of my visit, the implication being that if both she and Tim did not agree to the visit, I might not be allowed to see him. I ignored the fax, and they made the visit as uncomfortable for me as possible.

I first met with the social worker in a private office. She seemed pleasant enough as she reviewed Tim's progress during the two weeks he had been in the hospital. Then she told me the rules for our visit. There were no visiting rooms available. And because of "confidentiality rules," I would not be allowed to go anywhere in the hospital with Tim where I might see other children, including the indoor and outdoor recreational areas and the dining room. Despite those confidentiality rules, however, our own visits would be in a small public reception area, where our conversation could be overheard by anyone down the hall. We were told to enjoy ourselves.

I stayed for eight hours. Tim looked good. His eyes were bright, and he had been eating well for two weeks. He showed little or no anxiety, having responded well to the hospital routines. He was animated and happy. He told me stories about his life at the school, the wilderness program, and the hospital, and I told him stories about mine. We talked politics and reminisced about his childhood, our trips together, our drives to morning therapy sessions with *Imus* on the radio, and family picnics and parties. He wanted the details of Ben's, Lizzie's, and Larissa's lives, and I updated him about what they were all doing as they prepared for the school year. We discussed at length my planned move to Austin the following year. I was going to sell our house in the spring. Tim said he would miss the woods in our backyard, but he had visited Austin with his mother one time, liked it, and looked forward to seeing it again. We laughed about the Schlitterbahn T-shirt he had bought when he went to the well-known Texas water park. He had worn the shirt to his previous high school one day, and because no one there spoke German or knew much about central Texas, they worried that "Schlitterbahn" was some coded drug message. Tim laughed when he recalled this.

When I told him that the boarding school had never delivered the letter I had written to him about my engagement to Pam, he shook his head. "See what I mean about them?" he said. He reminded me of his warning that he didn't think the school was worth the money we were paying for it.

There was a normalcy to our conversation that was common to most of the conversations I had with Tim. When he was not in an acute phase of his mental illness, he was charming, happy, and sociable and enjoyed visiting, talking, and laughing. It was good for me to see him this way. We continued talking until five o'clock, with just a brief break for me to run out and pick up some sushi for lunch. Then I was told that I needed to leave so that Tim could have his supper and begin his evening routine. I told him I'd see him the next day for a few hours before going back to the airport, gave him a hug, and drove back to my hotel.

I got up early the next morning and drove to the school. I stayed only a few minutes. It was a quiet Sunday, and the campus was situated in a beautiful mountain setting. But in late August it also felt a little dreary, isolated, and cold. The campus was deserted, and there were few signs of life. No one said hello to me.

Then I visited with Tim at the hospital for another three hours. Our conversation was more subdued than it had been the day before. We were a little talked out and more focused on the here and now. As I got ready to go, I was certain I was going to get him back to Connecticut as soon as I could. But I did not want to get his hopes up too soon, so I encouraged him to try to make his stay a positive one. We hugged, telling each other "I love you." I went out to the parking lot, got into the rental car, and drove myself back to the airport.

A few days later, the hospital decided that Tim was no longer in need of acute inpatient hospitalization and moved him to a lower level of care. Tim stayed there for three more weeks, when my insurer decided that further treatment was unnecessary. He was discharged, and if he had a detailed aftercare treatment plan, I never saw it.

When Tim was released from the hospital, he was taking Zyprexa for bipolar disorder and "possible" schizoaffective disorder. He returned to his emotional-growth boarding school, and once again Rachel tried to be upbeat. She e-mailed me: "Tim has grown so much that we had to get him new jeans the other day. He could no longer button the ones he had when he arrived! You've seen him recently, but he almost seems to grow on a daily basis. He tells us that he is happy here, but he is quite routinely forgetting to go to the nurse to get his meds. We are working on a behavioral sequence plan that will help him organize to remember meds, as well as daily bathing, dealing with dirty clothes and attention to his dorm space cleanliness."

The return to the school's routine, however, with its regular confrontational "raps," was not what Tim needed. The behavioral sequence plan apparently involved other students getting on Tim's case in raps about his messiness and lack of cleanliness. At first, he was verbally confrontational in return. Then the situations escalated into minor scuffles. A week later, Tim was involved in a major fight, which resulted in another teenager breaking his collarbone. When Rachel gave me this news, she reported that Tim was "on the cusp" of being asked to leave the school. He was argumentative and confrontational, and increasingly he couldn't control his temper.

The next day, Tim was in crisis again. He was acting aggressively and couldn't calm down. He was readmitted to the hospital, and my insurer certified the stay. I had a long conversation with a case coordinator at the insurance company after this. She explained that Tim's bipolar diagnosis qualified him for extended mental health benefits under the Connecticut state parity regulations in place at that time. Otherwise, she reported, Tim would already have exceeded his lifetime cap on mental health benefits. He was only fifteen years old.

She explained that after reviewing Tim's history, the insurer believed that Tim's current needs could only be met in an inpatient setting. The insurer did not see a return to the boarding school as a viable option. I agreed, and I learned that day that the hospital in the northwest had come to the same conclusion. The insurer's case coordinator suggested that we transfer Tim closer to home, and she gave me a list of programs that she believed might be able to meet Tim's needs.

Linda and I began the process of trying to find an inpatient program that would admit Tim, but beds were in short supply. We asked the hospital in the northwest to check into the availability of beds in several Connecticut hospitals. Tim found out about this and grew excited about what he hoped was an imminent return to Connecticut.

In late October, we received news that a hospital just a few miles from our home would have a bed for Tim if we could wait three weeks. The insurer agreed to cover Tim's stay in the northwest until the bed in Connecticut opened, then cover his stay at the hospital in Connecticut. This was great news. I spoke with the Connecticut hospital's admissions director and began to work out the arrangements for Tim's admission.

In the meantime, Tim was transferred to the intermediate care unit at the hospital in the northwest. He was a little stir crazy waiting to leave, but for the most part he managed the routine—eating, watching television, attending group and individual counseling sessions, and getting a little exercise. He made no friends and was occasionally involved in scuffles, but so far as I knew there were no major incidents.

A couple of weeks later, I was disappointed to learn that the bed in the Connecticut hospital had fallen through. We discovered that none of the other hospitals in Connecticut had a bed for Tim, either. Linda and I redoubled our efforts, but before we were able to come up with anything, the insurance company found a placement. It was a program in western Connecticut, about an hour from our homes. I knew the program from my time in the state legislature. I liked it, but neither Linda nor I thought it was right for Tim. I understood it to be primarily a drug treatment program, not a mental health program, and Tim was not using drugs at the time. But I was assured by both the insurer and the program that this was a "myth" that the program had been "trying to debunk" for ten years, so they made plans to approve a stay for him there.

The insurer's plan was for Tim to start in the residential treatment component and then transition either to the intensive outpatient component or possibly a partial hospitalization program at a different facility (should a bed become available) that specialized in mental health treatment. When I told the insurer's case coordinator that the drug treatment program did not offer the round-the-clock supervision I felt Tim needed, she dismissed my worry.

In fact, she was so eager to place Tim there that she wanted him released from the hospital in the northwest on the day before Thanksgiving. I had to explain that I could not get flights for Tim and me on such short notice on the busiest travel days of the year. She relented and agreed to delay his discharge until after the holiday. I was to find out later that the insurer denied this portion of Tim's stay because it was not medically necessary. This was mental health coverage in a nutshell for me.

I booked a flight to the airport closest to the hospital on the Tuesday after Thanksgiving and a return flight to Connecticut for Tim and me on Wednesday. The new program expected Tim on Thursday. When I arrived at the hospital in the northwest I was shown to an office where a staff person gave me a copy of Tim's discharge plan and some papers to sign. No one else met with me or came to wish Tim well. We were shown to the door as if he were being released from jail. He and I looked at each other and agreed that it was long past time to go.

Tim had arrived in the northwest in April 2000 to attend an emotional-growth boarding school that promised him a comprehensive academic, social, emotional, and physical growth experience. He left a little over seven months later having attended the school for a total of ten weeks. He earned zero academic credits, made no friends, and regressed emotionally. He stopped taking his medications and acquired new diagnoses of bipolar disorder and possible schizoaffective disorder.

He came back home with no community-reentry or long-term treatment plan in place. He had technically exhausted his lifetime mental health benefits.

On the plus side, Tim had scaled a fifty-foot wall (though no mountains). I had parted with about $10,000 and felt no wiser for the experience.

But that high school was still better than the one that followed.

Tim arrived at his new program on Thursday, November 30, at eleven in the morning. The insurer had approved the first seven days of his stay. On Friday, the program enrolled Tim as a freshman in its on-campus school—I'll call it High School 3. It assigned him to a youth treatment center and provided him with a semiprivate dorm room.

On Saturday, the program reported Tim missing after he walked away from his unsupervised living arrangement. On Sunday, it discharged the still-missing Tim from its program. I actually received an official transcript for Tim from High School 3 a month later. Needless to say, he hadn't earned any credits. And the insurer did not even have to pay for all seven days.

Tim was missing for two days. He found shelter from the December cold in an abandoned building. His smoking fire attracted the attention of neighbors, who called the police. They brought Tim to the New Haven Juvenile Detention Center—his first experience in a correctional facility.

When Tim had flown back with me to Connecticut the week before, he was calm, well-fed, clean, and in good spirits, looking forward to seeing his siblings again. But by the time he arrived at the juvenile detention center, he was nervous, dirty, hungry, and upset. He had not slept well for several nights, and during his intake evaluation he reported that he was hearing voices again. He was transferred to a local hospital for a psychiatric evaluation. The hospital admitted him on December 5, just five days after his discharge from the hospital in the northwest. It felt like a month to me.

My insurer approved the stay and paid over $6,300 for the ten days he was hospitalized. Tim's case coordinator admitted to me that she may have been premature in pushing so aggressively for Tim's discharge from the hospital in the northwest and admission to the drug treatment/behavioral health program in western Connecticut. I had a queasy feeling that it would not be the last time a premature discharge or inappropriate placement would lead to another hospitalization for Tim.

During his ten-day hospitalization, Tim's doctors concluded that he needed a long-term mental health treatment program. The hospital offered such a program, but it did not have a bed available. These shortages are nothing new. A March 2008 Treatment Advocacy Center report (Torrey et al. 2008) characterized forty-eight of the fifty states, including Connecticut, as having a bed shortage in the range of serious to critical—shortages that have only been growing over the years. And this report was published just before states embarked on four years of deep cuts—totaling well over $4 billion—in state mental health services. So after ten days, Tim was sent back to juvenile detention to await a court hearing. Two days later, he again reported that he was hearing voices. Detention center officials sent him back to the hospital's emergency department. This time he was deemed stable and sent right back to detention.

To end this bouncing back and forth, we needed to find a bed for Tim as soon as possible. I learned that there might be one at the Riverview Hospital for Children and Youth, a state facility located behind the Connecticut Valley Hospital campus in Middletown. Riverview had a small, specialized program for young people referred from the juvenile justice system. An intake worker confirmed in late December that a bed would open by the end of January and that it could be Tim's if he would agree "voluntarily" to a three-month stay.

Tim did not want to make this commitment, but he weighed it against the alternative. If he said no, the court would probably still send him to Riverview for a thirty-day evaluation. Then he would be back at the detention center awaiting a court hearing. That could take days or even weeks, and from there he would probably still be required to go to a partial hospitalization program.

This cooperation between treatment and correctional programs to bring pressure to bear on people with mental illness to accept treatment "voluntarily" in lieu of incarceration is a strategy of today's growing number of behavioral health courts. For many, it is controversial because it can be considered forced treatment. Several studies (for example, Ridgely et al. 2007; Steadman et al. 2010) have found behavioral health court programs to be effective at lowering recidivism rates and improving treatment compliance. The challenge, of course, is having a treatment program available so the person doesn't just sit in jail waiting for a bed.

Tim waited about a month for the bed at Riverview to open. During this time, he received no educational or clinical treatment services. However, his stay at the juvenile detention center helped stabilize him—and even helped to reintegrate him into our home life again. He had a regular schedule and routine and ate and slept well. He was allowed frequent visitors and was also given day passes to spend time at home during the holidays.

Tim went to juvenile court in mid-January and was ordered into his "voluntary" Riverview program on January 17. He remained on "intensive probation" until mid-May, meaning that if he left Riverview during that time he would be taken back into custody. At the time of his Riverview admission, he was physically healthy, well-groomed, clean, and sober. He conversed easily with adults. He was interested in current events, cooking, rock music, comedy movies, and complex video games. He enjoyed conversations about religion and philosophy and often found humor in the ironies of life. He seemed, in many ways, like a typical teenager.

But Tim was far from a typical teenager. He brought with him to Riverview a kitchen sink's worth of labels. His preliminary or admission diagnoses at the time were listed as psychotic disorder, conduct disorder, cannabis abuse, ADHD, learning disabilities, and dyssomnia. He was also suspected of having bipolar disorder, schizoaffective disorder, PTSD, and possible cannabis dependence. Trying to treat all of these at once presented a buffet of possible drugs and therapies. Clinicians had continued to add diagnoses over the years, but I wasn't certain that we had found the correct one yet. And neither was Riverview. Its plan was to clarify Tim's diagnoses, determine the appropriate medications, and use individual and group counseling to help him manage his symptoms of mood instability, anger, low frustration tolerance, suicidal ideation, aggression, and auditory hallucinations.

Tim's hospital-based social worker reported that he adjusted well to the hospital routines. He was enrolled in a campus school for his first meaningful educational instruction in almost a year. I'll call it High School 4. He did well there at first as the school reviewed material he had previously learned and relied heavily on classroom participation, receiving A's in English, math, and health and B's in social studies, earth science, art, and computer technology. And as he still aimed to please adults whenever given the chance, his teachers reported that he displayed appropriate classroom behavior, interacted appropriately with teachers, and displayed good effort in class.

To determine where Tim was academically, the school also administered some standardized tests. When he took them, the school noticed the significant discrepancy in his oral and written abilities. Tim was reported to be "very lethargic" during the testing. The results included that "he was unable to tell time, had no knowledge of decimals or fractions, and appeared to be unable to compute math problems with the use of a paper and pencil."

Tim tested at nearly the same levels he had achieved three years earlier, and a lifetime ago, at his sixth-grade school in Middlefield. He had made no academic progress since then. We attended a PPT meeting during the second week of February. While his IEP acknowledged that his expected placement was tenth grade, in light of his test results he remained in ninth.

Tim's overall academic goal at Riverview was to earn credits toward a high school diploma. He ultimately earned three. His overall behavioral goal was to improve his interpersonal and social skills. He had less success with this. Tim's IEP called for him to receive instruction in a "regular" classroom with no more than seven students and to participate in a behavior-management program, which included positive reinforcement, cueing, a point system for tracking appropriate behavior, time-outs if needed, and removal from the classroom for unsafe behavior. Suspension wasn't used at this school because there was no place to send a suspended student.

Tim was not an entirely willing participant in his clinical program. He was always polite and never refused to attend his family counseling session. He and I usually had these sessions alone, without any of the other children present, and he had separate family counseling sessions with Linda because the issues he needed to work out with her were different from the ones he needed to work out with me. But he usually had little to say when I was there other than to complain about minor issues he had at the hospital with patients or staff or at home with his mother when he had a day pass, and to ask when his next day pass might be. To me, it seemed that he was just tired of talking about himself and his issues after years of counseling. Tim's social worker reported that he was also very cautious in his group counseling sessions but that he was a little more open in his individual counseling.

My insurer approved Tim's stay at Riverview, but we were still fighting about past bills. One day, I was summoned to a meeting to appeal a denial of payment. There were so many appeals pending at the time that when I arrived at the office, I had to admit that I had no idea which denial we were there to discuss. Neither did the people conducting the appeal. So we picked one—the denial of care for Tim's last week at the hospital in the northwest—because it was for the biggest amount.

The hearing board members listened to me with a sympathetic ear, especially when I explained how his early release had led to his jailing and rehospitalization the following week. The administrative aide who accompanied me from the hearing said that mine was one of the most compelling stories she had heard. Yet the appeal was still denied.

Denials of care were our norm. Before the Mental Health Parity Act was enacted in 2008, 90 percent of health insurers imposed restrictions on mental health treatment. Now, with even stronger mental health benefits under the Affordable Care Act (ACA), things are supposed to be different. Under ACA, insurers are supposed to make mental health benefits part of the "essential health benefits" offered in all insurance packages. And under the Mental Health Parity Act, these benefits are supposed to be equivalent to the benefits offered for the treatment of physical illnesses. But neither law is perfect. The "essential health benefits" in the ACA are in part determined by the historical record in each state (which means that they can still differ from state to state), and "parity" does not in and of itself prevent limitations on services—or guarantee that mental health providers will be reimbursed for services at the same level as other providers.

One day, Tim's Riverview social worker pulled me aside to talk about Tim's clinical profile. Tim was refusing to bathe. He was being aggressive toward other teenagers. There had been a couple of times when he needed to be restrained, and he seemed unable to manage either his thoughts or his emotions.

She said that Tim's clinical team had met, but they were not sure what his primary diagnosis might be because he was exhibiting so many symptoms, some of which might be side effects from medications. They proposed a "med wash," which involved stopping all of the medications Tim was taking. It would take several weeks for the effects of all the medications to clear his system, but the symptoms that were left would give a much clearer picture of his illness. And he would be safe in the hospital for the whole time. At this point, I thought that the most important thing after so many years of uncertainty was finally getting a clear diagnosis so we could get the correct plan of treatment with the most appropriate meds for Tim. I agreed to the med wash, as did Linda.

I was commuting between Austin and Middletown at the time. I had a new job in Austin running a community health and mental health collaborative called the Indigent Care Collaboration and was finishing up my old job in Hartford. I was also getting my Middletown house ready for sale while helping Pam settle into our new house in Austin. When I was in Connecticut, I visited with Tim at Riverview as often as I could, and we enjoyed talking, eating together, and playing Ping-Pong in the recreation area. Tim was also allowed to spend some days and nights at home. He was generally well behaved with me at home. He typically watched television, played video games, or spent time visiting with his siblings. I was running a Catholic Youth Organization basketball league at the time, and Tim also came happily with me to see his siblings play in their games. But I did not ever leave him alone or even let him far from my sight.

Over time, as he went off his medications, Tim's agitation increased. He became more hyperactive, short-tempered, and anxious. I didn't have too much trouble with him, but his social worker at Riverview reported that he occasionally had to be put in a time-out room. Linda also suffered through a challenge or two. One time, after Tim went to a friend's house and drank alcohol, she told him that this was unacceptable and ended the visit. But as she was bringing him back to Riverview, he jumped out of the car along busy Route 66 in Middletown. She called 911 and me for help. The police found Tim and took him back to Riverview, while I followed behind to check him back in.

After a month, the report from Riverview was a little frightening: "While off medication, Tim became grossly psychotic as evidenced by no longer showering or attending to his grooming, talking to himself, responding to auditory command hallucinations to hurt himself and others, marked thought disorganization, inappropriate affect, frank paranoia and delusions about people plotting to hurt him."

Later, the hospital reported that "at one point he tried to hang his clothing from the sprinkler in the time out room so that he could hang himself." I was astonished at how severe his symptoms were without medication, especially because I had never witnessed some of the worst of these symptoms myself.

His social worker scheduled a meeting with Linda and me in April and told us that the clinical team had come to a consensus. They believed that Tim had schizoaffective disorder. Diagnoses of schizo-affective disorder are rare, and there is some debate about whether it is simply the co-occurrence of schizophrenia and a mood disorder or a separate clinical condition with aspects of both schizophrenia and bi-polar disorder (Abrams, Rojas, and Arciniegas 2008). I didn't care about this debate. From my perspective, there were only two things that were relevant about the diagnosis. The first was that for the first time we had a clear clinical consensus that Tim might have schizophrenia. The second was that this afforded us an opportunity to try some drugs that had not been available to him before. The team at Riverview was rec-ommending that we try the atypical antipsychotic Geodon, a brand of ziprasidone.

Tim's condition improved after he began taking Geodon. Over the next several weeks, his fear, agitation, and anxiety levels decreased; his auditory hallucinations quieted down; his hygiene improved; and he was clearer and more rational in his thinking. I was thrilled to have the Tim I knew best back. He also seemed to be tolerating the drug well, without any side effects. By the beginning of May, we were mak-ing plans for Tim's discharge from Riverview. After some discussion, we decided that Tim would come to live with me when I moved to Texas in the summer. I began to look into services and schools for Tim and arranged for a weekend pass from Riverview so that he could ac-company me and the other children to Austin to attend Verena's high school graduation over Memorial Day weekend.

Tim had originally been scheduled to be discharged by then. But Riverview did not think he was ready, and I agreed. Unfortunately,

Riverview made a critical mistake in how it went about accomplishing this. Without telling me or Linda in advance, it contacted Tim's probation officer a week before his scheduled discharge and arranged for a finding that Tim had violated his probation on the day of the alcohol incident with Linda. Tim was locked in place until he could go back to court in June.

When the social worker told me this, I was not pleased. The alcohol incident was more than a month old, and Tim had stabilized considerably since then. She told me that Tim had remained calm and under control when they told him what they were doing. But they missed the point. They lost his trust, and he never really developed a close working relationship with a therapist again.

Tim remained at Riverview until July 17. He eased back into home life and played an important role in Pam's and my wedding in Middletown on July 5 as one of my two "best men" with Ben. It was Tim's first major family event in a year and a half. We had a big picnic on an estate owned by the city. He had a great time eating lobster and veggie burgers, playing volleyball and bocce, and listening to music.

Tim's discharge summary from Riverview noted that he needed "medication management of psychiatric symptoms of depression, anxiety, paranoia, auditory hallucinations, inattention, and disruptive behavior." He also required "constant prompting with his limited motivation for self-care, hygiene, and positive social skills."

Finally, with respect to illegal drugs, "Tim has a history of self-medicating with marijuana; he intends to quit for one year, but continues to glorify uses and 'business.'" Presumably, that meant that he thought drug dealing might be a lucrative career someday.

In summary, Riverview considered him to be "at high risk for re-emergence of psychiatric symptoms." He was discharged on ziprasidone and trazodone, the antidepressant he had been taking for some time to help him sleep.

His discharge diagnoses included schizoaffective disorder, PTSD, ADHD, learning disorder, and cannabis abuse. His mental illness was described as serious; his prognosis was guarded.

And Pam and I faced two more challenges as Tim came to live with us. "I'm institutionalized now," Tim joked, paraphrasing a line from *The Shawshank Redemption*. Tim would have a difficult adjustment to the freedom of living at home again and to the demands of attending a regular school.

The second was that Tim's biological and legal clocks were ticking relentlessly toward adulthood. If we did not do something in the next eighteen months to teach him some survival and living skills, he would turn eighteen with little or no prospect for a manageable life.

Tim left Riverview Hospital after six months of inpatient treatment. My insurer paid at least $141,000 for his stay—all of it just after its penny-wise, pound-foolish decision that Tim would no longer need hospitalization but only services in a drug treatment program when he came home to Connecticut. The State of Connecticut picked up most of the rest.

And just as everything else is bigger in Texas, soon these numbers would grow bigger there, too.

ten

TIM COMES TO AUSTIN

T IM FLEW TO Austin with his siblings in late July,
eighteen days after Pam and I were married. For the
first month of our marriage, we had all five children with us
—seventeen-year-old Verena, sixteen-year-old Tim, fifteen-
year-old Larissa, twelve-year-old Lizzie, and eleven-year-
old Ben.

We all had some adjustments to make. Tim had spent
most of the last year in locked facilities where all his daily
routines were regulated. Now he decided when to eat,
sleep, bathe, and come and go. Austin was a new community for him, culturally different from both central Connecticut and the northwest. Pam was also a new adult in
the picture for Tim. Her personality was very different from
Linda's, more low-key. He did not know how she would
respond to him or what our joint expectations of him would
be. Fortunately, though, Pam was willing to work to help
Tim be successful and prepare him for adulthood.

Pam and Verena were adjusting to what Pam said later was like "an invasion of aliens from Connecticut." Our lifestyle was much louder and more chaotic than they were used to. Austin was a big university city and was more diverse racially and culturally than central Connecticut, and that appealed immediately to my growing children. Lizzie observed that she saw many more people who looked like her than she ever had before. Larissa spent the month trying to decide whether she wanted to stay in Austin or go back to Connecticut. Lizzie and Ben were worried about being asked to choose between mom and dad. And I was getting used to being seen as a Texan, working at a brand-new job in a brand-new community.

We did not waste time getting Tim into treatment in Austin. We quickly made appointments for him with a new psychiatrist and a new mental health counselor.

At the first visit with his psychiatrist, Tim and I realized we weren't in Connecticut anymore. The psychiatrist was wearing cowboy boots with his suit. Tim grinned when he saw them and began to act a little silly. The psychiatrist didn't seem to notice. He invited us into his office, reviewed Tim's medical history, and then asked a question.

"Do you know you're adopted?" he asked my six-foot, three-inch African American son, as I, his five-foot, nine-inch white father sat there next to him. Still smiling about the cowboy boots, Tim could not contain himself. We always found the question a little absurd when it was asked, and usually irrelevant. Adoption, after all, does not cause schizophrenia.

"Adopted?" Tim said with mock astonishment. "I'm adopted? Dad," he said turning to me, "did you know I was adopted?"

I played along. "Adopted? You're adopted, Tim? I didn't know you were adopted," I answered. "It's news to me."

"It's news to me, too, Dad!"

We had our joke together, but the psychiatrist just sat there, stared, and entered something into his computer. We decided later that he probably didn't get our alien Connecticut humor.

Tim left the appointment without having established much of a relationship with the psychiatrist but with prescriptions for trazodone and Geodon in hand. The psychiatrist told him he'd see him again in a few weeks and warned him sternly against mixing his medications with marijuana or any other drugs. That warning bothered me because I knew that Tim would probably use marijuana again soon and because the psychiatrist didn't really take the time to do more than say "don't."

Tim's new counselor was a friendly, even-tempered, unpretentious, low-key woman. Tim liked her but went to sessions only reluctantly and infrequently after the first couple of months. He was tired of therapy and did not think that it had helped him much after he left Dr. D behind.

Meanwhile, we approached a small private school—I'll call it High School 5—to see about enrolling Tim. Verena had graduated from the school in May. While it had no special education program, its staff provided plenty of individualized instruction, and Verena had thrived there. Tim interviewed with the principal and several teachers. These interviews went well, and the principal told us that the school would admit Tim on two conditions. The first was that we pay for extra tutoring in math. The second was that we enroll Tim in the ninth grade once again—his fifth start on a ninth-grade curriculum.

During this transition, Linda took a trip to Austin and visited with the school's staff. While she came away with a favorable impression, she worried about Tim's transition to Austin in general. In particular, she wondered how we would manage to keep Tim away from drugs and alcohol. She was skeptical about his recent sobriety; he had admitted to staying "straight" only so that he could get out of Riverview.

I was worried about this, too. But based on Tim's history, I didn't think it was possible for us to keep Tim away from drugs and alcohol in any community. I replied to Linda in an e-mail: "Tim will not be able to function in society if he doesn't begin taking responsibility for his own sobriety. You and I can't protect him; we can just support him to make good decisions about who he hangs around with and what he does." At this point I was hoping we'd get a year of sobriety, if even that. I had long since learned to take things one day at a time.

Linda was also concerned that Tim might not be able to avoid being arrested in Austin. I thought that would be a problem anywhere, and I could only reply that staying out of trouble was Tim's responsibility. She also wondered if a small private school would be up to the challenge of educating Tim. The school had no track record of being able to handle a child with Tim's issues. "What if he had psychiatric symptoms? How would staff know what to do? Would they do the right thing?" she worried. Tim's psychiatrist and counselor were also recommending a specialized treatment program for Tim. But neither Linda nor I thought this would be a good choice because he had already spent so much time inside institutional walls during the past year. And we had both wanted to try a small private school a few years earlier to see if individualized instruction might work better for Tim after the debacle of his sixth-grade due process hearing.

I may have been grasping at straws, but I at least wanted to exhaust all the possible educational options before giving up on Tim.

Linda worried about Tim's social skills development and also wanted to know about his path to independence now that he was nearly an adult. We needed to start thinking about his learning to drive and getting a job. I told her I'd support his job search and drivers ed. so long as he remained sober.

Linda was satisfied enough with my replies to support Tim's enrollment at the school. Pam and I covered the $6,000 tuition cost and the cost of tutoring. His regular school district was not required to pay for it because the placement was not part of any IEP.

In late August, Linda met with Connecticut school officials to cobble together a transcript from Tim's time during his four earlier "freshman" years to send to Austin. All told, Tim had earned only 5.25 credits toward his high school diploma. This was discouraging enough, but things were actually going to get worse. The struggles of Tim's teen years—his ongoing battles with mental illness and drug use, the challenges in getting him an education, his desires for independence and to feel normal and accepted by his peers—all would come to a head during the coming school year.

The school was located in central Austin, about a mile north of the University of Texas campus. It was in an old, beat-up A-frame building on a couple of shady acres, next to an old estate house and not far from a municipal golf course and a shopping center. As a new school, it was just completing the accreditation process. The facilities may have been modest, but the academic program was rigorous. Tim would have to work hard to succeed there, but he and his teachers initially seemed committed to his success.

A week before school started, Tim began getting into trouble again. He started climbing out of windows to leave our house at night because he did not want us to know when he was coming and going. He didn't hide his tracks very well—he usually left the window open and the screen against the wall. We sat him down and told him he was free to go out at night so long as he honored his curfew and used the door.

He began dirtying and damaging the kitchen with his food preparation and cooking. He made small knife cuts in the Formica counter tops, forgot about food cooking on the stove, and forgot to turn off the burners after he finished cooking. We established some basic cooking rules and increased our supervision of him.

He began to lie and steal again. One day, Verena noticed that a large sum of money was missing from her room. Tim and Ben both insisted that an acquaintance of Verena's had taken it, but Tim was a prime suspect. We never found the money. Years later, Ben admitted that Tim had told him to lie about having seen someone else enter the house.

We began to realize that Tim was out buying drugs at night and using the kitchen to cook them. He denied this, but we insisted that he go to therapy more often and attend Narcotics Anonymous meetings. With the encouragement of his therapist, we also asked him to sign a behavior contract with us—even though these had not had much effect on Tim in the past.

Pam and I tried to make the contract simple and straightforward, and to enforce it as consistently as we could. We asked him to do six things—go to school, stay off drugs, not break laws, keep the house safe and clean, continue with therapy, and abide by a curfew. In return, we gave him permission to leave the school campus for lunch, as most of the students did because the school did not have a cafeteria. We agreed to consider letting Tim move out of his upstairs bedroom and make a "man cave" in the large heated and air-conditioned garage. We also agreed to reward Tim for good behavior by taking him on special food-shopping trips once a week and to teach him to drive.

There were three consequences for violations of the rules. He could be grounded for up to five days, he would have to accept the legal consequences of any law breaking without us bailing him out, and each time he was discovered using drugs there would be a three-month delay in his driver training.

Tim never did learn to drive.

He signed the contract but refused to comply with it. One night, he missed his curfew. We didn't hear from him for hours and couldn't reach him on his cell phone. It was close to three in the morning when he called us for a ride home, as if nothing were out of the ordinary.

Right after that, Tim went out three straight nights without permission, each time staying out past curfew. The second day, we brought him to appointments with both his psychiatrist and his counselor, and both said that he was not taking his treatment seriously. That night, he was gone for three hours and came home stoned and hostile.

Tim's mood swings were very wide. One day, he fixed himself a big plate of spaghetti and put it down on the coffee table in the family room, then went back to the kitchen to get a drink. While Tim was in the kitchen Pam's dog Jazz started happily eating away at Tim's dinner. After shooing her off, Tim surveyed the damage to his meal, shrugged his shoulders, and sat down to eat what was left. At other times, however, Tim seemed a completely different person—disengaged from the world, surly, contrary, defiant, and irrational. Whether this was the result of his mixing illegal drugs with his prescribed medication or not, Tim was showing full-blown symptoms of serious mental illness again.

The first weeks at school briefly interrupted Tim's downward spiral as he once again aimed to please the new adults in his life. He worked hard, but it didn't always show in his results, even with nightly support from me to complete his homework. When Linda e-mailed me to see how Tim was doing, I was able to answer truthfully: "Doing fine right now. Going to school every day, doing homework, going to counseling, and being good."

Tim's teachers were not as positive in their assessments. As with many of his previous teachers, they saw that he had a great deal of difficulty with spelling and math, was inconsistent in all his written work, and was not completing tasks on schedule. And they came to the same conclusion as others had before them—they interpreted this as evidence that he wasn't trying hard enough. I explained that this was not the case, that he was actually making a considerable effort, and I encouraged his teachers to focus on his classroom participation.

Tim was also having difficulty making friends at school, but he had no trouble making a few enemies. The friends he did make were not a good influence on him (nor he on them). They used drugs and alcohol and engaged in petty theft. Tim had to attend his first "Responsibility Committee" meeting at the school in mid-September. This was a joint student-faculty committee charged with resolving disputes between students and determining consequences when students broke school rules. Tim was upset and didn't tell me what the problem was. That night, however, it was clear that he took whatever criticism he had received to heart. He worked especially hard on his homework, logging two full hours on it. He asked me for help spelling every word correctly on his English assignment. But he also talked seriously for the first time about dropping out of school. I encouraged him not to make any rash decisions.

I knew that Tim was struggling. After so many disappointing educational experiences during the past few years, I was pessimistic about Tim's chances for success at his new school after only a month of observing his teachers' reactions to him. I tried to stay positive when I wrote to the principal that "it's way too early for me to predict how this will all come out, but, despite the struggle, I see a lot of good things."

Despite my optimistic words, I knew what was coming next.

Tim began skipping classes. At the end of September he went before the Responsibility Committee again for what turned out to be the third time in two weeks. I was invited to attend.

Recognizing that they were losing Tim quickly, one member suggested easing his academic load by having Tim drop one course and pick it up in the summer session. The committee members agreed, and together with Tim they decided that he would drop math because he felt most overmatched there.

Focusing on his remaining subjects, Tim improved his effort. He did not miss any classes during the next couple of weeks and did homework with me every night. At best, though, he maintained only a C average. He stayed close to home and continued to steer clear of most drugs. He also took his Geodon every day and met every other week with his counselor. While he still made big messes in the kitchen and needed constant reminders about his hygiene, he volunteered to help out around the house at times and used deodorant daily. It turned out to be a one-month respite.

Tim's first-quarter report card arrived at the end of October. His teachers' comments were more positive and offered insight into the type of student Tim could be. His English teacher wrote:

> I am happy to see the cloud of apathy beginning to lift. These last few weeks have allowed me to glimpse the intelligence and insight you have been carrying around in that head of yours. Of course, that's not to say that it will be all smooth sailing from here. I need you to take on the responsibility to arrive in class on time and awake. You will need to convince yourself to spend more time studying. There will be more independent work in this class as we move through the year and this means you will need to develop some strategies for staying on top of it. I know you can do this, it is just a question of how we can work together.

Over the next few weeks, however, Tim began to use drugs again, especially marijuana, and he occasionally drank alcohol. He had shied away from alcohol since the incident when he passed out in the park, so this was a new problem. We noticed it at home, his teachers noticed it at school, and Tim reported it to Linda when he talked with her on the phone.

In November, he was arrested for shoplifting. He went to a supermarket during school lunch hour and was caught trying to steal a bottle of wine. He was charged with three misdemeanor violations, and the police gave him a ride back to school. He had to appear in municipal court, pay a fine, and do community service. He also had to meet with the principal the next day. The school considered expelling him, but the principal offered an alternative. Tim could remain at school, but he would have to stay on campus during lunch period, participate in a drug treatment program, and have his urine tested. Tim's initial reaction was that he preferred to drop out of school.

Upon reflection, Tim came up with another option: he claimed that his mother had told him that she would welcome him back to Connecticut at any time, "no questions asked," and that she would have a more lenient attitude about his drug use. When presented with this plan, Linda said that of course he was welcome to return to Connecticut if he wished, but drug treatment was nonnegotiable. Fuming, Tim agreed to the conditions imposed by the school, and he grudgingly attended an NA meeting in Austin in addition to continuing his counseling.

Pam and I had a talk with Tim after this. We told him that no matter what we felt or believed, and no matter what his mental health issues were, others outside the family were going to look at him through the lens of what they considered to be normal and acceptable. His mental illness was not going to give him a pass about his "self-medicating." He was going to be held responsible for all of his actions as he got closer to adulthood. So that was how we intended to treat him while offering supervision, guidance, and boundaries appropriate to someone his age and with his needs and experiences. He was going to be accountable for living by the rules of our house, his school, and the city of Austin, no matter how he felt about them.

Unfortunately, Tim stopped taking his medication at this point. It was an exercise in poor judgment, and one that neither Pam nor I could alter. It was also the unintended consequence of a conversation he had with his psychiatrist. Because Tim was using illicit drugs, the psychiatrist said that he didn't want to give him more prescriptions and risk a drug interaction. So the psychiatrist stopped writing prescriptions for him. Tim interpreted this to mean that he had a free pass not to take his medications anymore.

"Why don't you just take them?" I asked him one day.

"Because they even me out too much," he responded.

"Even you out? Isn't that good?"

"No, they kind of make me feel like you, all even all the time, not like myself. I like being hyper sometimes." Illicit drugs, on the other hand, let Tim be Tim.

Treatment noncompliance has long been recognized as a significant problem in the recovery of people with schizophrenia. In fact, it has been estimated that as many as three-quarters of all people who are prescribed psychotropic medications will stop using them within a year (Mitchell and Selmes 2007). The reasons include unpleasant side effects, stigma, and a sense that the medications aren't helping. Having to take pills every day is also an inconvenience to some. So Tim's reaction was not unusual. On the other hand, we know that many of these same people self-medicate with illegal drugs. As marijuana becomes more available, either as a legally prescribed drug or as an entirely legal drug, it will be interesting to see what this means for people like Tim — and if it becomes part of the arsenal of drugs used to tame symptoms of mental illnesses.

Tim completed the fall semester in mid-November with a few C's and a few incompletes. The one bright note was in English, where he scored a 78 and his teacher commented: "Tim, what a rally! You really pulled through at the end. I think you are well on your way to making the transition from not being a student at all to being a good student. I've seen your writing skills improve and your study habits are even starting to take shape." I felt good about this; I had spent hours with Tim at our living-room desk facilitating those study habits.

Our family dynamics were changing. Larissa, who was turning sixteen, joined us in Austin in January to spend a year at Austin High School. She threw herself into school activities and made friends. While this gave Tim new opportunities to socialize with Larissa, whom he had missed, it also disrupted his routines. Larissa did not always give Tim the time he wanted, preferring to spend her free time with a boyfriend, girlfriends, or at school social events when she wasn't working on her homework. He had to fight for her attention, and he had another difficult period of adjustment.

Tim's bedroom was across the hall from Larissa's. He played music loudly, disturbing her when she was trying to study. He barged in on her without knocking or knocked loudly on her door when she was talking to friends, leading to squabbles and arguing, often when Pam and I were trying to get some sleep down the hall. After he broke Larissa's door one day, we finally agreed to let Tim move into the garage. We fixed it up with an old rug and moved Tim in with a bed, a chair, a couch, a stereo, and an old television. When it got dirty we just pushed everything aside and hosed the floor down.

We spent January swinging on a pendulum with Tim. On January 7 he was arrested for possession of alcohol. The principal at his school was not pleased, but since it hadn't happened during school hours he did not expel Tim. Tim had to appear in municipal court, where he was required to take part in an alcohol education program for minors. He completed that program in April. Mid-month, the pendulum swung back. Tim stayed up most of the night working on a major project for school and completed it. He was proud of it and got good feedback at school. On January 23, the same day he was due in municipal court for his alcohol possession arrest, Tim was arrested for shoplifting during school lunch hour again. Shoplifting was a Class C misdemeanor, and he was referred to youth court. He was assigned to do more than thirty hours of community service, which he completed by June.

As his volatility increased, Tim's capacity for good decision making declined. Early in March, Linda visited and took Tim to San Antonio. He left her behind on the River Walk, and she was unable to locate him for hours. That he was seventy miles away from home with no money and no means of getting back on his own made no impression on him.

He also attracted new acquaintances, some of them teenagers and some older, who showed up at our house at all hours of the night. More than once, when Pam and I went to wake Tim for school in the morning, we were startled to find some stranger also sleeping in Tim's room. His explanation was always that the person just needed a place to stay. Tim's older friends were often just there to use drugs and party with him. A few months later, Pam came home one evening to find a group of people in our family room, eating our food and getting high. She had to throw them all out of the house by herself. She was still shaking with fear when I saw her; Tim just shook his head.

Tim's interest in drugs did have one unintended benefit late that winter. It helped him to improve his reading, research, planning, and science skills. He told me that he had decided to grow mushrooms in the garage. He finally learned to use a computer while doing a tremendous amount of Internet research on the subject. He organized a list of supplies, including wood to build an incubator box, starter kits, fertilizers, and purifiers, and started acquiring these items using his allowance. One day, he asked if he could use a piece of old plywood. I heard sawing and hammering, and a couple of days later he had built a perfectly serviceable box. It still needed a lid, he told me, and a week or two later he had attached a plastic top with working hinges. An air purifier came next—something he badly needed in his room anyway—and then fertilizer. He put everything together, and after a few weeks, was finally ready to grow. Nothing happened. He made some adjustments and tried again. Still nothing. However, over a couple of months working on the project his reading and fine motor skills had improved, his focus was good, and he stayed mostly sober. He soon lost interest, decided that mushroom growing wasn't for him, and turned his attention to researching how to make a bomb. (He did not succeed in doing this, either.)

In late March, a few days after his seventeenth birthday, Tim met some people who were going to California. He asked if he could hitch a ride with them. They said yes and took him fifty miles to northern San Antonio, where they left him. He called us from a gas station looking for a ride back to Austin. He was upset when we picked him up not because the people had left him but because he really wanted to go to San Francisco.

Tim began to behave much more badly during March, after his mushrooms failed to grow. He repeatedly forced the dog into his room and tied her there so she wouldn't get away, then forgot about her when he left. He also collected knives and slingshots. He made no threats with them, but we were worried anyway. Whenever we found them lying around the house, Pam would bring them to work to hide them. She eventually acquired quite a collection. If Tim realized they were gone, he never said anything. He just went out and got more.

Tim's volatility finally got him expelled from school, just weeks before completing his freshman year. On April 1, he and another student got into a fight, which Tim had instigated. He was immediately suspended and was scheduled to go before the Responsibility Committee the next day. The committee recommended expulsion and asked Tim to suggest an alternative punishment if he wanted to stay. He declined to do so.

We immediately enrolled Tim in our local public high school— I'll call it High School 6—hoping that he could finally complete his freshman year. We didn't want him to know that he could refuse to go to school at his age. We also found a charter school run by a local nonprofit that was willing to consider admitting him in August. The nonprofit had a companion AmeriCorps work program for young people who had either dropped out of school or were at risk of dropping out.

If Tim qualified for both the charter school and the AmeriCorps program, he could complete his high school education while getting paid and earning up to $4,700 in scholarship money to use anytime in the next seven years for post-secondary education.

Tim was interested in the AmeriCorps program, and he interviewed for it in April. He learned that there might be some AmeriCorps openings as early as June and decided to apply for one of those. The program offered two types of jobs: in construction building energy-efficient houses in East Austin or landscaping work in county parks.

Tim arranged for a second interview to present his case to AmeriCorps. They told him candidly that his odds of getting into AmeriCorps were not high because they accepted only twenty-five of over eighty applicants. He put his best foot forward, however. He told them that the AmeriCorps program was his motivation for going to the charter school. He was willing to continue in the high school program in August if he could get into the AmeriCorps program in June. But he didn't think he would go to school anymore if he couldn't get the work assignment, too.

I admired his tenacity in negotiating, and while he awaited a decision I took stock of his situation. The clock was running out on his childhood and his time in school. He had been a student at the private school for a total of eight months. He had earned two credits there, giving him a total of 7.25 credits toward a high school diploma. He had significant learning disabilities and had not been successful in any of the schools he had attended.

He had been suspended from, or asked to leave, four different schools, and no dismissal had ever resulted in improved behavior.

Tim's illness was getting worse as he got older, and with inadequately integrated care he had regressed academically the longer he stayed in school. He didn't have much of a track record as he attempted to sell the nonprofit program on his strengths. All Tim had learned in school so far was how to fail. And, after he was surprisingly successful at convincing the nonprofit to accept him into both the AmeriCorps and charter school programs, he was about to be offered one more opportunity to put failure to the test.

eleven

AMERICORPS AND THE CHAIN OF NEGLECT

TIM ATTENDED HIGH School 6—our local public high school—for one month to attempt to complete his freshman year. It was too late in the year to schedule a PPT meeting, so the school enrolled Tim in the classes that most closely matched those he had been taking at the small private school and then filled in the rest of his schedule and forgot about him. Tim's favorite "class" at High School 6 was "office assistant," a period during which he sat in the main office and waited until someone gave him something to deliver to a classroom. He may or may not have found his way to his other classes because he never seemed to bring home any work. One day, he came home puzzled. "I went to one of my classes," he said, "and it wasn't there. There was a bunch of students and a different teacher, and they were taking a test." Tim had walked in on final exams, not knowing that it was finals week. He had missed his own finals.

On May 20 however, he received some good news. He had been accepted into both the AmeriCorps program and the charter school. He was very pleased, and I was proud that he had done so well in the interviews. This was a significant accomplishment he had achieved on his own.

He started his employment in June with the burst of energy and enthusiasm he brought to many of his new activities. He was assigned to a work crew building energy-efficient homes in east Austin.

He enjoyed working and earning his own money. He set his alarm so that he would be sure to get up by six and catch the six-thirty bus. He took his sleep medication. And on nights when he stayed up too late and knew he might not have time to get ready the next morning, he got dressed before he went to bed and slept with his clothes on. He spent over an hour on buses, transferring along the way, and arrived at the work site fifteen minutes early. In the afternoon, he reversed his commute, ending his nearly twelve-hour day when he arrived at our house close to six in the evening. He had Fridays off and used them to catch up on his rest. It was a joy to see him feeling, and being, successful for a change.

Tim's initial term of enrollment in AmeriCorps was six months. If those months went well, he could enroll for twelve more. He would earn high school credits for both school and work, and if he reached 900 hours of work and school combined during the first six months, he would also qualify for the first $2,300 of his $4,700 postsecondary scholarship.

On most summer days he came home animated, talking about the work and the other people on the work crew. One day, he found me outside looking at some cracks in the brick facade of our house. He volunteered to put stucco over them. "Where did you learn how to do that?" I asked. "At work," he responded proudly. "I do it all the time."

When Tim officially enrolled in the charter school—High School 7—at the beginning of August, he was finally assigned to the sophomore class. It was on a technicality, but I was willing to take it any way we could get it. The 7.25 credits Tim had earned before entering the charter school might not have been sufficient to place him out of the freshman class at his previous high schools, but they put him almost one-third of the way through his current high school program, which required 22.5 credits for graduation. Better still, he had the potential to earn 9.5 more credits between August and June if everything fell into place and he stayed on the pace he was on in the combined charter school and AmeriCorps program. He would be eighteen by then, but staying in the program for the full eighteen months would put him within reach of a high school diploma around the time he turned nineteen. It was a long shot, but the only one we had. The big "if" was that he actually had to complete a full year of school, something he hadn't done since the fifth grade.

The charter school scheduled its IEP meeting, in Texas called an Admission, Review, and Dismissal (ARD) meeting, in mid-August. Tim's new IEP recommended individualized instruction, special equipment, reteaching in math and spelling, instructional strategies geared to Tim's learning style, and monitoring of Tim's progress by the special education teacher. It did not recommend integrating his clinical treatment into his educational program. I thought it was a pretty typical plan, similar to the ones that had been tried and failed in the past. But there was something different—the staff recognized that Tim was nearly an adult and understood that his educational program at this point was secondary for him to the AmeriCorps work program.

I requested a number of evaluations to determine Tim's current levels of achievement. His academic achievement was nearly nonexistent. The school also conducted a comprehensive behavioral evaluation. I was asked to complete a Behavior Assessment System for Children, a rating scale to compare Tim to other students. Not surprisingly, I rated Tim below average in his social skills and significantly higher in aggressive behavior, conduct problems, and inattentiveness. Two of Tim's teachers also rated his classroom behavior during the first month of school. They reported that he had difficulty understanding the relevance of rules, adhering to social policies, and avoiding conflicts with other students. But both also described him as articulate, creative, and having a good sense of humor, strengths he had had since he was a child.

When school began in early August, Tim's work performance immediately began to suffer. He was supposed to work in the morning and attend three classes in the afternoon. But he was a little slower to get up and out in the morning, and his supervisor described him as less productive on the jobsite. He also didn't always manage to get from work back to school for his afternoon classes.

After four weeks, I got a letter from the school informing me that Tim had accumulated a total of seven absences and ten tardies. This behavior clearly jeopardized his position at both the school and the AmeriCorps work program. Tim complained that he didn't like school. I encouraged him to give it his best shot anyway and to recognize that he was still earning money for his troubles.

But Pam and I were losing heart. We tried to buoy ourselves by making a list of Tim's accomplishments from July 2001, when he arrived in Austin, through September 2002. To his credit, in fifteen months he had lost weight and was eating more healthily, had earned some high school credits and was still in school, had reduced his drug use (though he hadn't eliminated it entirely), had stayed out of the hospital and juvenile detention, had gotten a job, had made some friends, and was paying more attention to his grooming. However, we sensed something ominous on the horizon.

In October, we received our first concrete evidence that Tim was not going to be successful at the charter school. His first progress report was too weak, and he had failed several classes.

The school scheduled another ARD meeting, where it lowered its sights. His short-term objectives were now to "react reasonably when informed that he has broken the rules," "attend each class," and "maintain a class notebook, updating assignments and tests due." We had come full circle. After a decade, notebook maintenance was once again one of the keys to his school success.

That was what it took for me to understand that Tim was not going to finish high school. Until then, I had clung to the hope that if we could just push the schools to suspend him a little less, make his IEP do a little more, and help Tim to try a little harder and push him a little closer to graduation every few months, he might eventually pick up sufficient momentum to graduate. But now the clock was running out. Tim would be eighteen in five months, and notwithstanding his entitlement under the IDEA to stay in school through age twenty-one, the decision to leave at eighteen would be his. He was tired of failure. He had already decided to leave.

But what did him in was something more basic. When the symptoms of his disease reemerged in full force, his clinical, educational, and social services were not (and never had been) integrated. He lost the thing he valued—work—first. His supervisor lost trust in Tim as his psychosis reappeared, so he was transferred from the home-building program to the less intensive park-landscaping program. He was accused of harassing a young woman there, and she filed a complaint against him. The AmeriCorps staff dismissed Tim from that work setting, too. Without work, Tim had no desire to attend school, and the school had ruled out the one means it had of engaging him.

Tim showed new symptoms of paranoia at home. He refused to take his medications, claiming they would poison him and began to self-medicate almost daily. He became delusional and was hearing voices. He stayed up at night and was restless all the time. He brought weapons into the house to protect himself against imagined enemies. He then began using them. One night, he shot out a streetlight with a slingshot because he said it was too bright and allowed people to spy on him.

Linda e-mailed me to report that Tim was calling her at all hours of the night, not lucid and apparently high, sounding like he could endanger himself or us. One night, Pam awakened to a loud noise downstairs. Tim was using a leaf blower in the house. He had no explanation why. Another time, we both woke up at three in the morning to loud music. He was blasting his stereo to annoy Larissa. When he refused to turn it down, I had to unplug the equipment and lock up the speakers. We went back to bed. I slept for three hours and then got up to run in a twelve-mile road race. Pam was too stressed to go back to sleep. The next day, she asked me how I could do it. It was easy. By then, I was beyond stressed. I was numb.

Getting a good night's sleep was difficult because we never knew what to expect when we woke up. On more than one occasion, Pam and I came into the kitchen in the morning to find an electric stove burner red hot, with the metal spoon Tim used to cook drugs nearby, as Tim slept soundly in his room.

Pam went downstairs one night when she couldn't sleep to find Tim sitting at the kitchen table fingering a kitchen knife, looking menacing and muttering to himself. Larissa had a friend over that night. They were talking about him, he reported in a rhythmic, measured tone, and he was going to make them stop. Pam explained that Larissa and her friend were sound asleep upstairs and calmly took the knife away from him. She stayed up even after he went to sleep. We hid all of our knives, just as Linda and I had done years ago in Connecticut.

A few days later, Tim found a knife we had missed and announced that he was going to kill Pam because voices were telling him to do so. We knew then that he needed hospitalization.

We called the police, asking that mental health officers—who are in most areas the frontline responders to community mental health crises—be sent to our home. When the officers arrived, Pam and I told them what had happened. They asked us to leave the room so that they could talk with Tim. After ten minutes, one officer came back to us and reported that Tim was calm and in control of his faculties. Tim had denied making the threat, so the officer didn't think Tim was a danger to himself or anyone else. There was nothing more the officer could do.

I was incredulous. "But he just threatened to kill Pam."

"But I didn't hear it, sir."

"You can't take our word for it?"

"No, sir, it's a serious matter to deprive someone of his rights by locking him up, even if it's just for twenty-four hours."

"But you'd be locking him up in a hospital! What about his right to treatment for his mental illness?"

"Sorry, sir, I'm not going to do it."

I tried one more time. "What if he had told you he was going to kill you, but we didn't hear it. Would you think he was a danger then?"

"Yes, but he didn't threaten me." And of course, he had no access to any of Tim's prior history.

Tim sat smiling in the other room as the officers went out the door. Pam was so frightened that she packed a bag and considered going to her sister's house for the night. But she was even more terrified of leaving me home alone with Tim, so she decided to stay. Tim finally went to sleep and we went to our bedroom, locked the door, and stayed awake most of the night.

When Tim was dismissed from AmeriCorps during the first week of November, he was awarded a pro-rata scholarship worth over $1,600. He was told he could stay in the charter school if he wished. I knew what the answer would be, but we gathered anyway the following week for another ARD meeting.

Tim came with us to our next ARD meeting. He listened quietly as the school agreed to change his classes from the afternoon to the morning so that it would be more convenient for Pam and me to get him to school. It also added weekly counseling to his IEP that would focus on "boundary" issues. But when it came time to approve the plan, Tim abstained.

After that, Tim stopped going to school. He hoped that this would give him leverage to get back into AmeriCorps. Two weeks later, the school scheduled another ARD meeting, to try again. When he was told that he could not be readmitted to AmeriCorps until the following June at the earliest and would only be readmitted if he attended school until then, he insisted that he only wanted to work, not attend classes.

The school had one more option to offer. It proposed moving him from the traditional program to a vocational program. In this program, he would have only one hour of academics each day and could receive academic credit for work time, so long as he worked a minimum of twenty hours per week. But the offer came with a catch. Tim would have to find the job on his own, and he had no job skills and a poor work record.

Still hoping that AmeriCorps would change its mind, Tim tried to be accommodating. He agreed to return to school the next day and attend the next five days (the final five days of the semester). He also agreed to meet with a counselor and to submit to a new psychological evaluation. He attended school for the week before Christmas vacation.

Tim was hospitalized again on January 2, 2003, while in Connecticut during Christmas vacation. He was precertified for four days and discharged prematurely at the insistence of our insurance company, which did not consider a longer stay to be medically necessary. The insurance company approved just nine outpatient psychotherapy visits for Tim over the next six months.

When Tim returned to Austin, he was very ill. He was unable to sleep. He was paranoid and said he was hearing voices again. There was a cold snap in Austin that weekend, with the daytime temperature hovering around forty degrees. After two nights of limited or no sleep because the noises in his brain were keeping him awake, he got up on the third day, stripped down to his underwear, took a blanket and sleeping bag outside, and fell asleep on our patio because he was afraid to be in the house. Pam and I called the mental health officers again. This time they agreed that he needed hospitalization.

Tim was shaking, cold, and scared when he agreed to go voluntarily to a hospital in Austin. He was there for ten days, during which time he was finally diagnosed simply with schizophrenia. We had been circling around this diagnosis for years and had pretty much gotten there with the diagnosis of schizoaffective disorder, but this time it was clear. It did not shock me to hear it. The doctor explained that it was childhood-onset schizophrenia, and from Tim's history he said it was likely that Tim had had it at least since he was ten years old and probably longer. "It's somewhat rare for it to manifest that early," he said, "so it's not unusual that his doctors diagnosed other conditions first."

Tim was discharged from the hospital on Zyprexa and trazodone. He was almost eighteen. He decided that he did not want to return to school. He wanted to live on his own and was willing to accept supported housing to do so. We made a list of the services Tim would need, including some form of income, housing support, case management and care coordination services, access to health and mental health treatment and medication, and job training. We thought we could provide the rest—furniture, food, support navigating the service delivery system, and ongoing guidance. I spoke with an attorney at Advocacy, Inc., Texas's state-funded program working on behalf of people with disabilities, who advised that we should apply for Supplemental Security Income (SSI) and Medicaid for Tim. I also approached the Austin Travis County Mental Health Mental Retardation Center—now called Austin Travis County Integral Care—to obtain supported housing and case management services.

The school kept Tim on its roster for a few more weeks in case he had a change of heart. I received one more notice from the school in March informing me that it was transferring Tim's IDEA rights from me to him because he had turned eighteen. That was the last I heard from the school.

I also spoke with the aftercare coordinator at my insurance company who was assigned to Tim's case. He suggested that Tim might now be eligible for intensive case management. This was terrific, I thought. That decision had come down just as Tim was moving off my insurance and onto Medicaid.

Tim quit high school two months shy of his eighteenth birthday, in the same year he would have graduated had he stayed on course.

Over a four-year period, Tim had attended seven different high schools—a vocational-technical school, an emotional-growth boarding school, a drug treatment center's school, a hospital-based school, a small private school, a public high school, and a charter school. Altogether, he attended high school for thirty-five months, enough time to complete four full years of academic work. Throughout, he was eligible for special education services to help him achieve his academic objectives.

During that time, he was known to have one or more serious mental illnesses. He was in some form of treatment throughout the four years, often in structured, self-contained residential settings. His community-based therapists were available to consult with his schools at pretty much any time. His parents and step-parents were as involved in his education and clinical treatment as any parents could be.

In four years, Tim accumulated 8.25 credits, roughly one-third of the number required for graduation. He failed to reach most of his IEP educational goals and objectives. His last test scores in math and spelling suggested, incredibly, that he had no more mastery of those subjects when he left high school than he had when he entered first grade.

And for all of the special education services he was provided, the result was this: Tim never finished a full year of school after the fifth grade.

Many years ago, we put people with mental illnesses in chains in institutions and forgot about them. Nowadays, we shackle them with chains of neglect. What failed Tim? It was not his teachers or his parents. It was a chain of neglect that we have been forging for more than a generation that stretches from infancy to adulthood. Consider this: according to the National Institute of Mental Health, 49 percent of children with mental illness and 41 percent of adults with serious mental illness receive no treatment at all (NIMH n.d.b, n.d.c). These people are all worse off than Tim was.

Today's chain of neglect begins when children are very young. In 2011, only 389,000 children, teenagers, and young adults between the ages of three and twenty-one were enrolled in special education under the category "emotional disturbance" (NCES 2012). This was the lowest number in two decades and represented a reduction of more than 20 percent over six years. Only eight-tenths of 1 percent of all school children are, for the purposes of receiving special education services, identified as having an emotional disturbance, but according to the earlier NIMH data I cited, more than 20 percent of children have a "seriously debilitating mental disorder" at some point during childhood. This means that no more than one in twenty-five ever receives special education services *because of that mental illness*. In time, Tim eventually became that one child. What about the other twenty-four?

Tim was fortunate in another way, too. He was in foster care for only the first seven weeks of his life. Children who are in foster care for their entire childhood are two to four times more likely to have a mental disorder than their peers. However, less than half of them receive treatment. And after these children age out of the foster care system at eighteen, only a handful remain in counseling or other treatment (Havlicek, Garcia, and Smith 2013).

In 2012, Tim's former school district in Middletown, Connecticut, made national news for using isolation rooms to control children with mental illnesses (CBS New York 2012). The headlines referred to these as "scream rooms" because the children placed in them could be heard screaming by other students in the school. Removing children with mental illness from classrooms is nothing new. Tim was suspended from school repeatedly after the fifth grade. In New York in 2012, for example, special education students accounted for 12 percent of the student body but 32 percent of the suspensions (Lestch and Monahan 2013).

In its 2005 publication "Dismantling the School-to-Prison Pipeline," the NAACP Legal Defense and Educational Fund noted that while only 8.6 percent of children at that time had a learning disability, 32 percent of children in juvenile detention had one. The Children's Defense Fund puts the figure at 30 percent today. Six percent of our population has a serious mental illness, but 15 percent of adult male prisoners and 31 percent of adult female prisoners do (Steadman et al. 2009). By population count, the largest "mental health facilities" in our nation are Rikers Island, the Cook County Jail, and the Los Angeles County Jail (UPI 2010). The largest "mental health facility" in Texas is the Harris County Jail.

Incarcerating people with mental illness is not the same as treating them. It is simply neglect that leads to more neglect. A felony conviction is often all it takes for a person to be denied regular housing. According to data from the National Coalition for the Homeless, up to 25 percent of all chronically homeless people have a serious mental illness, and many more have addiction disorders as well (NCH 2009).

And still the chain of neglect grows longer, from homelessness to hospitalization. The Agency for Healthcare Research and Quality's recent Healthcare Cost and Utilization Project report (Pfuntner, Weir, and Stocks 2013) noted that mental illnesses are the leading cause of hospitalization for children between the ages of one and seventeen. Mental illnesses are the third leading cause of hospitalizations for people between the ages of eighteen and forty-four, and the fifth leading cause for people between the ages of forty-five and sixty-four.

And we neglect people with mental illness when they are in treatment by paying so little for their care. On average we pay only $4,800 for each inpatient stay for mental illness, about half the average cost for all hospital stays (Pfuntner, Weir, and Steiner 2013). AHRQ reports that we pay four times as much for a brief hospital stay for an acute brain injury than we do for a chronic brain disease.

And so the chain leads to early death. According to the CDC, serious mental illnesses can reduce life expectancy by more than twenty-five years (Colton and Manderscheid 2006) because they can lead to early death from a host of other undertreated and neglected chronic diseases.

As Tim left high school, I had no idea how far into adulthood he would carry this chain of neglect. But I was terrified of what might result. If Tim were to be ignored or even just treated like everyone else, he would not succeed in life because he would not be able follow the rules without assistance. And if he were left on his own, I might lose him.

twelve

TIM BEGINS ADULT LIFE

A T HIS LAST high school, Tim had completed an "Interest Profile" that examined what he might have become if he did not have mental illness. According to the profile, he had plenty of options. He could have been a military intelligence officer, a geological technician, a general farm worker, a fire inspector, a nuclear monitoring technologist, a movie camera operator, a physicist, a stone mason, a taxi driver, a private investigator, or a medical lab technician.

When Tim was discharged from the Austin hospital where he was diagnosed with schizophrenia in late January 2003, he was tall and handsome. He was six feet, four inches tall, and more than one person remarked that with his short afro he looked like a young Muhammad Ali. He had distinctive bright-brown eyes, an easy smile, and broad shoulders. And he had a serious, lifelong mental illness.

He had attended high schools for four years but had no diploma to show for it. He wanted to be on his own but could not live independently. He wanted to work but could not hold a job.

The harsh realities of his adult life would soon begin to emerge. He would be assigned to but receive little or no service from a case manager. He would find and lose his first supported living arrangement. He would experience homelessness for the first time. He would break a law and be introduced to the adult judicial system. He would have his first extended stay in jail.

The supported living arrangement we found for Tim was an adult cooperative group home in north Austin operated by the Austin Travis County Mental Health Mental Retardation Center (ATCMHMR). It was in a residential neighborhood, near a supermarket, and on a bus line. If it worked out he could remain there for an extended period of time. But it was not permanent, and so ATCMHMR advised us about the Section 8 voucher program sponsored by the Austin Housing Authority. It was available to people with disabilities and offered a long-term rent subsidy in regular rental housing. The waiting list was two years long, but ATCMHMR was taking new applications on behalf of the Housing Authority in late January. We made sure to file Tim's application at that time.

At the group home in north Austin the residents ranged in age from approximately twenty to fifty. They managed the home together, providing peer support to one another. They had private bedrooms and shared a kitchen and living room. They divided up chores and cooking and bought their own food. They had daily access to caseworkers and other professionals from ATCMHMR. Some of the residents worked; others went to school. Tim's rent was approximately $300 a month, and there was a onetime move-in fee of $170.

As long as he lived at the group home, Tim was supposed to receive services from ATCMHMR's Assertive Community Treatment (ACT) team. These included case management, clinical services, and supported employment services. The team was also supposed to help him apply for Supplemental Security Income, Medicaid, and food stamps.

He signed a three-month probationary lease and moved in during the first week of February. It was a big ranch house. Tim's bedroom came furnished with a bed, a dresser, a nightstand, and a few cleaning and grooming supplies. Pam and I gave him a computer, a video game console, a few cooking supplies, some clothes, and toiletries and made sure he had a supply of Zyprexa and trazodone. We paid his rent and also gave him a food allowance of forty dollars a week to hold him over until he was approved for food stamps.

Tim was clinically stable when he moved in and settled into semi-independent living. He rode his bike to the supermarket to buy food. He cooked his meals in the kitchen, sometimes sharing them with other residents. He socialized on occasion but generally kept to himself in his bedroom, playing video games or reading magazines. He took the bus downtown a few times to visit the charter school but confirmed that he did not want to return to school. He also used his bike and the bus to get to the "Drag," an area near the University of Texas campus, because he enjoyed being around people close to his age. Pam and I saw Tim frequently. I picked him up every Sunday to bring him to our house for dinner.

Tim had one good month at the group home. Soon, though, his housemates were complaining about the messes he left in the kitchen and living room. He was also dirty and wouldn't shower. Tim argued that they were too critical. And because some of them were twice his age, he thought of them as authority figures and refused to listen to them. He had not yet been assigned an ACT caseworker, so there was no one to run interference for him.

He stopped taking his medications and soon began bringing both drugs and acquaintances into the house. In late March he brought over a particularly disruptive group, and the other residents were afraid of them. They complained to ATCMHMR, and Tim was found to be in violation of his lease. His position in the house suddenly became tenuous.

Pam and I took him out to a sushi buffet as a treat for his eighteenth birthday, but he was tired and depressed. He ate only a few pieces of sushi and declined any desert or after-dinner activities. Because he still did not have a caseworker, I offered to take him to file his SSI, Medicaid, and food stamp applications a few days later so that I would have a reason to see him again soon.

I called ATCMHMR to urge that Tim be assigned a caseworker right away, but it was already too late for Tim to remain in the house. The other residents would not support the renewal of Tim's lease after April, and so I starting working with ATCMHMR to find other housing for him.

ATCMHMR suggested an efficiency apartment in a small apartment complex in a more central part of Austin; perhaps Tim could live more successfully if he had his own place. Also, because nearly everyone at the complex received services from ATCMHMR, someone's caseworker was usually around whenever there was a problem.

At first, Tim turned down the apartment because he did not want to leave the group home. But his anxiety level was increasing as he continued to argue with the other residents, and he finally left and headed to the Drag, where he became homeless for the first time. He spent a few days on the streets. I was panicked because I didn't think he could survive out there. But he quickly ran out of money, and this forced him to consider his limited options.

Tim was too imposing a figure to panhandle successfully, but he and another young man discovered that they could make some money by returning empty beer kegs to a liquor store near the college campus. The difficulty was getting the beer kegs. One day, they noticed some empty kegs in an alley outside a restaurant, so they helped themselves. The restaurant owner saw them and called the police.

Tim was charged with a felony count of burglary. It was his first serious offense, and if he was convicted it could result in a state prison sentence of up to a year. He would also have to disclose the felony conviction on housing and employment applications, further diminishing his chances of finding either one. All at once, we were faced with the possibility that at the age of eighteen Tim could become a convicted felon, unemployable, and homeless.

Tim was sent to the Travis County Del Valle Correctional Complex to await his court date. He asked Pam and me if we would post bail for him. We told him no, repeating what we had said many times: His actions had consequences, and he needed to understand this. Going to jail was the consequence of what he had done. From the day we signed his behavior contract with him almost two years before we had been clear that we were not going to bail him out if he landed in jail. It was much easier to say this than to carry it out in practice, however. But I believed that if I did not follow through, I would just reinforce his belief that someone would always be there to get him out of a tough situation.

What made it a little easier was that Pam had a good friend who worked at the jail. We knew from her that the jail was safer than the streets. Tim would be off drugs, and he would be housed and fed. We also knew that a majority of people in the jail had some form of mental illness and that personnel were experienced in interacting with people like Tim. A few weeks in jail also would buy us some time to work out a more permanent housing plan with ATCMHMR.

Tim's weeks at Del Valle were still not easy for any of us. There were many rules by which we had to abide, some of which seemed designed to isolate Tim from us. Tim could not receive any phone calls. If I wrote to him, I could send only a letter, with no cash, money orders, or anything else in the envelope. When Pam tried to send him a stamped envelope so he could write back to us, the envelope was confiscated and the mail returned to us as undeliverable. If we wanted to send reading materials they had to come straight from the publisher, and never more than two at a time. He also could not have any personal belongings. He could make purchases at the jail commissary, but we couldn't send money directly to him. Instead, we had to send a money order or cashier's check to the Inmate Trust Fund.

Tim was also limited to two twenty-minute, noncontact visits per week. These were on the jail's schedule, not ours; on specified days and at set times; and could change without notice if Tim was transferred to a different unit. Signing up to see Tim was also challenging. I had to present a photo ID and have my name checked against a list of approved visitors provided by Tim. I was not allowed to bring my watch, wallet, loose change, or cell phone into the visiting room. And I had to be patient—the wait could be as long as two hours before I got into the visiting room.

We visited through a glass window using telephones. Tim was in good spirits the first time I saw him at Del Valle. He said he was being treated well but admitted he was bored. He felt safe even though he was housed in a barracks-style unit. The food was fine, but he wanted some money deposited in his account so he could buy some soups from the commissary.

He told me that he had decided it wouldn't be worth it to post bail; he would be credited with two days served for each day he stayed in jail while he awaited trial and sentencing. He figured he would be in jail for two to three months before then. If he then pleaded guilty, he'd probably be sentenced to no more than six months, get time served, and be released. I was worried about a felony conviction, but Tim said not to be. He was certain that the felony charge would be reduced to a misdemeanor, and he told me to contact his public defender to tell him that Tim wanted to talk to him about this. In the meantime, he said, "I've got a roof over my head," and he left smiling.

I met with Tim's public defender, who said that Tim was correct about how his time served would be calculated. But he didn't see how the charge could be reduced to a misdemeanor.

He said that the judge would be ordering a mental health evaluation when Tim returned to court on May 27 and would want Tim to have a permanent residence when he was released—not for his own good but so his probation officer could find him. I conveyed all of this to Tim the next time I visited. He took it all in but was still anxious to see his lawyer, who had not yet conferred with Tim. He also stood his ground that the charge would be reduced to a misdemeanor and believed this could affect his sentence. I told him that in either case he would have to have a place to live when he was released, so he reconsidered and gave me permission to arrange for the ATCMHMR apartment for him.

He seemed especially tired, so I asked him how he was doing. He told me that his fatigue was just a product of the boredom of his routine. He got up and had breakfast around five-thirty each day, went back to sleep, got up and went to kitchen duty at around eleven-thirty, worked there until around six-thirty, then went back to his bunk and read until ten. He said that he had read and enjoyed *Red Dragon*, the first Hannibal Lecter book. But he was not getting much exercise.

After the visit, I talked again with Tim's lawyer. He was pleased to hear about the apartment but still thought that Tim was minimizing the significance of the felony conviction he was likely to receive. Then he finally went to see Tim. The lawyer came away from that meeting acknowledging that Tim was right about the charge because he did not go into the restaurant to take the kegs, just into the alley behind it. If he had entered the building, the crime would have been burglary. However, because the kegs were outside the building, the crime was theft—a misdemeanor. And the restaurant owner, who was the witness, had not seen Tim inside the building. Tim had reasoned all this out before the lawyers did by comparing notes with other inmates.

While we waited for Tim's trial, I put a deposit down on the $450-per-month efficiency apartment for Tim. A week later, I met with an ATC-MHMR staff member who told me that Tim was now being assigned to the ANEW program. ANEW would be more appropriate because it was for people with mental illness who were in the judicial system, and it offered a more intensive level of services.

Tim's charge was reduced to a misdemeanor, and he pleaded guilty. He received a sentence of two years of probation in lieu of one year in prison (which he would have to finish serving if he violated his probation) and eighty hours of community service. Tim was ordered to report to his probation officer once a month, receive services from ATC-MHMR, and take his medications. His new caseworker from ANEW was supposed to pick him up at the jail the day he was released, take him to a one-night overnight program, take him to his first meeting with his probation officer the next day, and then bring him to his new apartment. But Tim's release did not go according to plan.

I first realized that there was a problem when I did not hear from anyone by two-thirty in the afternoon. That was plenty of time for Del Valle to have processed Tim out. I called the jail to find out why Tim was still there. It turned out that Tim's release order wasn't in the computer because his release card had been misplaced. It took three more calls, to the clerk, central booking, and Del Valle, to confirm that Tim's release was moving forward. If I hadn't made those calls, Tim would have stayed in jail until someone finally noticed that he wasn't supposed to be there.

It was five o'clock when the mix-up was finally cleared up, and I was told it would take between two and six more hours to complete Tim's release. I called his ANEW caseworker, who explained that he did not work nights and that there were no night staff on duty who could handle the pick-up. There was a second problem: not only was there no one to pick Tim up, but the program to which Tim was supposed to go for the night might not hold the bed for him if he did not arrive early. And if Tim didn't make it to the overnight program, the caseworker did not know how he would find Tim the next morning to take him to meet with his probation officer. So I agreed to do it if he could arrange for the bed to be held.

The caseworker called me back to tell me that Tim would be released by ten-twenty-five that night. (I remember being amazed by the precision of the presumed release time after the problems of the day.) He also told me that the overnight program had agreed to hold Tim's bed and that when I picked him up I should bring him directly to the program. The caseworker promised to take over in the morning to make sure Tim made his probation appointment, signed his apartment lease, and completed the ANEW paperwork.

It was close to eleven when the jail door was finally unlocked and Tim walked out. It had been a long day. Tim wanted to make it even longer by going to the Drag. I told him no and bought him some food instead. Then I dropped him off at the overnight program and waited until he went into the building.

He saw his probation officer and signed his apartment lease the next morning. Pam and I gave him a bed, a dresser, a couch, another television, and some more dishes and kitchenware. The newly renovated efficiency apartment consisted of a combination living room/bedroom, a kitchenette, and a bathroom. It had new paint and a new floor. It looked clean and nice, and Tim smiled when he saw it. The morning Tim moved in, however, he promptly locked himself out and lost his key. His ANEW worker wasn't available, so I spent the rest of the day tracking down a master key. He never found his lost key, so he asked his caseworker to help him get the locks changed.

Tim had a number of tasks to complete that week. He needed to get a new photo ID because he had lost his old one, buy a new bike and bike lock because he had lost his old ones, apply for food stamps, arrange to get a phone installed, open a checking account so we could deposit money into it for him, and make an appointment with a doctor and get new prescriptions for his medications. The ANEW team was supposed to help him do all these things.

But none of this happened, because less than a week after he was discharged from jail, Tim went back to the Drag and purchased some marijuana. The police caught him, charged him with possession, revoked his probation, and took him directly to jail.

I called Tim's public defender and told him about Tim's new arrest. He listened politely and then explained that he was no longer representing Tim. Because of its heavy caseload, the Travis County Public Defender's Office contracted cases out to private attorneys. There were many attorneys in the rotation. Under the Public Defender's Office rotation system, the lawyer at the top of the list got the next client's case—even if a different lawyer had represented that client in the past. He told me that a different lawyer had been assigned to Tim for this offense. I had to give the new lawyer Tim's background information, but I did not know who it was. Tim wasn't able to tell me, either. He forgot to put me on his new visitors list, so I was not allowed to see him.

While Tim was in jail, I learned that he had been denied SSI a month earlier because he had failed to respond to a request from the Social Security Administration for additional information. I was surprised by this because I had filled out the application with him in March. The ATCMHMR worker who had helped us said she would keep an eye on it, and she had not reported any problem. I discovered that the request had been sent to his old group home address. He hadn't received it because ATCMHMR had not updated his contact information on the application it was managing for him. Tim had the right to appeal the denial, but the ATCMHMR eligibility worker told me that she didn't plan to file the appeal because she believed that Tim might be in jail for some time, and he wouldn't be eligible for SSI benefits while he was there.

I figured that Tim wasn't going to be in jail forever, so I decided to handle the appeal myself. I was more motivated than the eligibility worker anyway because I was paying Tim's rent and food bills. I made a call to the local Legal Aid office for advice. I learned that the next round of SSI appeal hearings for Austin would probably not take place until six months later. If Tim won the appeal, he would receive payments retroactive to his application date, but he would receive nothing in the meantime.

I next turned my attention to Tim's apartment. I called the ATC-MHMR housing specialist to find out if the apartment lock had ever been changed as Tim had requested and if the apartment was secure while Tim was in jail. Tim's caseworker had not arranged for the lock to be changed, and the apartment had been overtaken by squatters. The caseworker called the housing specialist to have them evicted. But the housing specialist said she assumed that the people in the apartment must have been there with Tim's permission. And she wanted me to know that they had broken a window, so Tim would have to pay $83.50 to have it replaced.

The judge decided to release Tim from Del Valle on July 18, after Tim, his lawyer, and ATCMHMR all agreed that he was stable enough to go back to his apartment. The probation officer disagreed, wanting to enroll Tim in a program called Cornerstone. (ATCMHMR pointed out that the Cornerstone program had closed down eight years earlier.) The judge toyed with the idea of sending Tim to an alternative incarceration center for people with schizophrenia but instead ordered him to attend a six-week outpatient program at a northern Travis County facility. The order was a hollow one as Tim had no transportation to get there.

Tim stopped by our house during the first week in August while I was visiting the other children in Connecticut to celebrate Ben's thirteenth birthday. He brought Pam up to date on his living situation: He was settled in his apartment but was not attending his program in the northern part of the county, was not seeing his probation officer, and had no contact with ATCMHMR. She drove him back to his apartment, and when they got there a man she didn't recognize offered her some marijuana. Tim was embarrassed. "That's my stepmother," he said, wincing.

Three weeks later, Tim was charged with possession of marijuana and destruction of evidence, a felony, after someone complained about the activities going on in his apartment. He returned to Del Valle for his third incarceration in five months. He was assigned a third public defender to represent him on the two charges.

The next day, I talked to his lawyer, who explained that Tim's felony charge was going to be scheduled for a fast-track system called the "rocket docket" on September 4. This would result in a plea agreement for Tim to consider.

Tim remembered to put me on his visitors list this time. When I saw him, I learned that he was feeling right at home at Del Valle. He joined the night cleanup crew and was assigned to the jail "honors" program, which gave him more time credits for good behavior. He was also running the clock on the one-year sentence he had received on June 16 for stealing the beer kegs and keeping close track of his days in jail. He calculated that at his current rate of three days credited for every day he served, he would have enough time served by the time he went back to court to fully satisfy that sentence. Tim also seemed to be aware of what was going on at his apartment. He said that he had a friend who was keeping an eye on things. I also spoke with the jail's mental health counselor, who had been seeing Tim weekly. (Tim had signed a release so she could talk with me.) He had reported to her that he was hearing voices again. He was not on any medications, and she did not recommend that he see a psychiatrist right away. She wanted to continue to monitor him. Unfortunately, I knew that none of her work would follow Tim out into the community when he was released because the care he received in the jail was not integrated with the care he received in the community.

I visited with Tim about a week later. As had been the case in the spring, Tim was well versed on his legal status. This was no small accomplishment. His relationship to the justice system had become very confusing to me over the past few months. He had been arrested in April, June, and August and had accumulated a number of charges related to one or more of his arrests, including violation of probation, marijuana possession, and destruction of evidence. Time-served clocks were running on some or all of these as he awaited his next court date and sentencing. He patiently explained to me how each one would be resolved. The felony charge for destruction of evidence had already been reduced during the court's "rocket docket" to a Class B misdemeanor charge for possession of marijuana. Tim pleaded guilty to this and was sentenced to six months in jail, which translated to a minimum of two actual months, taking into account the good behavior credits he was earning in the Del Valle Honors program. At sentencing, the judge also credited him with twenty-one days served, meaning that Tim had to serve a minimum of five more weeks in jail, beginning on August 24, the day he was incarcerated. As a result, his earliest possible release date on that misdemeanor conviction was September 27. Tim also calculated that he would be credited with additional time served dating from his incarceration in April. When his probation was revoked in June, his sentence for the April misdemeanor conviction had been reduced from one year to six months, and the sentences for the April beer keg theft and the June marijuana possession were to be served concurrently Since he earned six weeks' credit for the three weeks he was in jail in June and July, these weeks would be credited to both sentences, and so he was just about clear of his April sentence.

The only time that Tim couldn't get credited to the possession charge in June was the time he had served before he actually committed that crime. This turned out to be another small matter because the computer showed that he had already served that full sentence while awaiting his September court date. As a result, the good news was that based on the computer information, he had completed his sentences resulting from his arrests in both April and June, and these were now behind him.

There was only one additional charge from August that was unresolved. At the time he was charged with destruction of evidence (the felony), he was also charged with misdemeanor possession of marijuana. The original misdemeanor possession charge was pending before the county court, not the district court, which handled the felony destruction of evidence charge on the "rocket docket." However, once the destruction of evidence charge was reduced to the Class B possession misdemeanor and Tim pleaded guilty, he had effectively already been tried and sentenced on that charge. So he couldn't be tried on it again in the county court. I had no idea how he could keep all of this straight.

After the visit I talked with a couple of the guards, who looked up Tim's case and confirmed everything Tim had explained to me. I later spoke with an associate of Tim's attorney, who also confirmed that Tim was correct. The final possession charge was dismissed the next day.

Tim was discharged from Del Valle in late September, on what turned out to be a very good day for us. Not only was he free of the criminal justice system with no felony conviction on his record, but we learned that he was being approved for SSI.

This approval hadn't come easily. After learning about how long we would have to wait to schedule an appeal, I called a friend of mine who worked for Senator Chris Dodd to ask for help. Less than three weeks later, Senator Dodd's office called to say they had been notified that Tim was being recommended for approval for his SSI by the Disability

Determination Services of the Texas Rehabilitation Commission. We would not need to file our formal appeal after all—but it took a call to a senator's office to achieve this. How many people are able to do that?

I was hopeful that we were on track after an exhausting summer. But it was not to be. Tim's apartment, used by so many other people during the past few weeks, had been turned into a filthy, smelly, unsafe pigsty. And Tim's anxiety levels were clearly increasing as the weeks passed.

Tim's housing specialist seemed to be the only service provider who took any real interest in him, and that was mostly to complain to me about the damage to the apartment. In late October, she told me about another broken window. This time they found a "friend" living in a storage closet where Tim was allowed to keep his bike. They cleaned the friend and his possessions out of the closet and piled up everything on the balcony outside Tim's apartment door. They changed the lock on the storage room door and presented Tim with a bill.

Tim barely knew who his ANEW caseworker was. He wasn't taking his medications and couldn't handle the chaos of his living arrangement. He rejected overtures of help from ATCMHMR and became increasingly fearful of the people who dropped in and out of his apartment. His symptoms of psychosis intensified. He started calling Pam and me at least twice a day, telling us he was afraid to go in his apartment. I saw him toward the end of November, and he told me that he was afraid the people in his apartment were trying to kill him because he could "see it in their eyes." He said gravely that he was "ready to die."

I was very worried but tried using a little black humor to lift his spirits. When Tim was younger I would tease him about all the help he needed from me, saying, "I'm taking care of you now, but you'll have to take care of me when I'm old and decrepit."

"Dad," he would reply with a devilish grin, "I'm gonna put you in a home." I reminded him of this, then said with gravitas equal to his own, "If you die, Tim, who's going to put me in the home?" He smiled.

I called Tim's rehabilitation therapist at ATCMHMR, who agreed to see Tim and try to persuade him to go back on his medication. She also said that she wanted to refer Tim to the supported housing director to determine whether they had another housing option that could offer Tim more intensive services.

Tim received an early Christmas present when he was notified officially that his SSI payments would begin in January. But despite this and the efforts of family, friends, and service providers, he would soon become trapped in the revolving door of incarceration, hospitalization, and homelessness.

thirteen

TIM HITS THE REVOLVING DOOR

THE PHRASE "REVOLVING door" was already part of our mental health policy vocabulary in the early 1980s, but then it meant that when we released someone from a state hospital into the community, he or she often just went right back in again. Today, we have added a few more stops—courts, jails, the street, and community hospitals and services—but a lot of people still seem to end up right back where they began.

When Tim was a young child, I once asked him what he wanted to be when he grew up. "A hobo!" he exclaimed.

As a young teenager, he said that wanted to build a shack where he could be left alone to live off the land. "Where would you build this?" I asked him. "In the woods behind your house," he answered—the most expansive, remote, and private space he knew.

In fact, Tim always wanted to find a place where he could lead a life on his own, in which he could easily erase his rather large footprint and be accountable to no one but himself. In early 2004, I had a glimmer of hope that he still might find such a place.

His SSI money began to flow. At $564 per month it wasn't a huge amount, but it was enough for him to pay for necessities and establish a little independence. His disability was expected to be lifelong, and so he would not need to face a redetermination of eligibility for seven years. Along with his SSI came Medicaid, which would cover his basic health needs. Food stamps would help cover his food expenses, and he still had a tenuous hold on his apartment for shelter. Pam and I were close enough to look in on him regularly and to supplement his lean resources with some of our own. And when he needed even more help, the ANEW program was there.

On the surface, these seemed to be the pieces Tim needed to begin to move forward more independently in his life. But it turned out they were not.

He received the first blow to his independence when he was told that he would have to have a "representative payee" for his SSI benefits. This meant that the representative payee, not Tim, would manage Tim's funds. I was going to be his first representative payee, and I explained to Tim that all this meant was that I would set up a bank account into which his funds would be deposited directly. I would take responsibility for paying his rent and other regular bills. And after setting aside a few dollars each month for items like clothing, I would give him the rest of the money as a monthly allowance. This would not be a permanent arrangement; over time, he could take on more of the responsibility for managing his funds and eventually receive the funds directly. He was almost on board with this until he learned that he was also going to receive a retroactive payment of almost $3,000, dating back to his application six months earlier. When he learned that he wasn't going to be given those funds directly, either, he stormed out of the office in anger. I completed the paperwork without him.

I hoped that we would have a better result with his food stamps. After paying his rent and other expenses from his SSI, and holding back fifty dollars in reserve each month for clothes and other necessities, he was left with only fifteen dollars a week for food. This was far less than he needed, and he complained that I was forcing him to use soup kitchens or go hungry. I bought him some supermarket gift cards and scheduled an appointment at the Texas Health and Human Services Commission's office in charge of food stamps. Tim was notified in mid-January that he was eligible for $117 per month in food stamp benefits. He was mailed a "Lone Star" food stamp debit card. When it arrived, I told him to keep it in a safe place and use it whenever he went to the market.

But he could never keep track of his card. Within a few weeks of receiving his first card, he lost it. I contacted the food stamps office with him to get him a new card. He received it in March, used it a couple of times, and then lost it, too. We replaced it with another one in June, which he lost in July. He received yet another new card in August, but it disappeared shortly thereafter. We devised all kinds of strategies to help him keep track of it. I had him leave his card with me when he wasn't using it, but he lost it when he took it from me to use. I had him keep the card in his wallet and chain his wallet to his belt buckle, but he lost those pants. I even tried having him put the card inside his sock and shoe. The next time I saw him he was barefoot and had no idea where he had left the socks, shoes, or card.

For Tim, independence was elusive. And the SSI and Medicaid rules did not do much to facilitate his independence. Every time Tim entered an institution, his SSI payments were automatically suspended because he was presumed not to need them. But when he was released from the institution, reinstatement was not automatic. He had to bring a copy of his discharge or release papers in person to the Social Security office. The jail or hospital couldn't just fax or mail the paper and reinstate him automatically.

And, for reasons I never understood completely, the "housing" share of Tim's SSI benefits was paid on a two-month delay. I learned this when we received his first check in January and it was for $200 less than the $564 we expected. Because he was housed and I had paid his rent in November and December, his January and February checks were both smaller. Moreover, I could not reimburse myself for the rent payments I had made. This rule really took a toll whenever Tim went to jail. When he was released, the first two checks would always be too low for him to pay his bills.

And because Tim's Medicaid benefits were tied to his SSI, whenever his SSI payments were suspended he lost his Medicaid eligibility, too. This meant that whenever he was transferred from a jail to a hospital, in effect he was hospitalized with no insurance.

But the biggest blow to Tim's independence that year did not come from his poor money-management skills or from the bureaucratic rules of the benefit programs. It came when he entered the next acute phase of his disease.

Early in 2004 Tim began to destabilize. He became highly agitated and angry. His drug use, living conditions, and choice of acquaintances all got worse. His apartment became a flophouse, creating tension with Tim's neighbors. He increasingly lost track of the days, and when I went to his apartment to pick him up for Sunday dinner, more often than not he was nowhere to be found and some stranger would answer his door. When I did see him, at his best he was surly and uncooperative. At his worst, he was menacing. One time—after he had argued nonstop with me about his SSI money—I had to ask him to leave my house and not come back until he calmed down.

Linda visited with Tim during the holidays, and she was so appalled by his living conditions that she thought even jail was preferable. She contacted Pam, asking whether we all should consider having Tim arrested again so that he could at least have a cleaner, safer living environment.

Tim refused to let his current ANEW caseworker help him, so he was assigned another one. I called to tell her that I understood Tim was resistant to services. But I was afraid he might lose his housing or, worse, need to be hospitalized again if we could not figure out a way to help him. I asked if she could try to reach out to Tim and coax him back into treatment voluntarily. She promised to consider it and get back to me. A few days later she told me that she and her colleagues had decided that Tim's current "consumer directed plan" was not working. ATCMHMR was going to have several team members work together to try to convince Tim that he needed to accept more support. Her toolkit was limited. This was the only idea she had, but it did not work.

Tim's "friends" did not help matters. Someone identifying himself as Timothy Gionfriddo was caught shoplifting one day at a local grocery store called Fiesta Mart. The Fiesta Mart people took his picture and contact information and agreed not to press charges if he made full restitution. When he did not, Fiesta Mart sent a letter to Tim at our address informing him that it was going to prosecute him. Tim insisted that it was all a mistake. I visited Fiesta Mart and spoke with the manager, who showed me a photograph of a white man with light brown hair. When I showed him Tim's official ID, he agreed to drop the charges.

In the early spring, Tim's symptoms were intensifying. He was anxious, nervous, and jittery most of the time. He kept muttering that "people" were out to get him. He spoke vaguely about an injury and a visit to a hospital. I wasn't sure if he imagined this until I received insurance statements showing that he had been transported by ambulance to the hospital on March 11. I never learned for what.

At the end of March, Tim entered Austin State Hospital for observation and evaluation. He stayed for three days, and in my view he was not stable when he was released.

And then he lost his apartment. His ATCMHMR caseworker contacted me to tell me that a day-care center near his apartment had lodged a complaint about the people hanging out in the complex and that ATCMHMR was "considering" evicting Tim. Two weeks later, he was served with an eviction notice. Because he was unstable, I contacted ATCMHMR's housing specialist to find out if there was any alternative. She told me that she wished Tim well but had no other place for him to live.

I wasn't notified when, a few weeks later, Tim's few remaining possessions were put out on the sidewalk to be picked through by anyone passing by. Neither was Tim. He was on the Drag, being ticketed for "sitting or lying on a public sidewalk." An arrest warrant was also issued to him for leaving the scene of a crime because when he was ticketed he got up and walked away. I confirmed all this later with the prosecutor, who told me that Tim was being scheduled for a June jury trial on the charges.

When Tim returned to the apartment and saw everything he owned scattered all over the sidewalk and the street, he had a breakdown. He sat down in the middle of the road and refused to move, daring cars to hit him. When the police arrived he was incoherent, unable to explain what had happened or why he was sitting there. They brought him back to Austin State Hospital, but the hospital decided that he was not a danger to himself or others and released him that day. He was homeless again.

Over the next few weeks, Pam and I had difficulty finding Tim as he settled into his life as a homeless person. We drove up and down the Drag but rarely saw him. Whenever we did, we bought him some food and made plans for the next time. But he was seldom where he said he would be when we returned. We tried to convince him to stay in touch with his ANEW caseworker, but he was unhappy about the way he had been treated by the housing specialist. Although he obviously needed it desperately, he told me he did not want any more help.

He did, however, accept help from the squatters who had been part of the reason he was evicted from his apartment. Those who found other housing took Tim in. Then I understood how Tim's social support system on the streets worked. It was based on interdependence among the (usually) homeless people in his group, not on independence from services and supports. Whoever had housing at any given time opened his or her doors to the rest of the group. Those who had cash shared it with others, and those who had benefits also shared those. Sometimes they even shared identities. Privacy did not mean to Tim and his friends what it meant to me.

In mid-June, Tim landed back in the Travis County Jail, just in time for him to miss his June 23 jury trial for sitting or lying on a public sidewalk. The prosecutor told me not to worry about Tim missing the trial. The matter would be handled the next time Tim was in the system.

When Tim was released from jail, he expressed a willingness to receive services from ATCMHMR again. I talked with an ATCMHMR official, who told me to follow up with someone new—the agency's homeless coordinator. The coordinator had a group of outreach people who were not pushy, and Tim liked them. They explored some ideas with Tim to help him get off the streets. Tim had a new friend who was also encouraging Tim to get his own apartment. He was a little older than Tim and came from northern Texas. He had no family in the area and very few possessions of his own. But he came across as mature, thoughtful, and even-tempered. He said that he would provide peer support to Tim in return for being able to stay with him from time to time.

With the blessing of the homeless coordinator, Tim and his friend searched for an apartment. They found one in north Austin, and Tim was more excited about moving in than I had seen him in months. I was skeptical about whether the management company would rent to Tim, but he insisted that the company was aware of his circumstances and was still willing to rent to him. Tim told me that I didn't have to take his word for it; he wanted me to meet with representatives of the company to verify that, as his representative payee, I would be paying Tim's rent each month.

The two people with whom I spoke were very pleasant. They confirmed that they knew Tim was homeless and had been evicted from his last apartment. They also understood that he was a client of ATCMHMR. So long as the rent was paid and there was someone at ATCMHMR to call in case Tim had a problem, the apartment was his for $445 per month. I said I would pay the rent and called the ATCMHMR homeless coordinator, who assured me that he would endorse Tim's application when the management company called.

However, when the call came it did not go to the homeless coordinator. Instead, it went to the ATCMHMR housing coordinator who had evicted Tim from his apartment. And she—who was not in contact with the homeless coordinator that day—gave a terribly damaging report about Tim to the management company. She claimed, among other things, that he did not pay his rent on time. The management company representatives called me back to tell me that they were turning down Tim's application because he failed to pay his rent, had unauthorized guests in his previous apartment, and had damaged the apartment. I was stunned because the rent had been paid and Tim had disclosed both of the other issues when he applied. So I knew that there must have been another reason.

I called the ATCMHMR housing coordinator for an explanation. She had always been pleasant to me in the past, but this time she hung up on me after refusing to say more or to correct the misinformation she had provided about the rent.

All Tim knew was that his apartment had fallen through because of ATCMHMR. So he refused to cooperate any longer with the homeless coordinator and went back to fending for himself on the streets. This decision helped land him back in jail.

In early September he entered a restaurant through an unlocked back entrance, took a bolt cutter, and left. He was arrested for the sixth time in eighteen months, this time for burglary, and was returned to Del Valle jail. He was assigned his sixth public defender. His projected stay at Del Valle was 120 days, probably in anticipation of a one-year sentence with credit for time served. In October, I received notice of yet another outstanding arrest warrant for Tim. It was for failing to appear—while he was sitting in jail—in court in June for his trial relating to sitting on the sidewalk and leaving the scene. I figured the sheriff knew where to find him.

Tim did not respond well to this stay in jail. His psychosis worsened, he showed signs of paranoia, and he reported hearing voices again. He was also involved in at least one fight. A mental health counselor evaluated him and decided to admit him to Austin State Hospital for treatment in mid-October. Tim spent several weeks there.

At the hospital Tim was put back on Zyprexa and trazodone. His social worker at the hospital told me that Tim would stay there until he was able to stand trial. I visited with Tim several times—a much more pleasant experience than visiting him in jail. He was soon stabilized and once again explained that the charges would probably be reduced by the time he got to court. He predicted that he would be released shortly after he returned to Del Valle, sometime in December.

With Tim off the streets, I had some time to find him housing. There was some urgency to this. If Tim wanted to avoid being ordered into a halfway house when he was released from jail, he needed someplace to live. I talked with the Section 8 people at ATCMHMR and received some good news. After waiting two years, Tim would be at the top of the Section 8 list by January; he would be able to get a Section 8 subsidized apartment. There was just one minor, technical matter that his lawyer would have to explain in court. Tim's Section 8 certificate was reserved for someone who was homeless; in other words, Tim would have to be released as "homeless" in order to be eligible for this housing.

I contacted Tim's attorney to give him this information, but he did not return my call. When Tim went back to Del Valle during the first week of December, he couldn't reach his attorney either. We both tried repeatedly to reach him over the next three weeks with no success.

Linda finally got through to him. She called me to report that the lawyer told her that in addition to the burglary charge, Tim had to deal with the October arrest warrant for "failure to appear." I brought her up to date about my earlier conversation with the prosecutor and called Tim's lawyer to leave him a message that he did not have to worry about the failure to appear charge—he just needed to talk with the prosecutor. Again, he did not return my call.

I learned from the court clerk during the last week in December that Tim had a court date for January 5 at nine-thirty in the morning. I called his lawyer, and the receptionist told me that he was on vacation and would not return until January 3. I was upset and let her know that I thought it was wrong for the attorney not to answer calls or interact with his client for weeks. I suggested that his lack of attention might be related to the fact that the client wasn't paying the bill. She assured me that he wasn't treating Tim any differently from the way he treated any other client.

I was frustrated and vented my frustration to the receptionist. The prosecutor was still pushing for a felony conviction, and Section 8 landlords weren't renting to felons. The lawyer had to make certain that Tim was released as homeless in order for him to be able to use the Section 8 housing voucher, which meant that the lawyer would have to explain this to the prosecutor and the judge. There was more, but when I stopped to take a breath the receptionist told me politely that she would share all this information with Tim's lawyer when he came back from vacation.

On the day of Tim's hearing I still had not heard from his lawyer. I left two more voice mails for him in the morning. He finally called me shortly after nine, as he was rushing to court for Tim's hearing. I told him quickly about how the voucher worked. He said he understood and would take care of it. I also told him that ATCMHMR was willing to provide services to Tim, and he asked me to secure that commitment in writing. I arranged with a senior administrator to send the lawyer a letter by noon. He hurried off the call, assuring me that he had everything under control and that the process in court could take hours. He would call me back as soon as he had something to report.

He did not call me back. I was still waiting at the end of the day, so I called his office and spoke to his receptionist again. She said he was in a conference, but when I gave her my name she asked me to hold for a minute.

The lawyer came on the line and told me that Tim had had his charge reduced to a misdemeanor and was given a sentence of one year's probation. Just as I expected, he said that the judge would not agree to release him unless he had housing. But then he reported that since no one understood about the voucher, she sentenced Tim to a halfway house. Tim's attorney described this halfway house as "inappropriate" for Tim.

I was livid. I asked him how anyone could have misunderstood the nature of the housing voucher, which required simply that Tim be released as homeless to qualify for it. I told him that he said that he understood this when I explained it to him in the morning.

He replied that he knew a lot more about how to do his job than I did. I responded that I wasn't so sure and asked who I needed to call at the court to renegotiate the agreement. He gave me the names of the judge and Tim's probation officer. Then he told me to "take a deep breath" and not to give them the attitude I was giving him.

The next day, I talked with Tim's probation officer. She was perfectly reasonable, knew about the voucher program, and understood immediately why we needed to have Tim released as homeless. She suggested that I give the judge a call, too. I spoke directly with the judge, who also understood immediately. She said that she had not been informed by Tim's lawyer about the housing voucher. She changed her release order and wished Tim well.

A year that had begun with the hope of independence ended pretty much back where we had started. Tim was released on January 11 into the custody of ATCMHMR, and two days later I took him to the Housing Authority to pick up his Section 8 voucher. We obtained a list of Section 8 approved apartment complexes, and Pam and I set out with Tim to see if we could find one that was willing to rent to him. Within a week we found an apartment near Town Lake, about a mile from our home. It was close to shopping, fast food, a pharmacy, and a supermarket and near the bus line, a couple of primary-care clinics, and ATCMHMR services. Tim moved in at the end of January. His monthly rent was $459, but under the Section 8 program he paid only $109 and the Housing Authority paid the rest. I arranged for an automatic payment to the landlord from Tim's bank account so that the rent would always be paid on time.

Pam and I moved him in and held our breath.

fourteen
LAUNCHING TIM

I WASN'T GOING to make the same mistake I made the year before. Tim needed help to succeed on his own. And by now, I had a pretty good idea about what that help should be. First, Tim needed to rely more on mental health professionals to help him meet his day-to-day needs and less on his homeless friends. Second, these professionals needed to facilitate a formal collaboration of housing, legal services, law enforcement, and community-services providers in arranging for and carrying out services for Tim. In other words, Tim needed integrated services, led by a mental health professional. And third, we as parents had to play our role, supporting Tim as needed and working productively with all of these people on his behalf.

On the day Tim moved into his Section 8 apartment, I thought we might be on track. ATCMHMR was back in the picture on the clinical side as a result of Tim's probation and finally seemed ready to help organize and coordinate

Tim's care. Tim's homeless friends were a few miles away. We had a new housing provider that understood his basic needs, and Tim's probation officer seemed willing to advocate for services that could prevent his return to jail. And Pam and I were close by, able to work to connect him with a neighborhood bank, drug store, and supermarket and other resources to facilitate his independent living.

Then I received an unexpected out-of-state job offer, and Pam and I were making plans to move from Austin to Florida by the summer. I was reluctant to leave Tim behind, but he wanted to stay in Austin. We had six months to arrange Tim's supports. I thought that would be plenty of time.

We started by making a list of the things Tim would need to live on his own when Pam and I moved away. He had an apartment and food shopping and preparation skills, and he knew how to take the bus to get around town. He needed a telephone he wouldn't lose, so we installed a landline in his apartment. He also needed a new ID card, which we got for him.

The rest of the things he needed were going to be a little more challenging. Two in particular were a high priority. Tim had to be able to manage his money and his mail so that he could pay his bills and respond to important correspondence on time. He also had to be able to work with ATCMHMR to manage his mental illness and his medications. He needed a caseworker he could count on at ATCMHMR and someone to run interference for him with the criminal justice system, including his probation officer.

To improve Tim's money-management skills, I arranged to have a fifty-dollar check drawn from his account and sent to him by mail each week. I told him that he could use the fifty dollars any way he wanted. I wanted to help him begin to manage money—something he also wanted to do—and to have an incentive to check his mail regularly. Then I brought him with me to the bank branch office where Pam and I did our regular banking. I introduced him to the branch manager and tellers. I explained that Tim would be coming in each week to cash a check drawn on his own account. They agreed to cash the check for him even if he forgot his ID card.

With money management checked off our list, we paid a visit to a Walgreens pharmacy near his apartment. We made sure that the pharmacy had his Medicaid number and address on file so that Tim would be able to fill prescriptions there without needing to bring either money or identification.

I was feeling upbeat about our progress, but there was one thing that did not happen right away. ATCMHMR did not assign a new caseworker to Tim, and so no one from ATCMHMR accompanied us on our visits and started getting to know Tim. And when I asked if ATCMHMR could find Tim a representative payee, there was no one available for this, either.

No problem, I thought; we'll make do. But one Sunday in mid-February, Tim came for dinner showing signs of active psychosis. Fearful and anxious, he couldn't tell me if a caseworker had checked in on him. He hadn't gone to the pharmacy to fill any of his prescriptions. He hadn't slept for a couple of days but refused to take any of the trazodone we had in the house. He was irritable and he didn't want any food. "Just coffee," he said, because he wanted to stay awake. When Pam and I said no to the coffee, he cut short his visit.

The next day proved to me both how elusive the idea of collaborative services driven by mental health professionals would be for Tim and how inadequate my plan for his independence was. Nothing went according to plan.

Tim's probation officer called me as I was getting ready for work. I had not heard from her since just after Tim's release from jail, and she told me that Tim had missed two scheduled appointments. She did not have Tim's address or phone number, and her office was issuing a warrant for his arrest. I gave her Tim's contact information and told her that I did not think he was actively avoiding her. He was just holed up in his apartment and not feeling well and had not been assigned a new ATCMHMR caseworker yet. She seemed to understand as we strategized about how she might encourage him to ask for more treatment services from ATCMHMR.

I told her I was concerned about the arrest warrant because I didn't want him back in jail. I asked if it could be withdrawn if I brought Tim to see her right away. She said that it could not because her supervisor said that it had been ninety days since they had had contact with Tim. I reminded her that Tim hadn't been released from jail until the first week of January, so it could not have been more than forty days. She told me that the wheels of the system were turning and there was nothing more she could do but that she did want to see Tim right away anyway.

I skipped work and went to get Tim. It was a challenge getting him out of bed; he complained that he was too tired to leave his apartment. I told him about the arrest warrant and said that if he did not go to see his probation officer with me, the police might come for him instead.

He reluctantly agreed to come with me. We left his apartment around ten-thirty and arrived at the probation office a few minutes later. His probation officer spent about forty-five minutes with us. Tim was barely able to keep his eyes open. He was unwashed and incoherent in his responses to her questions. She judged that he was in need of treatment. She asked about the level of support that ATCMHMR was providing, and when I described it as inconsistent she immediately put in a call to the agency.

She demanded a more intensive level of treatment, either through ANEW or ACT. She told Tim that she was making it a condition of his probation that he take his medications and asked him if he was willing to go immediately to the ATCMHMR emergency services center for an evaluation. Tim said yes and agreed to take any medications they gave him. She asked him if he was drinking or using drugs; he said no to drinking but yes to marijuana. She asked him if he was using marijuana because it made him feel better, and he said yes. She said she appreciated his honesty and just let it go.

Before we left, she called ATCMHMR emergency services directly and demanded that a nurse see Tim as soon as we arrived. When she hung up she reported that she got "attitude" from the person on the other end of the line but that we should still go right to the emergency services program. She made a follow-up appointment for the end of the week to meet with Tim in his apartment and promised that she would follow up with ATCMHMR before then.

When we arrived at the ATCMHMR emergency services center, I let the receptionist know that we had been sent directly from the probation office for an evaluation and medication. She asked us to take a seat. Despite the call from the probation officer, we waited nearly an hour before seeing a counselor. Tim's agitation increased, and he occasionally muttered to himself. He also whined repeatedly that he wanted to go back to his apartment to sleep. He twice tried to leave the center, forcing me to follow him out the door and coax him back.

We finally saw a mental health counselor. Tim answered his questions in a monotone. Then the counselor turned to me and said that we shouldn't be there because Tim didn't need emergency services; he just needed a medication order. He handed it to me and told us to go to an ATCMHMR clinic a mile or so away that would fill the order. Just to be sure, he called the facility before we left to tell the staff that he was sending us there and why.

As we were being ushered out, I told him I was concerned about Tim, who appeared to me to need more than just medication. He was becoming more and more agitated and was still muttering incoherently. The counselor asked Tim if he was hallucinating, and Tim said yes. The counselor hesitated for a moment and then repeated that he did not think Tim needed immediate treatment. We should just go to the clinic to get the medication order filled.

I was worried that we might have to wait again at the clinic. If the only service we were going to get there was filling a prescription, couldn't he just call it into Walgreens so we could pick it up there on the way back to Tim's apartment? He said no, that the order had to be filled at the clinic.

Over Tim's objection, I drove directly to the clinic. When we got there Tim was asked to take a number. We waited. Finally, we were called into an office where a young woman said that she would register Tim in the system and issue him a card so that he could receive medication dispensed from the clinic. But when she looked up Tim's name in the computer, she said he was already on Medicaid. The clinic only dispensed medications to uninsured clients. Tim needed to take a prescription to a regular pharmacy, such as Walgreens, to get his medication.

I took a breath. I told her that I had already asked the emergency services center counselor to call in a prescription to Walgreens but he had refused. And now all we had was a medication order the clinic was refusing to fill, not a prescription that we could take to a regular pharmacy.

She asked us to wait a minute while she went to get a supervisor. He came back holding the order in his hand. He brusquely informed us that there were no refills permitted on the order. I had no idea what he was talking about. "We're not trying to get a refill," I explained, "just the medication order filled or a prescription we can bring to Walgreens." All the while, Tim was sitting next to me moaning, begging to be taken back to his apartment so that he could get some sleep.

Finally, the supervisor agreed to call in the prescription to Walgreens. I thanked him, thinking that our hours-long ordeal finally might be ending. He glanced over at Tim, who was moaning, and said that we should leave because he was very busy and it might take him some time to call in the prescription.

I thought we might get a quicker result if we stayed put. I told the supervisor that we would just wait in the clinic until he could call it in. He told me to give him an hour and went back to his office and closed the door.

At that point I didn't want to deal with Tim, who kept begging me to leave so he could go home to bed. And no one at the clinic wanted to deal with me. So I used the time to call the CEO of ATCMHMR, who was a member of the board of the nonprofit for which I was executive director. I left him a brief voice mail explaining the situation. A short time later, the supervisor returned from his office and told me he had called in the prescription to Walgreens. He said it should be ready for us when we arrived there. He gave me a copy for my records and sent us on our way. I checked my watch. It was three-fifteen. It had taken us nearly four hours to get a prescription called into a pharmacy. I wondered how Tim was supposed to manage any of this when he was on his own.

But our day wasn't close to being over. When we arrived at Walgreen's a few minutes later, Tim told me he wanted to wait in the car; he had been asked to leave the store a week earlier and told not to come back. I took a deep breath and asked why. He wouldn't say but insisted that he hadn't done anything wrong. I figured that the day was already a loss but that this was something we had to straighten out, so I made him come in with me. I asked to speak to the manager, who confirmed that she had asked Tim to leave because he had been "hanging out" in the store a few days earlier. Tim hadn't said or done anything to arouse suspicion; his presence just made the cashier nervous.

I was too tired to be diplomatic. I asked whether it was Tim's height, race, or apparent mental illness that made the cashier nervous. The manager hesitated for a minute and then replied that while Tim was welcome as a customer at any time, "homeless people milling about" (she had just assumed, on the basis of his appearance, that Tim was homeless when she told him to leave) made other customers nervous. I told her that Tim wasn't homeless. He lived in an apartment in the neighborhood, and we had made arrangements for him to shop at this Walgreens. She finally relented, saying that he was welcome to shop there at any time.

The truth was that she hadn't treated Tim any differently from the way he was often treated in Austin. Tall, black, and usually unkempt, Tim was a target for discrimination, and it bothered me. Once I took him into a mall department store to shop for clothes. We went to the men's section, but to different clothing racks. He found a shirt he liked right away, but I was still looking. I noticed a salesperson watching Tim as he took the shirt from the rack and walked closer to me to wait. After a few minutes, she approached Tim and told him he needed to put the shirt back. Tim just smiled and shrugged as he started to comply; he never enjoyed confrontation. But I didn't mind defending my son and chimed in that Tim had as much a right to purchase a shirt in her store as anyone did.

Tim was embarrassed. He said, "Dad, don't make a big deal, it happens to me sometimes." It finally dawned on the salesperson that Tim and I were father and son and were shopping in the store together. She apologized for the "misunderstanding," offering a lame explanation that she was just trying to make sure we paid for Tim's shirt in the "correct department." "Of course you were," I said.

I was thinking about this as I handed the Walgreens manager my business card and told her to call me if she ever had any real problem with Tim. Then I told Tim privately not to hang out there anymore.

Finally, I thought, we were ready to pick up Tim's prescription. We went to the counter, but the prescription wasn't ready. The supervisor at the clinic had implied to me that he had spoken to someone at Walgreens when he called in the prescription, but all he had done was leave a voice mail, to which the pharmacist had not yet listened. So we waited some more.

While we were waiting, I received a call from Tim's probation officer, who told me that she had scheduled two more meetings for Tim. One was an interview with the ANEW program for the following Monday. She made it clear that she expected me to take the day off from work to be there with Tim. She had also set up an appointment for Tim for the following Thursday afternoon at her office. She wanted me to be there, too. In return, she said, her supervisor "might be willing" to pull the arrest warrant. I thanked her for her efforts and began to think about how I could revise my work schedule to accommodate these appointments.

When the call ended, the pharmacist called me back to the counter. She said that the prescription could not be filled because Texas Medicaid required "prior authorization" from a physician from the clinic. We did not have one and so would have to go back to the clinic to get it. Tim looked as if he were about ready to fall over. I took another deep breath and offered to pay for the prescription in cash if she would fill it. The pharmacist agreed, and twenty minutes later we finally walked out of the pharmacy with the medication it had taken us all day to get.

Drained of all energy, I brought Tim back to his apartment in silence. I took out one of his pills and filled a glass with water. As I held out the pill to him, he said that he did not want to take it. "It makes me sleepy," he said, before heading to bed.

Tim's intake interview for the ANEW program the following Monday was very long, and I sat through it all. He talked freely about himself, including where he was born, where he had lived, where he'd gone to school, what he'd accomplished so far in his life, and what his interests were. He also gave as much information about his medical history as he could. Toward the end of the session, the interviewer inadvertently went down an unintentionally existential path.

"The next question may seem silly," he said, "but I have to ask it anyway. Do you know who you are?"

After a long, reflective pause, Tim sighed. "No, not really."

"You don't know who you are?" the interviewer asked again, a little surprised by Tim's answer.

Tim thought a few seconds more. "No, I don't really think I know who I am yet."

The nature of the miscommunication dawned on everyone present. "I meant," the interviewer corrected himself, "do you know your name?"

"Yes, it's Tim Cionfriddo—but I don't really know who I am."

The interviewer moved on. "Okay. Do you know how old you are?"

"Nineteen," Tim answered correctly.

"Very good," said the interviewer. "And do you know what year it is?"

"I don't know. Nineteen-eighty-five or eighty-six. I think eighty-five."

I tried to help. "Not your birth year, Tim. He means what year is it now?"

"Oh," he said. "I don't know."

The interviewer made a note. "Do you know what day it is?"

"Uh, Monday?" Tim guessed, playing a one-in-seven chance that he would be right. He was.

"Do you know what month it is?"

"March."

"March?"

"No, wait, the month before March."

"And what month is that?"

"Uh, I don't really know my months."

"Do you know what time of day it is?"

"About three o'clock, right?"

It felt like three o'clock to me, too. "What time is it?" Tim then asked.

"Eleven A.M.," the interviewer replied.

I couldn't help it; the melody just started to run through my brain. "Does anybody really know what time it is? Does anybody really care?"

After that tedious day, I got a call back from the CEO of ATCMHMR. A caring and thoughtful man, he was as gracious as always, referring to our day's runaround as "unconscionable." He then asked what I wanted for Tim besides more intensive services. Nothing, I told him—just some actual service. The next morning, a caseworker left me a voice mail. He wondered if he should ask the Austin Police Department mental health officers to assess Tim. If that was the caseworker's idea of service, I wondered if Tim might need a different caseworker.

Tim mostly rested at his apartment over the next few days, recovering from his latest bout of psychosis. I paid him frequent visits to be sure that he took his medication and got some sleep. I cleaned his apartment with him before his probation officer visited so that it was as presentable (and free of illegal substances) as possible. The meeting went well, and the next day he made a successful trip to the bank by himself to cash his check. He came over for dinner a few days after that, rested and medicated. We had our meeting with his probation officer, who praised Tim for his progress. She did not, however, pull his arrest warrant.

The ANEW program did not accept Tim after his lengthy interview and evaluation. The counselor did not think that Tim would be able to show up for weekly appointments at the ATCMHMR clinic on his own, as was expected of all ANEW clients. If he did not, he would be discharged from ANEW. A discharge would result in a parole violation, and Tim could be returned to jail. He advised that Tim apply again for the ACT program, which provided more daily supervision.

But we ran into a snag. To qualify for ACT, Tim had to have had at least two stays in Austin State Hospital within the previous six months, or three within a year. He had been at the hospital four months earlier, but that was the only time during the last six months. Neither Tim nor anyone at ATCMHMR knew whether he had been admitted once or twice the previous spring when he was evicted from his efficiency apartment.

The ACT team suggested that to resolve the matter, Tim check himself into the hospital for a day. In recent weeks he had been hearing voices, feeling paranoid, and wondering how he could protect himself from people trying to harm him, and they guessed that the hospital would probably admit him if he said so. But Tim refused to do this.

As he was stuck between ACT and ANEW, Tim received no services from ATCMHMR, though both the agency and his probation officer were pushing him to accept some. Pam and I were traveling between Austin and Florida and could not keep a twenty-four-hour watch on him by ourselves. Tim's apartment manager discovered four additional people living in his apartment, and in late March Tim was cited for two lease violations — one for the unauthorized occupants and another for an unclean apartment.

After that, Tim agreed to admit himself to Austin State Hospital. He thought this would get his probation officer and ATCMHMR off his back, but his plan backfired when he signed himself out again four days later against the hospital's advice and mine. Instead of referring him to ACT, his probation officer responded by having him arrested immediately using the still-outstanding warrant, thinking that Del Valle jail would just send him directly back to the hospital for treatment. But her plan also backfired when the psychiatrist who evaluated Tim discounted his entire medical history. He decided that Tim did not have a mental illness and bounced him right back to Del Valle.

Tim was sitting in jail again, awaiting another court date. With time on his hands, he began to think seriously about moving back to Connecticut. He talked with Linda to see if she would help. She told me that she thought she would have time to put some services together for Tim.

Tim was released from Del Valle a few days later, but soon we were dealing with more immediate concerns. First, his illness worsened, but he denied that it was happening. Next, he was involuntarily admitted to the hospital—his third admission in a little over a month. Finally, while he was hospitalized he received a second notice of a lease violation from his landlord, this time for having too many "unauthorized persons" in the apartment, "urinating in the hallway," and "throwing up just outside of the entrance way." Tim had not been in his apartment when these things happened.

I contacted the apartment manager and explained that Tim was in the hospital. She said that she sympathized, but she would not withdraw the notice. In her view, Tim was not receiving the support she had expected from ATCMHMR. Also, she knew Pam and I were moving, and she did not want to have to deal with Tim's issues directly when he was released from the hospital. Instead, she said that she would evict him if things did not improve immediately.

I visited with Tim in the hospital. He told me what he had told Linda—that he would move to Connecticut "for a while" after he was released. I was relieved and contacted Linda. Unfortunately, the window in which she would have been able to arrange for services on her own in Connecticut had closed, and she told me that she needed me to figure out his health care and insurance. She was also concerned enough about Tim's failure to take his medication that she wanted to see if he could be put on an injectable medication first (which at the time only required dosing every three months). The problem was that Tim's psychiatrists had been unwilling to use an injectable unless he agreed not to self-medicate, too.

Also, there were some new logistical issues to resolve. Linda was vacationing on Memorial Day weekend, so she did not think it would be possible for Tim to come to Connecticut until June 1 at the earliest. But Pam and I would be in Florida by then. She suggested that I fly up to Connecticut with Tim from Austin and then go back to Florida.

I couldn't really blame her for wanting help. I knew from experience that assisting Tim was nearly a full-time job. But Pam and I were also busy. I had already squeezed in two trips to Connecticut that spring, one for Lizzie's confirmation and another to meet with Ben's teachers. When we were in Florida, I was working full-time at my new job while Pam searched for a place to live. And when we were in Austin, Pam and I were packing up the house and wrapping up our work obligations at the same time that we were running interference for Tim. I just didn't have the time, resources, or energy to do everything Linda asked as well. But our situation was by no means unusual—family caregivers of people with serious mental illness are often simply burned out by the effort.

When Tim was discharged from the hospital he temporarily put his plan to move to Connecticut on hold. Austin was looking better to him. He had a new girlfriend and a tenuous hold on his apartment. What he lacked was money. So while Pam and I were in Florida, he and some friends broke into our house. They helped themselves to hundreds of dollars' worth of computer equipment, a bike, jewelry, and other items and pawned them all. When we discovered what had happened, we were livid. We told Tim that he could not come by our house anymore when we weren't there and that if he did he would find himself back in jail.

He then decided he would move to Connecticut. Linda relented on some of her conditions, and Pam and I arranged for Tim to leave for Connecticut by bus during our last full weekend in Austin. But Tim was torn about leaving his girlfriend behind. Linda briefly entertained the idea of letting them both come north.

On the heels of the break-in at our house, I discouraged her in an e-mail. "These days," I wrote, "neither Tim nor his friends are to be trusted or taken at face value. You can take on whatever you want in inviting them into your home, life, and the life of your family, but be careful, and keep your eyes open. Also, Tim is legally an adult, and not your financial or legal responsibility in any way. To whatever extent you involve yourself in his affairs, others (in my experience) will attempt to make you partially responsible, and you may at times be tempted to do so yourself. It would be a mistake for you to let either happen." This was advice from experience—if I had learned anything since Tim had become an adult, it was that to get anything done for him, I always had to be right by his side. And that just wore me out.

On moving day, Pam and I brought Tim to the Greyhound station in Austin before we set out on our drive to Florida. All of his possessions fit into three bags. We sat at the bus station waiting for the bus, and I gave him some cash, his ID, and his birth certificate. I had paid the rent on his Austin apartment through the end of June, so the apartment was still his. We had locked it up together, and we agreed that he would wait until after he got to Connecticut to give his landlord notice that he was vacating. We talked a little about his two-day itinerary and reviewed the towns in which he would be stopping.

He left Austin at one-thirty in the afternoon. He transferred to another bus in Houston, leaving there at six-ten P.M. He was supposed to travel from there through Baton Rouge, New Orleans, Mobile, Montgomery, Atlanta, Charlotte, Richmond, Baltimore, and New York on his journey to Connecticut. He never made it out of Texas.

Pam and I were in Mississippi when Linda called to say that Tim had gotten off the bus during a stop in East Texas and the bus had left without him. His money, ID, Social Security card, birth certificate, and other possessions were still on the bus. For reasons that were unclear to Pam and me, Tim decided that he should return to Austin instead of taking the next bus and catching up with his possessions. He was already on his way back there. We had not anticipated this contingency. He had no cash, no ID, no parents, and no means of support in Austin. He did, however, have a girlfriend and an apartment waiting for him.

Linda flew to Austin the next weekend to try to convince Tim to return to Connecticut with her, but by then he was settled back into his apartment. He refused to leave, and Linda returned to Connecticut without him.

It was too bad that she had not been more persuasive. Two weeks later, Tim was arrested for misdemeanor assault with injury after getting into a fight with his girlfriend. He was assigned to another defense attorney, who had never represented him before. He received an eviction notice for domestic violence while he was in jail. He stayed in jail for a week and was released after someone posted bail for him. Tim agreed to a family-violence evaluation and was ordered to stay two hundred yards away from his girlfriend. Pam and I flew back to Austin at the end of June and tried, unsuccessfully, to convince him to go back to Connecticut.

I didn't hear from Tim for several weeks after that—the first extended period during which Pam and I were unsure of where he was. There would be many more in the future, and I would have to learn to live with this uncertainty. But I was very anxious until he turned up again. When he did, I learned that he had been arrested again just a week after we had last seen him and had been sent back to Del Valle jail. Because we had no landline in Florida and Tim was not permitted to call cell phones from jail, he could not contact us. But he did call Linda, who contacted me near the end of July to tell me that Tim was going to be released soon.

Tim's SSI benefits had been suspended while he was in jail, and when I got a copy of the notice I let Linda know so that she could get a message to Tim. He would need to bring his release papers in person to the Social Security Administration office in downtown Austin to apply for reinstatement. He would also need to remember that when his benefits were reinstated they would be lower at first because of the two-month delay in the housing portion of the payment. In the meantime, I had paid all of Tim's outstanding bills from the apartment and had previously sent Linda $400 to help with his move to Connecticut. The funds in his account were low, but between these and the $400, I figured that we might be able to put together a security deposit if Tim could find another place to live. He would need one soon if he wanted health care. Because his Medicaid benefits in Texas were linked to his SSI, he would lose them if we transferred his legal address to Florida or Connecticut.

Tim was now charting his own path in Austin, but he still had to make a decision. Should he stay in Austin, where he had friends and something of a support system, but no job or housing, and constant reminders that he was just one step removed from jail? Or would it be better for him to return to Connecticut, where he had family, housing, and assistance but no friends or other support system?

Because he was not thinking about coming to Florida, I withdrew as Tim's representative payee in late August, transferring the responsibility to Linda. My control of his money had always been a source of friction between Tim and me, and I was happy that we would no longer have to fight about it. I encouraged Linda not to remain as Tim's payee for long. I thought that she would have a better relationship with him if she could get someone else, preferably a service provider, to do it. Why invite more tension into a relationship that had plenty of tension in it already?

Almost as soon as he was released, Tim was arrested again and found his way back to jail. He waited there until November for a hearing. From Connecticut, Linda tried to bring Tim's new public defender up to speed on Tim's history and situation. In addition, she asked that the lawyer help Tim get the copy of his release papers to the Social Security office when he was released so that his SSI benefits could be restored. She also asked the lawyer to help Tim obtain a new photo ID and a referral back to the social services delivery system. His lawyer had no interest in doing any of these things; his job was simply to represent Tim in court.

When Tim was released from Del Valle after a hearing on November 3, he returned once again to the streets without any supports. I talked with Linda about getting Tim back to Connecticut as soon as possible, but again events with Tim moved more quickly than we could. He located his girlfriend, with whom he reconciled, but he got only as far as the Drag. A couple of days later, he was cited for criminal trespass. For the third time in his life—just as he had at the wilderness program and when he was evicted from his apartment—he sat down on the spot, would not say a word, and refused to move. The police brought him directly to Austin State Hospital.

During his first days there, he carried a quotation with him that read "He who knows, speaks not; he who speaks, knows not," and showed it to any staff members who questioned him. They contacted Linda, but he would not talk to her either. He did, however, agree to respond to yes-no questions she asked by scratching the phone receiver once for "yes" and tapping it for "no."

Fortunately, Pam was in Austin visiting Verena, and they went to see Tim at the hospital. Tim had started talking again by the time they arrived, and the three of them had a pleasant visit, during which Tim was calm and contemplative. He told them that he was trying to practice Buddhism and that his refusal to speak was part of an effort he was making to surround himself with peace and tranquility. This is when, on his own, he began studying Buddhism and Eastern philosophy and religion in earnest.

This more tranquil Tim was deemed to be stable and discharged from the hospital a few days later. He went back to the Drag, staying with his girlfriend or other friends in the evenings. He also began to use some services voluntarily, but not from ATCMHMR. During the day he hung out at a youth drop-in center, where he got food, health care, and supervised companionship with his peers. But he soon had another run-in with the police, which resulted in his being transported by ambulance to a different hospital, where he was treated for cuts and bruises and released. Pam and I saw him that weekend when we returned to Austin for Verena's December graduation from college. We arranged to meet him for lunch at a local sub shop near the Drag. I was surprised by the extent of his facial injuries. He had a black eye, a bruise on his cheekbone, and a variety of small scrapes and scratches.

"What happened to you?" I asked. "The police did it," he answered. His story was that they had accosted him for loitering on the Drag, and when he tried to run away he was tackled from behind. The officers ground his face into the sidewalk. We had no way of verifying his story, but we did confirm that he had gone to the hospital and that he had not been arrested. This was the last straw for Tim. The year had been a far too difficult and challenging one for him. He now believed that the Austin police were out to get him, and he decided that it wasn't safe for him there anymore. We bought him a bus ticket before we left, and he was back in Connecticut in time for Christmas.

fifteen

TIM RETURNS
TO MIDDLETOWN

TIM'S RETURN TO MIDDLETOWN was not the homecoming he had hoped it would be. His old school acquaintances had moved on into their adult lives, his family was scattered, and the neighborhoods in which he had grown up were no longer his home. Nor was he free to do as he pleased. Service providers and the police were an ever-present part of his life.

To get him started, we found him a local service provider, River Valley Services. It offered short-term shelter and a drop-in center, along with case management and other services for people with mental illness. I appreciated this; I had provided its start-up funding twenty years earlier when I was a state legislator.

River Valley Services gave Tim a bed, assigned him a case coordinator, provided him a place to go during the day, and let him know that it would work with him to obtain either permanent supported housing or a bed in the regular twenty-four-hour Middletown shelter program located a short distance away. I also appreciated that; I had provided the start-up funding for the shelter when I was mayor of Middletown fifteen years earlier.

Tim tried with mixed success to carve out a life for himself in Middletown over the next two years. That first winter, he spent many of his nights at the shelter and most of his days either in downtown Middletown or on the Wesleyan campus. He especially enjoyed Wesleyan. Full of people his own age, it housed an expansive library, to which he could retreat and read philosophy and religion texts for hours—much as I had as a student there in the early 1970s—without being bothered.

Tim found the rules of the shelter too constraining, and so his case manager suggested a supervised apartment. Tim declined the offer because he was using drugs and drug use was not permitted in the supervised apartments. He did not want to risk another arrest and eviction, so instead he searched for a place on his own. One February day, he knocked at the door of a student house near the Wesleyan campus. When the students living there told him they did not have a room for him, they discovered that he was storing some of his possessions under the porch, including a propane stove. The students alerted Wesleyan public safety officers, who called the Middletown police. The police questioned Tim, but because he had done nothing wrong, they let him go.

One of the students said that she did not feel especially threatened by Tim. "Had I not met [him] I might have been more worried," she later told a newspaper reporter. "He was our age, and he seemed honest and scared. I trusted Public Safety when they said he wouldn't be back there. [He was] just trying to survive . . . not to say I appreciated that there was a stove, propane, and a box of matches under my porch. I was shaken up but wasn't really afraid of him."

Four years later, I asked her about the encounter after explaining a little of Tim's history. She recalled, "Timothy was strikingly honest and warm given the circumstances. Now having some context for what he was going through and what he may have been thinking, I wish I could have done more for him."

She was one of the few people at that time who said that she wished she could have done more for the six-and-a-half-foot tall, two hundred-plus-pound barefoot young man with the wild afro and torn, dirty clothes who needed all the help he could get.

After this incident, Tim's caseworker found him a room at a local motel while they searched for something more permanent. This seemed like a good idea at the time, but, as had been the case with so many previous interventions in Tim's life, it would turn out to do more harm than good. I visited him in mid-March. He was too thin, I thought, but was enjoying the privacy of the motel and looking forward to getting his own apartment. He reported that he had his stove with him and was acquiring a few more essentials. Linda added that she had taken him to the pharmacy, where he made some small purchases with the allowance she provided him.

On March 24, a few days after his twenty-first birthday, the police knocked on Tim's motel room door while investigating an incident elsewhere in the motel. When he invited them in, they noticed his stove and also found a butane cylinder, sodium hydroxide, a beaker, coffee filters, and plastic containers.

Believing that they had discovered a methamphetamine lab, the Middletown police arrested Tim for criminal attempt to operate a drug factory, criminal attempt to possess methamphetamine, and possession of drug paraphernalia. It was reported by the *Hartford Courant* as the first crystal meth lab bust of the year in Connecticut, and the first ever in Middletown. Reading the headlines from my home in Florida, I just shook my head. Whatever his intent, Tim was no closer to operating a meth lab in Middletown than he had been to growing mushrooms in our Austin garage. But with this arrest in the news supportive housing in Middletown was no longer an option.

Tim did, however, get housed for several weeks in a prison facility in Connecticut for inmates with mental health problems. Because he was lucid and feeling well while he was there, both prison and court officials seemed uncertain about the extent of his illness. Tim was assigned to a public defender in Middletown, another attorney who did not know him or his history. Linda attended his court appearance during the first week in May and called me afterward to ask me to write his public defender a letter describing Tim's history. I wrote the following, a brief history of Tim:

Timothy first showed signs of schizophrenia when he was ten years old. His first diagnosis of schizoaffective disorder occurred when he was hospitalized at the age of 14 and when he was hospitalized at Riverview for a period of six consecutive months when he was age 15–16. Later on, about the time he turned 17, he was diagnosed with schizophrenia at a mental health facility in Austin. As his psychiatrist explained at that time, while diagnoses of schizophrenia are most commonly made when people are in their twenties, schizophrenia itself is not uncommon in children. With his schizophrenia confirmed during three separate hospital admissions two years apart, I hope there is not confusion that he has it, and that it has a profound effect on his life.

Though he has struggled throughout the last ten years, and certain allowances may have been made by medical professionals, law enforcement, and the courts because of his mental illness, he was never "bailed out" either literally or figuratively, when he got in trouble in Austin, but always paid a price.

Timothy is at bottom a bright young man with a good soul. He needs, and has needed, treatment for many years now.

But Connecticut was no different for Tim than Austin had been. He soon experienced the same revolving door. He was released from prison after several weeks without an adequate aftercare plan, and he destabilized within days. He was brought to a local hospital showing full-blown symptoms of schizophrenia, including auditory hallucinations, high anxiety, and paranoia, and was discharged before he was stabilized. He was readmitted to the hospital a few days later, after police responded to a 911 call when he had a severe delusional episode at a local Hindu temple where he had gone to meditate.

It was summer when Tim was released from the hospital, and he spent the warm days in downtown Middletown. He resisted formal services from River Valley, which he believed had failed to deliver on its promise of housing, and he also steered clear of Wesleyan. He passed his time reading in the Middletown Public Library during the day, usually taking his meals at a local soup kitchen. He occasionally found ways to earn a little money. For example, at the end of the summer he was paid to unpack textbooks and put them on shelves at the Wesleyan bookstore. He excitedly reported to me that he had done well at this and hoped he would be hired again the next time they needed help.

A few weeks later, as the weather cooled, Tim moved in with some young people in a downtown Middletown apartment. When I asked him how he had met them, he said "dumpster diving." One of them became Tim's representative payee. Tim stayed with them for a few months. I visited him early that winter. He was in good health and spirits, thin but in good shape. When I took him out to lunch, he avoided one of his old favorite herbs, garlic, telling me it was "dirty," and he reported that he was a vegetarian again after eating meat for several years. His eyes were bright, and his mind was quick. He was staying away from drugs—"they're unnatural and bad for you," he reported—and was still meditating and reading up on Eastern religions when he could.

Pam and I shipped him books, clothes, and a bag for his meditation mat that Christmas because we could not come together to see him. Pam had wanted to come to Connecticut with me but was being treated for melanoma and not up to the trip. She was in treatment for a full year, which curtailed my travel, too. It was a tough year for both of us and absolutely draining for Pam.

We did not know what to say when Tim called to tell us that he was going back to Austin for a brief visit after Christmas. We tried to talk him out of it, but I couldn't fly to Middletown to try to stop him. When he arrived in Austin during the second week in January, it was cold. His old friends were gone, and he had no place to stay. He decided to return to Middletown right away, and his caseworker at River Valley

Services arranged to help pay for his return bus trip. But he destabilized before the arrangements were complete. He acquired what he believed to be a fifteenth-century religious artifact—a sheathed knife that he imagined he could use to forage for food. The police found him with it on the University of Texas campus and arrested him on a weapons charge (illegal carrying) and for trespassing.

Tim went back to Del Valle jail, where he was evaluated and found to be incompetent to stand trial. As Tim waited for a bed to open up at Austin State Hospital, his public defender told Linda that when Tim was stable enough to stand trial he might not be a candidate for time-served release because of the seriousness of the weapons charge.

It took two weeks for a bed to open up at the hospital. His lawyer was working on a "religious artifact" defense for Tim. As I understood it, his theory was that if everyone agreed that the knife could be an artifact, then the weapons charge might be dropped. I thought this was a nonstarter and that it was more likely that Tim would be released if he agreed to treatment for his mental illness. I suggested that the public defender ask the prosecutor for time served and arrange for Tim to be released to ATCMHMR, so that it could coordinate with River Valley Services to get Tim back to Connecticut for further treatment. Tim's lawyer did not want to do this. He suggested as an alternative that Tim plead no contest, in which case he might still be sentenced to time served and receive a prepaid bus ticket back to Connecticut. But we needed the cooperation of ATCMHMR and River Valley Services, and the lawyer did not want to play a role in connecting Tim to either one. In other words, it turned out that the lawyer had not arranged for them to be notified when he secured Tim's release so that they could coordinate their efforts to keep Tim off the streets.

After a month in the hospital, Tim was transferred back to Del Valle jail. By then, ATCMHMR and River Valley Services had both indicated to Linda and me that they were ready to coordinate their efforts to get Tim back to Connecticut as soon as he was released. However, when Tim was released from jail after serving his time, neither ATCMHMR nor River Valley Serivces knew about it.

Our plan had disintegrated around us. Linda sent me an e-mail a couple of days later. "Tim's already psychotic," she wrote. "Hasn't slept for 2 days and is repeating 'Ya hear what I'm sayin'?' staccato-like so often he sounds like a scratched CD. . . . I'm so tired of this, Paul. I am SO sick of people not listening. Someone needs to send a message and maybe that's Tim's purpose on this earth."

Tim called me a week later. He reported that he was staying with a friend at the Sandstone Apartments in Austin, about a fifteen-minute walk from the University of Texas football stadium, and was going regularly to the Phase program, which offered social and health services to youth along the Drag. He was not taking his medication. He had applied for a job at a sandwich shop. He had also gotten a copy of his release papers from the court so that he could go back to the Social Security Administration office and have his SSI reinstated, and he still had his Lone Star food stamp card. He said that he intended to stay in Austin for a while longer.

But he was back in jail within a month, and that finally convinced him that he was ready to return to Middletown. Fortunately, on the July day he was released, Pam, Lizzie, Ben, and I were in town for Verena's wedding—the first trip Pam had felt up to taking in months. In spite of this, and despite all of the other family obligations attached to this celebration, we took time to arrange for his trip back to Connecticut before we left for Florida.

When Tim returned to Middletown in August, what was supposed to have been a brief vacation in Austin had turned into an eight-month odyssey through Austin State Hospital and Del Valle jail. He used his time in those institutions to deepen his focus on spirituality and meditation. He said that this gave him a sense of peace and comfort, and he was eager to share his experiences with me. He wrote to me in mid-August:

Hey Dad,
   Loving Jesus, I see, how's the bible reading go?
   Oh, yeah, almost forgot, very important for you, please read the

autobiography of a yogi. I'll send you the link as I'm too busy to send you the book. With kind regards, Tim.

And after I replied, he wrote again: "I really want you to check out Kriya. I know you might not have the time, and I can see it's not something you might know about. Who knows? Maybe you would like it. I am very certain that it would help you and Pam become closer to God. With Kind Regards and Divine Love, Tim."

He added a few days later: "Dear Dad, oh I haven't been up to too much. I went to the food pantry the other day, it was very nice and I do go to the library every day it's possible." He also told me that he wanted to audit a course a Wesleyan.

When I look back at that brief exchange, I realize how far off the mark we are when we assume that people with mental illness don't want to make their lives better just because they are noncompliant with treatment. The two are unrelated. Tim may have lived in the moment, but he continually looked to the future and sought out ways in which he could improve himself. He did not lack willpower. He lacked the tools and resources to advance his will.

I visited with him again at Christmas. I met him in downtown Middletown, gave him some gifts, and took him to lunch. It was a nice visit. We spent most of our time talking about religion, and Tim told me that he was planning a trip to Arkansas in January 2008 to attend a religious convention.

He enjoyed the trip to Arkansas but called Pam while he was on the road, stranded and without money. He talked to her because he thought I would be too disappointed in him to help him out. We wired money to him so that he could buy a ticket back to Middletown. He didn't want any extra; he had earned thirty dollars "holding a sign" for someone during the day and took pride in the fact that he had earned his own spending money. A few weeks later, I received an e-mail from Tim: "How are you? I'm fine, I meant to call you. Hey, I think I'm going to be in your neighborhood soon, maybe we could hook up and do something? I've been okay just getting back to normal; nothing really new to report except its probable I'm going to India soon for 5 to 8 months, then Tokyo and Ireland all this year. Cool, right? Love, Tim."

Tim's grasp exceeded his reach, but I applauded his reach anyway. He did not make it to Florida, India, Tokyo, or Ireland that spring. He made it as far as New York, where he completed another religious workshop. "Hi dad," he wrote, "I just got done completing this workshop. I got a certificate and everything. It looks real nice. I've been feeling a lot better lately. I'm still really impressed with the work you and Pam have done over the years and continue to do. What could be more important?? Not really trying to think about what's not new, and beyond this seems like a dream. Wishing you well. In love, Tim."

Anything beyond this seemed like a dream for me, too. But at last, as the weather warmed in Middletown, Tim seemed to be finding himself and learning who he was. And he seemed happy. He soon reported that he had found a job at the youth hostel in New York where he had stayed when he went to his workshop. But he wasn't ready for nonsupported employment yet. He was let go after only a few days and returned to Middletown before setting his sights a little farther. He wrote: "I hope to see you soon any way on my way to . . . San Francisco CA. Maybe soon. I'm going to stay away from TX for a Long Time. How's Pam doing? Well, I hope. I'm praying for her. Love to see you soon. Love, Tim."

Shortly thereafter, his brief, peaceful respite ended. He had some run-ins with Wesleyan Public Safety and argued with Linda over money. So he decided to move on.

On May 25, 2008, I saw Tim on my fifty-fifth birthday, when Pam and I were in Middletown for a visit to celebrate Larissa's graduation from Southern Connecticut State University. We arrived a day after her graduation because Ben graduated from Lake Worth High School in Florida on the same day.

It was commencement weekend at Wesleyan, and we decided to walk over to the campus to sit on Foss Hill and listen to the commencement speaker, Senator Barack Obama. He gave the perfect speech for a

Wesleyan crowd—a call to political and social action for a new generation that echoed Ted Kennedy's call at the 1980 Democratic National Convention and honored Kennedy's legacy to the nation.

Pam and I made arrangements to meet Tim a couple of blocks from the campus after the speech ended. But the ceremony ran long, and we were more than forty-five minutes late as we hustled to the church we had chosen as our meeting place.

There was no sign of Tim, and I was afraid he had not waited for us. But as we hurried around the corner, we saw a tall, thin, somewhat disheveled African American man patiently walking barefoot down the sidewalk several hundred feet ahead of us. We called to him, and Tim turned around and smiled. "I was thinking you'd be here," he said, "but you were pretty late." When I told him we were listening to Obama's speech, he just laughed. "I don't think much about politics anymore."

We walked a block to a downtown bagel shop. A few people stared as we stood in line to order. We enjoyed our food, laughing and joking about *Imus in the Morning* and a host of other memories we shared. He turned to Pam, told her she looked good, and recounted in detail some of his favorite memories of her. As our visit ended, Pam and I walked back up the hill to the campus, the start of our brief journey back to my childhood home, where we were staying. Tim set off in a different direction, taking the next steps on his own path.

EPILOGUE

TWO WEEKS AFTER Pam and I visited with Tim in Middletown, he was featured in the local newspaper as a "downtown neighbor," one of the colorful local characters whom people recognized along Main Street. My sister sent me a copy of the newspaper. It published Tim's picture and job status—"always looking"—as he gazed skyward. I tried to reach Tim to congratulate him, but I couldn't locate him. Neither could anyone else.

I finally received an e-mail from him in late June. He was not in Middletown, but he wouldn't say much more. "Oh noble one," he wrote grandly, "see it is that I had to go away and leave the state for good. This, I hope, will be the best thing for a good life. So thus it is, love, yogi."

I understood his need to move on, but I needed to be sure he was okay. I wrote back and told him I was worried about him. His response was a bit more direct and down to earth. "So, okay, DON'T worry about me, Dad. Anyway, the best thing you could do is figure a way to wire me the monies. God willing, my hope is I'm never going back to Connecticut, not in this lifetime. Thanks, with all the best, kid."

I still wanted to know where he was. "Tim," I replied, trying to keep the conversation going, "I'll try not to worry, and I'm glad you're okay for now. To have money sent to you, we'll need to know where you are. I'll be happy to contact River Valley Services for you so they can send it, if you can give me a place."

He finally sent me an address. He was in San Francisco, the city of his teenage dreams. He told me where he could be reached, and I sent e-mails to him periodically, trying to stay in touch. In August he was homeless and finally wrote back to me.

"Dear dad," he wrote, "Hi, what's best in your world? Been okay, still working on check stuff. Slept on the beach coast for the last week or so. I've been thinking about you, all good thoughts and Pam, too. I'm praying for mom, Linda, please pray for her, too. Peace. Love. Tim."

I wrote to Tim at least once a month for the next year, but he never replied. As the months went by, I passed through worry that he might not be well to anxiety that he might not be alive and began listening carefully for any news reports of untimely deaths in San Francisco. Finally, Linda called me on Easter Sunday. She had just spoken with Tim, and he had given her a phone number where he could be reached. I called him, and we had our first conversation in almost a year.

He told me that he was fine and liked his life in the city. He said that he found San Francisco to be warm and beautiful and that he occasionally went to a drop-in center for homeless youth when he wanted to socialize. He had been in some trouble with the law, but nothing serious. He told me he was managing his disease through meditation, not medication. Most important, he felt as if he were finally in control of his life.

This was not what I wanted for him. But I understood that after surviving years of serious mental illness and the unrealistic expectations of others, including me, he had earned the right to lead his life as he wished.

Tim's problems did not end in San Francisco at the age of twenty-four. He did not find stable housing, nor did he manage to stay out of jail. He did not find a service provider he trusted, nor did he take his prescribed medications or stay away from illegal drugs. He did not avoid hospitalization or escape the revolving door.

And in the tally of his life's achievements, he would not be considered a success. He did not become a chef or a football player. He could not hold a job or keep an apartment. He did not graduate from high school. He could not do math above a fifth-grade level or spell above a third-grade level. He was never even able to organize his notebook. He made no lasting friendships and alienated most of his family. He could not follow rules and was not a "productive member of society."

But in San Francisco he did feel safe and alive. And independent. And as a result, he also found a quiet, unhurried place in his otherwise noisy brain in which he could reflect, meditate, and be at home with his own thoughts. Before we ended the phone call that Easter Sunday, I asked if he needed anything at all. He said no, and I believed him.

I did not hear from him again until June, when he wrote me an e-mail to wish me a belated happy birthday. He didn't respond to my e-mails again for several months after that. I waited anxiously until I finally heard from him in September. He had just one thing to say: "This is the most beautiful place. With great kindness, Yogi Gionfriddo."

Tim was hospitalized briefly toward the end of the year. Then I heard from him out of the blue in January 2010. He told me he needed a little money for food. I asked him how he had gotten my phone number. He said, "Dad, you put it in every e-mail you send me"—all of the e-mails I thought he was ignoring.

I heard from him again on March 18, his twenty-fifth birthday. He borrowed a cell phone from a stranger at a Laundromat to make the call. There was life in his voice as he asked how I was doing. I wished him a happy birthday and asked if I could send him some money as a gift. He was a little surprised and said, "Of course! Can you send me eighty dollars?"

I said eighty dollars would be fine, and Pam got on the phone and reminisced with him about their shared memories—Tim remembered only the good ones—while I made the arrangements with Western Union. "How are you going to spend the money?" I asked.

"I think I'll have some sushi," he answered.

It was another year to the day before I had contact with Tim again. By then, I had learned to manage my worries about him, and he had a new service provider working with him. I called Tim's caseworker and left a voice mail for her.

She called me back almost immediately, explaining that for reasons of privacy, she could not confirm whether or not she was working with Tim. He would have to sign a release first. Fortunately, he did, so she could now report that he was managing reasonably well, with some good days and some bad. On his good days, he was as delightful as any client she had—personable, well informed, intuitive, and mature. On his bad days, he was contrary, agitated, and unclear in his thinking and appeared to be self-medicating.

He had been revolving in and out of treatment and jail during the past year and had also spent time on the streets. His clothing wasn't always appropriate, she said, and he needed shoes, but those were small things. His SSI had been restored, and he had a representative payee. He was living in a supported apartment, but she told me that he was about to lose it because he could not follow the rules.

He wanted to talk with me, and I said that would be terrific. But he never called. So I sent him an e-mail on his birthday, wishing him well and giving him news about Pam and me. I told him that I wanted to hear from him and said that I would send him a present if he got back in touch with me.

That was all it took. He called that night, using a friend's cell phone. But this time it wasn't an easy conversation. Tim seemed to struggle with his thoughts, and although we had done this many times before, he asked me to repeat the details of how he could receive cash through Western Union. Finally, he put his friend on the phone to get all of the information straight.

When Tim returned to the call, I asked how he was doing. He said he was doing well but then launched into a fantasy story of seeing and talking to my brother Michael in San Francisco a few months earlier.

My brother had never been to San Francisco, but Tim was insistent. Through the haze of this confusing conversation, I asked him again how he was.

Then he admitted how he really felt. "I feel like I can't get out of this level, but I need to get out of this level, Dad."

I wasn't sure what he meant.

He explained: "You know how in *Final Fantasy II* there are a lot of levels? There was a level I could always get to. It was like in a house, but to get out of that level you had to go through a window or something, and I could never figure out how to get out of that level. That's how I feel now. I need to get out. I just don't know how to get out of this level."

Neither did I. I went to visit him a few months later, in August 2011. I caught him during one of those rare moments when he was not in jail, not in a hospital, and not living on the streets.

I drove to his caseworker's office in the Mission District. As I walked the couple of blocks up the street, I passed scores of people who appeared homeless. And too many of them looked like Tim at various stages on life's way.

Tim gave me his familiar grin when he saw me in the caseworker's office. He was gaunt and dirty and wearing old clothes that barely fit. But his eyes still had their sparkle. He wanted to go for a ride. "I haven't been in a car for years, Dad," he explained. But first he invited me back to his rooming house to show me where he lived.

The rooming house was half a block from the office. When we arrived, Tim rang the outside bell. We were buzzed into a small entryway leading to a narrow flight of stairs up to a second-floor office. I signed in as Tim's guest and gave up my ID to the young man at the desk. Tim then led me up another flight of stairs, which smelled of disinfectant. We passed a small sitting room and walked down two dark hallways toward the back of the building. Near the end of the second hallway, just before we reached another staircase, Tim pointed out the communal bathroom to our left. A rat raced out from under the door of the last room on the right. That was Tim's room. Tim turned to me and said matter-of-factly, "There are rats here."

When he opened his unlocked door, we were greeted by a cloud of flies. I stared at a bare, stained mattress on the floor, lying on a carpet of ramen noodle wrappers. A dirty sink with only a cold water tap sat on top of a broken cupboard next to the mattress. The room was filthy and had no furniture. A plastic bag with some snacks in it hung from a hook on the door. "I keep them up there so the rats don't eat them," Tim said. There were a few pieces of broken wood on the floor, probably remnants of the bed frame that had once been there. Tim used them as sketch pads. The room smelled of sweat, stale smoke, and half-eaten salty junk food.

Tim took contented pride in these surroundings because they were his. "What do you think?" he asked. I breathed slowly through my mouth and praised his drawings. "Let's get lunch," he said. If this was Tim's "level," I could see why he couldn't find a way out. There was a small window in the back stairway through which we could see a beautiful blue sky and some elegant rooftops just a block or two away. But that sky and those rooftops were just too far away for Tim.

Tim was arrested again shortly after my visit. He spent six months in jail. When he was released in May 2012, he entered a residential treatment program. He was supposed to stay there for sixty days. His new caseworker was cautiously optimistic that this program might be the right fit for him. I wanted to wish Tim well and hear his voice again, so I called two days later to introduce myself to the program manager. Once again, I was too late. The person who answered the phone told me cryptically that I should call Tim's caseworker immediately.

The caseworker explained that Tim had disappeared the previous day. He had left the program to go to a court hearing. Courthouse cameras verified that Tim found his way there, but when his case was called he was missing. He was back on the streets, where he remained until he was jailed again two months later. Finally, in August 2012, he agreed to go into treatment to get out of jail.

It seems to me that Tim is not the only one stuck at this level. On any given day, there are thousands of people just like Tim, also stuck on the streets, in rooming houses, in hospitals, and in jails. And all of us who have made mental health policy are stuck at this level, too, because we all helped build this chain of neglect that we refer to as our consumer-driven "system of care." Consumer-driven care is good, but ours is not really consumer-driven. This system has no drive. I am sure that some policy leaders today think they are on the right course, but recent evidence suggests that they have only succeeded in repeating the same mistakes we made more than thirty years ago. State policy leaders cut $4.6 billion from mental health services between 2009 and 2012 (Miller 2012). My generation could argue that we did not know any better. But what possible excuse for this neglect could lawmakers have today?

We could break this chain of neglect.

But first, we have to change the way we think about mental illness. It is not simply a failure of effort or will or a failure to follow the rules. It is a set of chronic diseases of the brain. And as a matter of policy, we must think about mental illness the way we think about other chronic diseases, like cancer, heart disease, hypertension, and diabetes. To me, our attitude toward mental illness has too long been akin to telling someone with congestive heart failure that willpower is all he needs to complete a marathon. And sending Tim to drug rehabilitation when what he needed was inpatient hospitalization for his mental illness was like offering a smoker with lung cancer a nicotine patch instead of surgery.

Next, we must recognize that, as is the case with any chronic disease, there are a number of paths we can follow in the progression mental illness. Mental illness can be prevented in some people if we address their risk factors early enough. For others, effective treatment can lead to full recovery. For still others, effective treatment will not lead to a full recovery but will lengthen and increase the quality of their lives. And, despite our best efforts, in some cases people will still head to a too-early death. We can offer support along all of these paths.

Finally, we must recognize that a single policy approach—removal from the mainstream, stigmatization, isolation, or whatever you wish to call it—repeated over and over again will not work for any of these people.

If there is one thing to be learned from Tim's story, it is that playing the blame game misses the point. While it is possible to point a finger at any given caregiver and argue that he or she was the weak link in the chain, is it really possible to argue that every school, every hospital, every provider, every advocate, and every family member failed Tim in spite of a system that was fundamentally sound? The system needs changing, and the way we can do this is to change our public policies.

We could break the chain of neglect in childhood through universal screening for mental health and early intervention. We screen for vision, hearing, communicable diseases, and genetic conditions. The problem with screening for mental illness is that some people fear that this would lead to stigma, discrimination, and the over-prescription of drugs. Some might think that Tim's problem was that he was prescribed drugs and wouldn't take them. But that's naive. Perhaps the reason that he didn't take them was because he learned that many of them didn't work. And while in hindsight one could argue that if he had received the right antipsychotic medication as soon as his symptoms emerged, the fact remains that there is still a ten-year gap between the emergence of symptoms and getting the right diagnosis.

We gave Tim more drugs than I can count when a simple screening could have helped his pediatrician rule out the wrong ones from the start and get him on the road to a correct diagnosis sooner. For example, when Tim was five, if he had been screened for mental health using evidence-based tools that are available today (these tools have names like PHQ-9, PHQ-15, and SBIRT; each screens for something different; some are for use with adults; others for children), anxiety, depression and perhaps even ADHD are conditions that would probably have been ruled out. In that case, we would never have wasted time starting down the Ritalin path later on. But some other possibilities, like PTSD and even childhood schizophrenia, would still have been in the mix, and Tim could have been referred to a child psychiatrist for follow-up years earlier than he was. In Tim's case, this could have changed the course of his life as far back as kindergarten.

Drugs are an important component of many treatment plans, but they should never be prescribed in the absence of a clear diagnosis and never used as a substitute for an integrated and well-funded system of care. In December 2011, the U.S. Government Accountability

Office noted that in five states, children in the foster-care system who had Medicaid were being prescribed psychotropic drugs more frequently than children in the general population who also had Medicaid. Worse, some children under the age of one were receiving these drugs. (Kutz 2011) That at least got the attention of some policy makers. But will it lead to widespread improvements in our state foster care systems, more screening of children and youth, or better integration of care? Not if we do not call for a change in our public policies and better systems of care.

Even if we fail to change the policies that affect our children when they are young, we still have time to intervene. At some point in the life of nearly every child with a serious mental illness, the situation deteriorates to the point where someone feels the need to remove the child from the classroom. For Tim, that time came in the sixth grade. This is an opportunity to change the IEP that everyone knows is not working and add the services that might. I still think that we can offer these services in regular schools, but I am open to alternatives. After all, we tried pretty much every type of school with Tim. But none distinguished itself from the others—not because they were inept or uncaring but because they all followed pretty much the same educational protocols. So I don't believe we can throw out the right to education in the least restrictive environment just because we don't always have a clear picture of how to modify the educational environment effectively. We just need to try a little harder and work a little more creatively and collaboratively.

No matter where we offer educational or community services, we may not always get them right. But integrating the recommendations and treatment of the child's therapists into the IEP would at least give us a fighting chance. We did not do this for Tim. Instead, we wasted months on planning and, when that failed, in a due process hearing. And as we wasted those months, Tim was not being educated. The immediate result was that he failed to progress to the next grade level. The midterm result was that he never mastered any more educational content. And the long-term result played itself out on the streets of Austin, Middletown, and San Francisco.

In spite of how we may write IEP goals and objectives, we fail our own test of accountability when we do not put all of the resources a child needs to succeed into his IEP. Because the reality is that when we fail to integrate a child's therapy and treatment into his IEP, we fail to educate the child appropriately. And this failure haunts the child for the rest of his or her life. And it haunts the rest of us, too, in wasted dollars and lost lives.

But our opportunities to break the chain of neglect do not end in school. Young adults with mental illness may not always appear grateful for our help, but we have more time to act as they age. And there are many obvious things we can do. We must fund our community mental health services adequately, just as we promised we would when we emptied our institutions. We must stop relying on the police to be our emergency mental health service providers and on our jails to be our twenty-first-century mental health facilities. We should let mental health professionals, not sheriffs, decide who is and who is not a candidate for hospitalization and treatment. We must let hospitals and clinicians, not insurers, decide when people are ready to be discharged from care. We must be willing to offer supported employment opportunities for people with mental illness who, like Tim, want to work. We must support them in their housing, even if it sometimes means curtailing their freedom just a little by providing them with housing support specialists who can help protect them from others who prey on them, and we can give them the freedom to break a few rules, such as forgetting to secure the premises, without punishment.

Perhaps most important, we should reduce the isolation of people with mental illness by giving them access to peers and role models whom they can trust. Professionals and caseworkers who worked with Tim were so overworked that they seldom had the time to get to know him. There is an easy alternative. We can provide more peer services to people with mental illness. These involve expanding programs that are led by people in recovery from mental illness to provide services to other people with mental illness. They include formal peer drop-in and support centers and less formal ones such as navigation support, education, and even those offered by Tim's Austin friend who sought housing together with him. Mental Health America calls peer support "a unique and essential element of recovery-oriented mental health systems," a sentiment that is echoed by the National Alliance on Mental Illness, SAMHSA, and many other private and public providers and advocates. We know that these services—which cost a fraction of the price of hospitalization—can be effective. In 2013, a group of researchers reviewed all the published literature pertaining to peer services and concluded that these can be as effective as professional services in helping people with mental illness to recover (Pitt et al. 2013).

Our current environment for people with mental illness did not happen by itself. We created it in 1981 when we repealed the Community Mental Health Act of 1963 and replaced it with an underfunded block grant to the states. We have fostered this environment for more than forty years and continue to do so whenever we cut back our mental health services without offering any alternatives. We have created our own revolving door by excusing ourselves today in much the same way we excused ourselves back then—by arguing that taxpayers are so overburdened that they can't spare a few more dollars for proper mental health services. What do we think the result of this neglect will be?

It does not have to be like this. Perhaps the Mental Health Parity and Addiction Equity Act of 2008 will eventually give us what we lost with the repeal of the Community Mental Health Act. Maybe it will give us true equity in care. Maybe it will mean that mental health providers in the future will be paid more for their skills, and maybe it will mean that people with mental illness will receive as much treatment as they need. But can we really count on this happening all by itself—without our attention and advocacy—when both providers and people with mental illness were still waiting after five years for the law to be implemented fully?

In the future, we need to focus on prevention, treatment, recovery, and—for those for whom effective treatment and recovery are not yet possible—meaningful and compassionate long-term care. Tim may be among this last group, though I hope he is not. My one reason for optimism is that, after more than twenty years, we still cannot say that no treatment would have been effective for Tim. We can only say that the treatments we did offer were ineffective.

There are elements of a better approach emerging at the national level on which we can build our policy advocacy.

For example, Mental Health America has developed and promoted a public health model for mitigating risk factors (such as violence and abuse) that can contribute to certain mental illnesses. Twenty to thirty years ago, this public health focus was unheard of in the mental health advocacy community. It was left to the public health advocacy community to explore and measure the impact of these root causes of mental illness.

In addition, the Affordable Care Act and the Mental Health Parity Act have the potential to assure that private insurers and government funders pay fairly for mental health services. But perhaps even more important, they could facilitate the integration of health and mental health care services in a single treatment system—because diseases of the brain are also diseases of the body. But we still have a long way to go to make parity a reality. And it will not happen unless we demand it.

There is also SAMHSA, the lead federal agency promoting the mental health of the nation, which has built much of its recent agenda around recovery—because it knows that many people with mental illness can and will recover if they are given the proper supports. But many laypeople never associate the word "recovery" with mental illness. So there will be a steep public education hill to climb before most of the population embraces recovery from mental illness as a possibility. And there will probably be another steep hill to climb before people understand the true value of recovery—when the life expectancy of people with serious mental illness begins to rise significantly.

But our dollars are always limited, and where should these limited dollars be spent? Should we favor prevention or put more money into treatment? Should we focus on recovery or on long-term care for those for whom recovery may not now be possible? Should we put more resources into our communities, so people can stay at home and in the neighborhoods in which they grew up, or into hospital beds? Should we be focusing on moving people out of hospitals as quickly as possible—especially when they do not want to be there in the first place—or adding new beds for those who need long-term treatment and support?

My answer is that these are not either-or questions. What we really need is a both-and approach. We need to do them all. How about biting the bullet and paying for a system of care that will actually work?

The money is there. Fifty years ago, it was spent on hiding people with mental illness behind the bolted doors of our state psychiatric hospitals. Today, it is spent on hiding people with mental illness behind the bolted doors of our county jails and state prisons. It does not need to be this way. It is time to unbolt the doors. And maybe to empty our pockets a little more, too.

Tim's mental illness has affected everyone close to him in ways I could not have imagined when I was first introduced to mental health policy making in 1979.

I have continued to work in related fields for thirty years, most recently serving as a board member of the Jerome Golden Center for Behavioral Health in West Palm Beach, Florida. The Golden Center provides services to hundreds of people like Tim. For three straight years between 2010 and 2013, the state of Florida reduced its funding. I was also appointed to the twelve member National Advisory Council to SAMHSA's Center for Mental Health Services in 2013. I am committed to SAMHSA's vision, in part because of Tim and in part because it's personal. I, too, was diagnosed with a mental illness in late 2009—generalized anxiety disorder—thereby becoming part of the 50 percent of all Americans who receive a diagnosis of mental illness at some point during their lifetime. And in 2014, I was named president and CEO of Mental Health America, the oldest U.S. mental-health-advocacy organization. Its mission is to promote prevention for all, early identification and intervention for those at risk, integrated health and behavioral-health treatment for those who need it, and recovery as a goal.

In 2009, Pam became the CEO of the Mental Health Association of Palm Beach County. Under her direction, MHAPBC became a national leader in promoting the integration of health and mental health services, winning the 2013 Innovation in Programming Award from Mental Health America. MHAPBC also operates a peer support center, Peer Place, used by hundreds of people just like Tim. In 2010, the Palm Beach Board of County Commissioners voted to discontinue funding for Peer Place. The county sheriff, who knows what the alternative is, stepped in to restore part of the money.

Linda has continued in her career as a consultant and advocate for people with disabilities. Verena began her career in Austin as a Child Protective Services caseworker and supervisor, and carried that career with her to Florida in 2013. Larissa began her career in Middletown as an outreach and advocacy director for a nonprofit organization serving people with multiple disabilities. Lizzie's first full-time job after graduating from college in 2013 was as a direct service worker with the Mental Health Association of Connecticut. And in 2012, Tim's best friend, Ben, started a family of his own, becoming the father of a beautiful baby girl.

As for Tim, after agreeing in August 2012 to go into treatment, he sat in jail for four months waiting for a bed to become available. When none did, he got tired of waiting and in early 2013 went back to the streets. I traveled to San Francisco in April to search for him but could not find him in any of the places he was known to frequent—the Panhandle of the Golden Gate Park, Buena Vista Park, Haight Street, or several downtown BART stations. He was keeping a low profile.

Can you really blame him? I can't.

But here's what haunts me. We are not as naive today as we were more than thirty years ago. If nothing changes, we all now know how this will end.

ACKNOWLEDGMENTS

I WANT TO OFFER MY GRATITUDE to many who helped bring this story to life.

Tim and Pam, my heroes.

Larissa, Lizzie, and Ben, whose central roles in my life are far too diminished in this story, but who give me joy every step of the way.

Verena, who joined our family late but became an essential part of it from the start.

My brother Michael, who inspired me to write.

My other siblings, Lisa and Victor, who endured all my political endeavors.

Linda and Mark, who experienced everything Pam and I did.

My friend and colleague Joe Coatsworth, who helped make this all possible.

My friend and colleague John Atkin, whose encouragement extended across continents.

Lee-Lee Prina, Sue Ducat, Ellen Ficklen, and everyone at *Health Affairs* for inviting me to write the "Narrative Matters" essay that brought Tim's story to the attention of so many.

Carol Gentry and Christine Stuart, two fine editors who give me regular feedback on my policy writing.

Carolyn Lumsden, editor of the opinion page at the *Hartford Courant*, whose invitation to write a piece in the aftermath of the Sandy Hook horror helped me crystallize my thinking about the chain of neglect.

Jennifer Perillo, Stephen Wesley, and Michael Haskell, whose editorial support and encouragement at Columbia University Press helped shape this story.

David Shaw and John Shaw, two lawyers who advised me well.

David Russell, who gave me hope.

Dave Audette, Rosemary Shea, Joanne Magner, John Niemczyk, and Joan Cardella, who demonstrated that the best educators are those not bound too tightly by the rules.

And the workers of the Connection, the Rushford Center, River Valley Services, Austin Travis County Integral Care, and Citywide Case Management, who too often bore the brunt of my frustrations while working under impossible constraints.

REFERENCES

Abrams, Daniel J., Donald C. Rojas, and David B. Arciniegas. 2008. "Is Schizoaffective Disorder a Distinct Categorical Diagnosis? A Critical Review of the Literature." *Neuropsychiatric Disease and Treatment* 4 (December): 1089–1109. http://www.ncbi.nlm.nih.gov/pmc/articles/PMC2646642/.

CBS New York. 2012. "Parents Furious Over Apparent Use of 'Scream Rooms' Inside Middletown, Conn. Elementary School." January 11. http://newyork.cbslocal.com/2012/01/11/parents-furious-over-apparent-use-of-scream-rooms-inside-middletown-conn-elementary-school/.

Collins, Chris, et al. 2010. *Evolving Models of Behavioral Health Integration in Primary Care.* New York: Milbank Memorial Fund. http://www.milbank.org/uploads/documents/10430EvolvingCare/EvolvingCare.pdf.

Colton, Craig, and Ronald W. Manderscheid. 2006. "Congruencies in Increased Mortality Rates, Years of Potential Life Lost, and Causes of Death Among Public Mental Health Clients in Eight States." *Preventing Chronic Disease* 3 (April). www.cdc.gov/pcd/issues/2006/apr/05_0180.htm.

Elbogen, Eric B., and Sally C. Johnson. 2009. "The Intricate Link Between Violence and Mental Disorder." *Archives of General Psychiatry* 66 (February): 152–61. http://archpsyc.jamanetwork.com/article.aspx?articleid=210191. doi: 10.1001/archgenpsychiatry.2008.537

Felitti, Vincent J., and Robert F. Anda. 2010. "The Relationship of Adverse Childhood Experiences to Adult Medical Disease, Psychiatric Disorders, and Sexual Behavior: Implications for Healthcare." In *The Impact of Early Life Trauma on Health and Disease: The Hidden Epidemic*, ed. Ruth A. Lanius, Eric Vermetten, and Clare Pain, 77–87. Cambridge: Cambridge University Press.

Gionfriddo, Paul. 2012. "How I Helped Create a Flawed Mental Health System That's Failed Millions—and My Son." *Health Affairs* 31 (September): 2138–42. http://content.healthaffairs.org/content/31/9/2138.full. doi:10.1377/hlthaff .2012.0248.

Harris, Katherine M., and Mark J. Edlund. 2005. "Self-Medication of Mental Health Problems: New Evidence from a National Survey." *Health Services Research* 40 (February): 117–34. http://www.ncbi.nlm.nih.gov/pmc/articles /PMC1361129/. doi:10.1111/j.1475-6773.2005.00345.x.

Havlicek, Judy R., Antonio R. Garcia, and Douglas C. Smith. 2013. "Mental Health and Substance Use Disorders Among Foster Youth Transitioning to Adulthood: Past Research and Future Directions." *Children and Youth Services Review* 35 (January): 194–203. http://www.sciencedirect.com/science /article/pii/S0190740912003647.

Hawkins, J. David et al. 2008. "Effects of Social Development Intervention in Childhood Fifteen Years Later. *Archives of Pediatric and Adolescent Medicine* 162 (December): 1133–41. http://www.ncbi.nlm.nih.gov/pmc/articles /PMC2593733/. doi:10.1001/archpedi.162.12.1133.

Insel, Thomas. 2011. "Understanding Severe Mental Illness." *Director's Blog*, National Institute of Mental Health. January 11. http://www.nimh.nih.gov /about/director/2011/understanding-severe-mental-illness.shtml.

Kessler, R. C., et al. 2005. "Lifetime Prevalence and Age-of-Onset Distributions of DSM-IV Disorders in the National Comorbidity Survey Replication." *Archives of General Psychiatry* 62 (June): 593–602. http://www.ph.ucla.edu /epi/faculty/detels/PH150/Kessler_DSMIV_AGP2009.pdf.

Kutz, Gregory D. 2011. "Foster Children: HHS Guidance Could Help States Improve Oversight of Psychotropic Prescriptions." GAO 12-270-T, December 1. http://www.gao.gov/assets/590/586570.pdf.

Lee, Deborah, and Gwen Foster. 2008. "Mental Health and Universal Coverage." California Endowment. January. http://www.calendow.org/uploaded

files/publications/by_topic/access/mental_health/mental%20health%20
and%20universal%20coverage.pdf.

Lestch, Corinne, and Rachel Monahan. 2012. "Dozens of Four- and Five-Year-Olds Suspended from New York City Schools Last Year." *New York Daily News*, November 16. http://www.nydailynews.com/new-york/education/dozens-4-5-year-olds-suspended-schools-year-article-1.1203575.

Merikangas, K. R., et al. 2010. "Lifetime Prevalence of Mental Disorders in U.S. Adolescents: Results from the National Comorbidity Survey Replication—Adolescent Supplement." *Journal of the American Academy of Child and Adolescent Psychiatry* 49 (October): 980–89. http://www.ncbi.nlm.nih.gov/pmc/articles/PMC2946114/. doi:10.1016/j.jaac.2010.05.017

Miller, Joel E. 2012. *Too Significant to Fail: The Importance of State Behavioral Health Agencies in the Daily Lives of Americans with Mental Illness, for Their Families, and for Their Communities.* Alexandria, VA: National Association of State Mental Health Program Directors. http://www.nasmhpd.org/docs/publications/Too%20Significant%20To%20Fail.pdf.

Mitchell, Alex J., and Thomas Selmes. 2007. "Why Don't Patients Take Their Medicine? Reasons and Solutions in Psychiatry." *Advances in Psychiatric Treatment* 13:336–46. apt.rcpsych.org/content/13/5/336.full.pdf. doi:10.1192/apt.bp.106.003194.

NAACP. 2005. "Dismantling the School-to-Prison Pipeline." NAACP Legal Defense and Educational Fund. http://www.naacpldf.org/files/publications/Dismantling_the_School_to_Prison_Pipeline.pdf.

National Center for PTSD. 2014. "How Common Is PTSD?" U.S. Department of Veterans Affairs. Updated January 30. http://www.ptsd.va.gov/public/pages/how-common-is-ptsd.asp.

National Research Council. 2006. *Improving the Quality of Health Care for Mental and Substance-Use Conditions: Quality Chasm Series.* Washington, DC: National Academies Press.

NCES. 2012. "Table 48: Children Three to Twenty-One Years Old Served Under Individuals with Disabilities Education Act, Part B, by Type of Disability: Selected Years, 1976–77 Through 2010–11." National Center for Education Statistics. http://nces.ed.gov/programs/digest/d12/tables/dt12_048.asp.

NCH. 2009. "Mental Illness and Homelessness." National Coalition for the Homeless. July. http://www.nationalhomeless.org/factsheets/Mental_Illness.html. Modified February 21, 2012.

NCHS. 2012. *Health, United States, 2011: With Special Features on Socioeconomic Status and Health.* Hyattsville, MD: National Center for Health Statistics. http://www.cdc.gov/nchs/data/hus/hus11.pdf.

Federal Education Budget Project. 2013. "Individuals with Disabilities Education Act—Funding Distribution." New America Foundation. November 8. http://febp.newamerica.net/background-analysis/individuals-disabilities-education-act-funding-distribution.

NIMH. n.d.a. "Any Disorder Among Adults." National Institute of Mental Health. http://www.nimh.nih.gov/statistics/1anydis_adult.shtml.

NIMH. n.d.b. "Use of Mental Health Services and Treatment Among Children." National Institute of Mental Health. http://www.nimh.nih.gov/statistics/1nhanes.shtml.

NIMH. n.d.c. "Use of Mental Health Services and Treatment Among Adults." National Institute of Mental Health. http://www.nimh.nih.gov/statistics/3use_mt_adult.shtml.

NIMH. 2005. "Mental Illness Exacts Heavy Toll, Beginning in Youth." Press release. June 6. http://www.nimh.nih.gov/science-news/2005/mental-illness-exacts-heavy-toll-beginning-in-youth.shtml.

O'Connell, Mary Ellen, Thomas Boat, and Kenneth E. Warner. 2009. *Preventing Mental, Emotional, and Behavioral Disorders Among Young People: Progress and Possibilities*. Washington, DC: National Academies Press.

Office of the Surgeon General et al. 2001. *Youth Violence: A Report of the Surgeon General*. Rockville, MD: Office of the Surgeon General. http://www.ncbi.nlm.nih.gov/books/NBK44294/.

Pfuntner, Anne, Lauren M. Weir, and Claudia Steiner. 2013. "Cost of Hospital Stays in the United States, 2010." Agency for Healthcare Research and Quality, Statistical Brief no. 146. January. http://www.hcup-us.ahrq.gov/reports/statbriefs/sb146.jsp.

Pfuntner, Anne, Lauren M. Weir, and Carol Stocks. 2013. "Most Frequent Conditions in U.S. Hospitals, 2011." Agency for Healthcare Research and Quality, Statistical Brief no. 162. September. http://www.hcup-us.ahrq.gov/reports/statbriefs/sb162.jsp.

Pitt, Veronica, et al. 2013. "Consumer-Providers of Care for Adult Clients of Statutory Mental Health Services. *Cochrane Database of Systematic Reviews* 3 (March). http://onlinelibrary.wiley.com/doi/10.1002/14651858.CD004807.pub2/abstract. doi:10.1002/14651858.CD004807.pub2.

Ravo, Nick. 1990. "The Talk of Middletown: 1950s Town Now Battles 1990s Woes." *New York Times*, April 2. http://www.nytimes.com/1990/04/02/nyregion/the-talk-of-middletown-1950-s-town-now-battles-1990-s-woes.html.

Ridgely, M. Susan, et al. 2007. "Justice, Treatment, and Cost: An Evaluation of the Fiscal Impact of Allegheny County Mental Health Court." RAND Corporation Technical Report. http://www.rand.org/content/dam/rand/pubs/technical_reports/2007/RAND_TR439.pdf.

SAMHSA. 2011. "Violence and Mental Illness: The Facts." Substance Abuse and Mental Health Services Administration.. http://promoteacceptance .samhsa.gov/publications/facts.aspx. Updated February 16, 2011.

Sharfstein, Steven S., and Faith B. Dickerson. 2009. "Hospital Psychiatry for the Twenty-First Century." *Health Affairs* 28 (May–June): 685–88. http:// content.healthaffairs.org/content/28/3/685.full. doi:10.1377/hlthaff.28.3.685.

Steadman, Henry J., et al. 1998. "Violence by People Discharged from Acute Psychiatric Inpatient Facilities and by Others in the Same Neighborhoods." *Archives of General Psychiatry* 55 (May): 393–410. http://archpsyc.jamanetwork .com/article.aspx?articleid=203874. doi:10.1001/archpsyc.55.5.393.

Steadman, Henry J., et al. 2009. "Prevalence of Serious Mental Illness Among Jail Inmates." *Psychiatric Services* 60 (June): 761–65. http://psychiatryonline .org/data/Journals/PSS/3881/09ps761.pdf.

Steadman, Henry J., et al. 2010. "Effect of Mental Health Courts on Arrests and Jail Days: A Multisite Study." *Archives of General Psychiatry* 68:167–72. http://archpsyc.jamanetwork.com/article.aspx?articleid=211027. doi:10.1001 /archgenpsychiatry.2010.134

Torrey, E. Fuller, et al. 2008. "The Shortage of Public Hospital Beds for Mentally Ill Persons." Treatment Advocacy Center. March. http://www.treatment advocacycenter.org/storage/documents/the_shortage_of_publichospital _beds.pdf.

Torrey, E. Fuller, et al. 2012. "No Room at the Inn: Trends and Consequences of Closing Public Psychiatric Hospitals, 2005–2010." Treatment Advocacy Center. July 19. http://tacreports.org/storage/documents/no_room_at_the_ inn-2012.pdf.

UPI. 2010. "Jails Are Top Mental Health Institutions." United Press International, July 12. http://www.upi.com/Health_News/2010/07/12/Jails-are-top -mental-health-institutions/UPI-27621278982109/.

U.S. Census Bureau. 1935. *Statistical Abstract of the United States.* http:// www2.census.gov/prod2/statcomp/documents/1935-02.pdf.

U.S. Code. 2014. Assistance to States for the Education of Children with Disabilities. 34 U.S.C § 300.322. http://www.ecfr.gov/cgi-bin/text-idx?SID=eod 2dbafb1f85ac63e8f2d5ef9203472&node=34:2.1.1.1.1.4.58.15&rgn=div8.

Yoon, Jangho, and Tim A. Bruckner. 2009. "Does Deinstitutionalization Increase Suicide?" *Health Services Research* 44 (August): 1385–1405. http://www .ncbi.nlm.nih.gov/pmc/articles/PMC2739034/. doi:10.1111/j.1475-6773.2009 .00986.x.